PRAISE FOR

The Rope

*

"Brisk and cinematic writing . . . the stories are so vividly told, so filled with velocity."

—*The Wall Street Journal*

"[A] riveting read."

The New York Times Book Review

"Compelling."

—*The Guardian*

"This outstanding, meticulously researched book will serve to commemorate [Marie Smith's] stolen life, as well as the countless Black lives stolen by lynch mobs."

—*The Washington Post*

"Fascinating, important, and colorfully reported. When a white detective and a former slave work separately but toward the same goal in an unspeakable murder case in 1910—justice is served. Their moral audacity and persistence highlight a question relevant to today: What kind of America do we want to live in?"

—Walter Isaacson, #1 *New York Times* bestselling author of *The Code Breaker* and *Steve Jobs*

"In Alex Tresniowski's brilliant and kaleidoscopic retelling of the infamous Marie Smith murder investigation, we see crack detectives, the bravery of anti-lynching crusader Ida B. Wells, and a civil rights organization gaining its footing, all linked in an effort to bend justice unto a white child—and a Black man. Riveting and quite relevant for the society which we inhabit today."

—Wil Haygood, author of *Showdown: Thurgood Marshall and the Supreme Court Nomination That Changed America*

"Tresniowski has breathed new and incredibly relevant life into an obscure and largely forgotten murder mystery with *The Rope*, a page-turner of historical true crime that transports readers to the turn of the century in a legendary New Jersey shore town. The shoe-leather detective work at the center of the narrative is gripping on its own, but what makes this story all the more compelling and timely is the backdrop of civil rights and racial justice, carried along by none other than Ida B. Wells. It's a book to make Bruce Springsteen proud."

—Joe Pompeo, journalist, *Vanity Fair*

"This book is a timely and powerful history lesson wrapped inside a compelling true-crime thriller. It examines the persistent and devastating inequalities between races in America, but also highlights the heroism of activists who fought to bend the country away from hate and toward justice. It takes a unique look at the early days of the NAACP by drilling into the courageous and often unheralded efforts of Ida B. Wells, a writer turned revolutionary who believed mere protests were not enough to challenge entrenched racist practices like Jim Crow, Black Codes, and lynching, and whose bold actions laid the groundwork for a century of Black American activism. Vividly and dramatically told, this story of two ordinary citizens who refused to buckle under the weight of systemic racism and instead struggled mightily to spare a single Black life, is especially relevant and powerful in today's regressive political times."

—Ben Jealous, former NAACP president

"This thrilling true-crime story documents a critical chapter in the crusade against racial violence in America."

—*Publishers Weekly*

"Gripping and powerful, *The Rope* is an important piece of history that gives a voice to the voiceless and resurrects a long-forgotten true-crime story that speaks to the very divisions tearing at the nation's fabric today."

—*Bookreporter*

"This suspenseful, well-written true-crime tale will be an eye-opener for anyone who assumes that after Reconstruction, lynching remained a serious threat only in the South. High-velocity historical true crime."

—*Kirkus Reviews*

"Engrossing . . . An indictment of lynching on a stark, personal level."

—*Booklist*

"Tresniowski breathes life into a largely forgotten murder mystery in this gripping true-crime story . . . An important reminder of the many layers of injustice still present in the United States . . . Timely, relevant."

—*Library Journal*

"In this riveting true story, Alex Tresniowski tells the intertwined stories of a crusading reporter, an innovative detective, and a man unjustly imprisoned . . . You'll read this in a night, I promise!"

—*CrimeReads*

"There are some parts here that'll make you gasp with cliff-hanging movie-worthiness, and reach for more. Why you'll devour *The Rope* should be no mystery."

—*The Philadelphia Tribune*

The Rope

A True Story of Murder, Heroism, and the Dawn of the NAACP

*

Alex Tresniowski

37INK

SIMON & SCHUSTER

New York   London   Toronto   Sydney   New Delhi

37INK

SIMON &
SCHUSTER

Simon & Schuster, Inc.
1230 Avenue of the Americas
New York, NY 10020

First 37 INK/Simon & Schuster trade paperback edition February 2022

37 INK/SIMON & SCHUSTER and colophon are trademarks of Simon & Schuster, Inc.

For information about special discounts for bulk purchases, please contact Simon & Schuster Special Sales at 1-866-506-1949 or business@simonandschuster.com.

The Simon & Schuster Speakers Bureau can bring authors to your live event. For more information or to book an event, contact the Simon & Schuster Speakers Bureau at 1-866-248-3049 or visit our website at www.simonspeakers.com.

Interior design by Kyle Kabel

Manufactured in the United States of America

1   3   5   7   9   10   8   6   4   2

Names: Tresniowski, Alex, author.
Title: The rope : a true story of murder, heroism, and the dawn of the NAACP / Alex Tresniowski.
Description: First 37 INK/Simon & Schuster hardcover edition. |
New York, NY : Simon & Schuster, [2020]
Identifiers: LCCN 2020046660 (print) | LCCN 2020046661 (ebook) |
ISBN 9781982114022 (hardback) | ISBN 9781982114039 (trade paperback) |
ISBN 9781982114046 (ebook)
Subjects: LCSH: Murder—New Jersey—Asbury Park—History—20th century. |
Murder—Investigation—New Jersey—Asbury Park—History—20th century. |
Heroes—New Jersey—Asbury Park—History—20th century. | National
Association for the Advancement of Colored People.
Classification: LCC HV6534.A62 T74 2020 (print) | LCC HV6534.A62 (ebook)
| DDC 364.152/3092—dc23
LC record available at https://lccn.loc.gov/2020046660
LC ebook record available at https://lccn.loc.gov/2020046661

ISBN 978-1-9821-1402-2
ISBN 978-1-9821-1403-9 (pbk)
ISBN 978-1-9821-1404-6 (ebook)

To Lorraine Stundis
Rainey, your support, intellect, silliness, and beautiful heart
make everything possible. The history of me is you.

This book is in memory of the 3,446 African Americans
lynched in the United States between 1882 and 1968—
people who lived and mattered.

ASBURY PARK

— 1910 —

Preach as if you had seen heaven and its celestial inhabitants, and hovered over the bottomless pit and beheld the tortures, and heard the groans of the damned.

—*Francis Asbury*

Contents

*

CONTENTS

CHAPTER 1

Black Diamond

*

November 1910
Asbury Park, New Jersey

For Thomas Williams, it was better to be no one than someone in Asbury Park.

Williams lived in a city that was not meant for him. It was designed as a haven for godly and wealthy white people. The purest air in the bluest sky, the gentlest spray from a perfect ocean, wide boulevards and candy-colored homes—the very best America. Williams lived there, but only in the shadows of other people's lives, a peripheral figure, a black man for hire, no one of note. This was how both he and the city wanted it. Williams took all kinds of jobs—chopping wood, painting houses, corralling hogs and cows for widows. He did these jobs and then he was gone, to somewhere on the edges of town. He was forty years old and complained of lumbago—chronic back pain—but there wasn't any kind of work Tom Williams wouldn't do, if it meant a few dollars for him.

He was not from Asbury Park, or even New Jersey. He came from Lynchburg, Virginia, where he'd been an amateur prizefighter and went by his ring nickname, Black Diamond. He had a boxer's build— six feet tall, broad shoulders, hard hands—and he wore a sweater coat that was dark with grime and pants held up by suspenders. He liked his liquor—gin and whiskey—and many mornings he could be found in the barroom at Griffin's Wanamassa Hotel, out past Wickapecko Drive, eating his breakfast and taking his drinks as early as 8:00 a.m.

In New Jersey, the record of Williams's life was a crime sheet, though not a violent one. In 1907, a state prison supervisor riding a train spotted a six-shooter sticking out of Williams's coat. He had him searched and turned up several gold watches and $375 in cash. Williams confessed to larceny and served eighteen months in state prison. He served a separate, shorter stretch for being drunk and disorderly.

For the fourteen months he'd been in Asbury Park, though, he'd had no trouble with the law.

That is, until an unspeakable crime happened in the fall of 1910, and Tom Williams became someone in Asbury Park.

*

Wherever he went, Williams carried with him the long, heavy history of racism in America, and in 1910 no part of his life would have been unaffected by it.

Education, land ownership, voting rights, due process, equality, self-determination—Williams would have been guaranteed none of these. By 1910, black people had been free from bondage for forty-five years, but the dark-hearted mentality behind slavery remained in place, not in the corners and fringes of the country but on its main streets and in its town halls and courtrooms. One race fought steadily and openly to keep another race as near to a state of subjugation as possible. The weapons used—black codes, Jim Crow, disenfranchisement, segregation, lynching—were insidious, suppressive, and terrorizing.

Williams lived in a time the historian Rayford Logan called "the nadir of American race relations"—a period from the late 1800s to the early 1900s that saw a violent, bloody backlash against any gains made by black Americans after the Civil War. During this half century some states identified crimes and passed laws "specifically written to intimidate blacks—changing employers without permission, vagrancy, riding freight cars without a ticket, engaging in sexual activity, or loud talk, with white women," wrote Douglas A. Blackmon in his Pulitzer Prize–winning study of the era, *Slavery by Another Name*. Black landowners lost billions in wealth as white mobs drove them from their homes and stole their land from beneath them. Many thousands of black men were lynched, many tens of thousands of families displaced, black neighborhoods purged or burned down, death sentences passed for stealing bread or "acting too white."

A voice in the world, dominion over his body, the barest of dignities—people like Tom Williams were denied these things, and had to fight for them every day.

They were often alone in this fight, but not always.

The story of Tom Williams is also the story of two individuals, a man and a woman, one white, one black, born at different times in different parts of the country, fated never to meet but linked by a passion for justice, and by a single legal case in a town called Asbury Park.

One of them, Raymond C. Schindler, was a cerebral private detective who never once shot a gun or even carried one, the son of a preacher and a prison librarian, a believer in redemption but relentless in pursuit of the criminals who needed it—a gentleman bloodhound.

The other was Ida B. Wells, a black woman born a slave and driven by personal tragedy, a crusader against racism and a champion of her race, barely five feet tall but towering in her righteousness and influence—the most famous black woman of her time.

Schindler was a raw-boned rookie only a few years out of high school when he crossed paths with Tom Williams; by then, Wells had been an activist and reformer for decades. Schindler came to know the dark corners of Asbury Park; Wells never set foot there. They were unaware of each other's efforts, and neither foresaw the full impact of the case that united them. Today, they are not linked in any textbooks, or in any telling of the crime and its aftermath.

Yet both Ray Schindler and Ida B. Wells, in their resolute pursuit of equal justice for all, emphatically answered the question posed to every citizen, every day—what kind of America do we wish to live in?

Their efforts demonstrated the power of an individual—a single, steadfast warrior—to collide with history and meaningfully shift its course. Their separate heroism, in the form of small, principled decisions and actions, day after day, against all odds and resistance, in service to the unheralded and the vulnerable, had a clear impact on one specific case, but also helped give shape to an ongoing struggle that was bigger than any one man or crime. They were part of a chain of unlikely events in 1910 and 1911 that galvanized the fledgling National Association for the Advancement of Colored People and set it on its way to becoming the most powerful force in America's long battle for civil rights.

Those events—and the moral audacity and persistence of Raymond Schindler and Ida B. Wells—are the story of this book.

*

"In small towns, such crimes are not soon forgotten," declared the sheriff of Asbury Park, in the days after the terrible crime. "There must be punishment. The man must be made to pay."

So it was that they came looking for Black Diamond.

When they found him and brought him in, some people had bad things to say about him. One woman told a reporter she always locked her doors when Williams was around; she didn't like him because "he was so black and dirty." Others said he was shifty, lazy, a drunk. The *Asbury Park Press* called him "a bad man generally."

Most people had no opinion of him at all.

Emma Davison, a key witness in the sensational case that was to come, could recall only a single prior incident involving Tom Williams—an innocuous encounter relayed to her by her young son.

According to the boy, he was playing with a little hop toad on a dirt path in the Wanamassa woods, on the northern edge of Asbury Park, when Williams walked by. The boy announced he planned to kill the toad.

"Don't do it," Williams told him.

"Why not?"

"Because it would be cruel."

The boy considered his choice, and opened his hand and let the toad go, and watched it spring and scoot away, into the indifferent woods.

CHAPTER 2

The Flower

*

November 1910
Asbury Park, New Jersey

The young girl woke up happy in the dark of early dawn. Happier than usual, her father noticed, though it was not a special day, not her birthday or a holiday. It's true that she was a sunny child, the way some children are sunny, but on this day she was even more cheerful than usual, which was fine by her father, even if he didn't know why.

Little Marie Smith, ten years old, hopped out of bed in her family's white frame home on West Monroe Avenue, in the roughneck Whitesville section of Asbury Park, and sat at the kitchen table for a hot breakfast. Marie was hungry and ate heartily—fried smoked beef bologna, wheat bread, and a cup of baker's cocoa.

It was a sharp fall day, but her mother, Nora, dressed her for winter—a fleece-lined cotton undershirt and cotton underdrawers, a green Scotch plaid dress, black stockings, and a brown winter coat Marie had long since outgrown. Her black leather shoes were boys' shoes with the clunky metal hooks cut off and the laces slipped through slits in the leather. Marie's light, sandy hair, trimmed short just below the ears, had a blue satin ribbon in it, covered up by her gray knit skating cap.

Just before she left for school, at 8:00 a.m., Marie took her favorite bracelet, made of shiny red plastic, and slipped it on her slender wrist.

Marie was pretty, with blue eyes and fair skin. She was small for her age; most people mistook her for seven or eight. Her life was hard and plain. Peter, her father, stocky and mustached, was a driver for a local rendering plant. His job was to visit butchers and gather leftover fat, bones, hides, tallow, skin, and grease and take his haul back to the plant to be made into soap. He kept the noxious smell of the plant in his nose around the clock, and at night he brought it home with him on his clothes and hair and skin.

Marie's mother was also pretty and fair, but she was frail and drank too much. Sometimes she sent Marie to buy bottles of beer off John Griffin's wagon, or whiskey from an Italian on the shadowy outskirts of town. At home, little Marie did much of her mother's work—cooking, cleaning, mending. She had an older brother, John, who died at eighteen months after swallowing horse liniment. Now she had two younger brothers, Thomas and Joseph, whom she helped to care for.

Marie's parents fought often, mostly over her mother's drinking, but sometimes because, when Peter Smith drank, he became cruel and violent. Six weeks earlier, Peter came home drunk and hurled a fork and plate at his wife. Before he could do any further harm, Nora's sister Delia stepped up and stopped him.

"I told him if he didn't let his wife alone, I would hit him myself," Nora would later testify. "That's when the trouble ended."

Yet as lacking in grace as Marie's life could be, she remained bright and cheerful. She was mature and strong-minded beyond her years. "Marie could not be coaxed in doing things she would set her mind against," one neighbor said. "She was a dutiful child." She went to Sunday Bible school and she knew to stay away from strangers, and she was properly frightened of the dark woods just behind her elementary school. After classes, Marie and her aunt Delia's mixed-race daughter liked to skip through the town dumping grounds on their way back from school, like a lot of kids did, but she was never, ever late getting home.

"She still had her first licking to get from us," her father would say. "She had no immoral habits. We never had to correct her for anything. She was too good for that."

"Her family were hard people," another relative said. "Marie was the flower."

At 8:00 a.m. on November 9, 1910, Marie and her brother Thomas left their home, bound for school. They walked up West Monroe Avenue, past a row of modest folk Victorian homes much like theirs, and took a right turn onto wide, curving Whitesville Road. They climbed up a small hill and crossed Asbury Avenue, onto the narrow sidewalk of Third Avenue. They followed Third all the way to the three-story, redbrick Bradley School on Pine Street. The walk was one mile long and it took Marie twenty minutes. She made the same walk every day she had school.

Marie led Thomas by the hand to his kindergarten class, then hurried off to her all-girls class, taught by Miss Wilde. Two hours later, at 10:30 a.m., the bell rang for morning recess. Some mornings, Marie's mother would slip a few pennies in her skirt pocket for buying lunch at the school, but on that day Marie had instructions to come back home at recess. She would eat lunch there and then drop off her father's lunch at the plant near her school, before going back for afternoon class.

At 10:30 a.m., Marie walked out of the Bradley School and headed down Third Avenue, toward her home. She was skipping and singing.

Emma Davison, who lived in the town across Deal Lake, along the northern border of Asbury Park, was turning onto Third Avenue just a few paces away from Marie. A dog jumped out from behind a hedge and barked at Davison, and she hit it on the nose to make it stop.

"I turned after hitting the dog and looked around, and when I looked around I saw this little girl coming," Davison later recalled. She heard Marie singing and watched her skipping and wondered whose child she was. She watched as the dog barked at Marie, too. But after that, Emma said, "I throwed my fur around my neck, for it was cold, and I didn't look around anymore." She walked away in the opposite direction and didn't give the child another thought.

And then, little Marie Smith disappeared.

*

She did not make it home. Not after morning recess, not after school was over. Her mother expected her back no later than 11:00 a.m., but figured the school had held all the children back for some reason. It was only when Marie didn't return from the afternoon session that Nora began to worry. "I thought she should be home around 3:00," Nora said. When she wasn't, "I walked out as far as the schoolhouse."

On her way, Nora stopped by the rendering plant to tell her husband, Peter, their daughter hadn't come home. He said to go to the Bradley School and ask her teacher about Marie. Miss Wilde told Nora she saw Marie leaving the schoolhouse at 10:30 a.m. Nora asked if her daughter looked as if anything was wrong. "She said she seemed to be all right," Nora said. "She didn't say she was sick or complaining."

Nora left the schoolhouse and ran down Third Avenue, toward the Asbury Avenue home of Marie's aunt, Delia Jackson. Perhaps the girl had gone there. But no, Delia told her, she hadn't seen her. Nora ran back home and called the Asbury Park Police headquarters to report that her daughter was missing. Then she called her husband, who came straight home and phoned the police, too.

It was almost dusk. Peter and Nora joined the Bradley School's principal, Helen Emery, and two of their neighbors—Tom Dean and Ed Ayres—and set out on a door-to-door search of the houses along Third Avenue. Peter carried a lantern and searched every bush and hedge and stretch of woods. "I went up through Whitesville Road because I seen the track of an automobile and I thought maybe it hit her and chucked her into the bushes," Peter said. The search lasted until 2:00 a.m.

Early the next morning, her eyes red and swollen from crying, Nora Smith dressed in black and stood woefully in the cold outside the girls' entrance to the Bradley School, watching students file in for morning class. She looked at their faces, desperate to see Marie's. Maybe her daughter had slept over with a classmate, she thought. It wasn't likely, but it was possible. But then, so many things were possible. Marie might have crossed one of the bridges over Deal Lake and stumbled off and drowned. She might have been hit by a car and ferried away to cover up the accident. She may have even tried to walk all the way back to Brooklyn in New York City, where Marie and her parents had lived before moving to Asbury Park eighteen months earlier. She could be anywhere.

That day, November 10, marked the beginning of the official investigation into the disappearance of Marie Smith.

Asbury Park police chief William H. Smith assigned two officers, Thomas Broderick and Walter Ireton, to lead the case. It began as a search mission. Peter Smith teamed with dozens of friends and neighbors, firemen and volunteers, police officers and even schoolboys let out of class, to comb the dreary woods around the schoolhouse. Swimmers dragged Deal Lake, while officers in heavy coats and rubber boots scoured the sand hills and backcountry, in automobiles and horse-drawn carriages, beating at the underbrush and looking in every house. The footprints of an adult and a child were found in the soft mud along the lake banks at the old Drummond brickyard on Asbury Avenue, but it was determined the smaller footprints were too large to belong to Marie.

Two days later, November 12, Police Chief Smith summoned every able man in Asbury Park to meet on the corner of Ridge Avenue and aid in the hunt. The police announced a two-hundred-dollar reward for information about Marie. At night, the jittery beams of flashlights sliced through the dark woods and side streets. In her home, Nora Smith wept and stayed awake, into her fortieth hour without sleep, and neighbors worried for her sanity.

There was nothing to show for any of it. No piece of ripped fabric, no blood on the ground. No sign of little Marie at all. The girl was simply gone—"vanished," one newspaper put it, "as thoroughly as though the earth had opened up and swallowed her."

Then came Sunday, November 13—the Lord's Day.

CHAPTER 3

A New Eden

*

June 1870
Ocean Grove, New Jersey

Forty years earlier, on a spot not far from the Wanamassa woods, two men stripped off their clothes and lay naked in the sand by the Atlantic Ocean.

One of them, a white man, thought about wading into the water, but the tide and the darkness of night scared him off the idea, and this was the best he could do—lie safely where the waves ebbed and the surf gently lapped his body. This was enough for him to feel what he had come to the ocean to feel.

Cleansed by God.

The white man, James Adam Bradley, was tired. Not just from the journey to the seaside, which had rattled his forty-year-old bones— across New York Harbor in the steamer *Red Bird*, a train to Eatontown, and from there a horse-drawn carriage over eight miles of a new "turnpike" that was little more than rocks and planks of wood.

Bradley, a burly man with a soft expression, was exhausted by life, physically and spiritually broken.

He grew up in Manhattan's Lower East Side, on its dense streets and dirty alleys, in the 1830s. His father, an Irish farmer, and his mother, who was English, were poor. Bradley fell into the lawless life of a Bowery Boy, skipping school to drink wine and sneak into playhouses with chums,

13

and this, it seemed, would be his lot in life—"drifting upon the rocks of intemperance," as a newspaper later put it.

That, however, would not be his fate. One day, one of Bradley's young running mates drunkenly offered to fight anyone brave enough to come forward. As a joke, the mischievous Bradley accepted. He put up his fists and, at the last moment, turned and fled, certain he could outrun his drunken friend. He made it a half block before a blow to the head knocked him down. His chum, it seemed, had only pretended to be drunk. Sober, he beat Bradley bloody.

The beating knocked Bradley straight. After that, he took his first job at fourteen, earning a dollar a week monitoring a pot of boiling lead in a brass foundry. At sixteen he answered a "Boy Wanted" sign in the window of a brush manufacturing plant, and apprenticed for the brush-maker Frances Furnold. Over the years he rose to shop foreman, and, with several hundred dollars saved from his wages, he opened his own small brush factory in Manhattan, at the age of twenty-seven.

But now he was forty, and despite his vast wealth—the result of a surge in demand for military brushes during the Civil War—he felt drained. The long hours in the factory, the stench of horsehair and bleach and glue, had got to him. Bradley's doctor told him he was suffering from nervous exhaustion. Even his quiet, Boston-born wife, Helen, who otherwise stayed out of her husband's affairs, urged him to take time away, not only from the brush business, but from New York City.

By chance, around this time, in 1869, Bradley ran into a friend on Broadway.

The friend was leasing undeveloped lots in Ocean Grove, a bare-bones summer campground site founded by Methodist clergymen on the rugged New Jersey seashore, sixty miles south of Bradley's Brooklyn home. Bradley saw it as his chance to escape the soullessness of urban life, and impulsively bought two lots for eighty-five dollars each.

It would be there, in the roughness of nature, Bradley hoped, that "my wearied body and brain might rest, lulled to sleep by the murmuring sea at night, and awakened in the morning by the songs of birds in the pine trees"—the dream of a tenement boy turned factory man.

It was also the aspiration of a God-fearing soul.

Bradley was baptized Catholic—the immigrant religion—but as an adult he left behind his church, and the poverty of his youth, and became a Methodist. He saw it as a step up in class. Here was an evangelical movement that stressed living a life of purity and holiness, which struck Bradley as a more refined and middle-class pursuit, and more in line with his hearty self-discipline. To be Methodist was to seek a purer, closer, more authentic connection with God.

So, in 1870, Bradley took his first trip to his new property on the Jersey shore. He brought along John Baker, the assistant, cook, and companion he called "my colored man." Formerly enslaved, Baker escaped a Virginia plantation at the start of the Civil War. As a free man in his mid-forties, he learned to read and write. To Bradley, their partnership was not unlike the Daniel Defoe novel *Robinson Crusoe*, with him as the fictional adventurer stuck on a desert island, and he saw John Baker as Crusoe's companion, Friday, the uncivilized black native Crusoe converted to Christianity.

Yet Bradley also considered Baker a friend. "Though his black face and his unmistakable African features left no doubt as to his origins, he completely refuted the argument of some who say the colored man is thick-skulled and stupid and only fit to be used as a servant," Bradley wrote. Their friendship surprised many, including one reporter who "was struck by Mr. Bradley's manner and treatment of his colored servant." Just a few years after the Civil War and the emancipation of four million enslaved people, their bond was not a common one, neither in the North nor South.

Yet there they were, together reaching the nothingness of Ocean Grove at nightfall on June 9, 1870.

They parked their horses in the barn of a local, Charles Rogers, and made their way on foot through a half mile of briar and bush, finally emerging into a man-made clearing. It was too dark to search for wood to use as poles for a tent, so they slung their tarp over the roofless beams of a structure under construction near the ocean. It was the first and only structure in all of Ocean Grove, soon to be the two-story building that housed the Ocean Grove Association. For now, it was a fine makeshift shelter for the two men, who ate a few crackers in the dark before going to sleep on carriage cushions they used as beds and pillows.

In the light of morning, John Baker awoke to the full realization that his boss's dream destination was a wasteland.

"Mr. B," Baker said forlornly, "this is a wilderness place."

"Oh, don't be cast down," Bradley answered.

That day they pushed farther south, through desolate sand dunes and marshes, and arrived at Bradley's two empty lots by a lake that bordered the ocean. They pitched their tent and dug a hole in the ground to use as an icebox. They spent the next several days in the almost complete solitude of Ocean Grove, occasionally spotting workers in the distance. Sometimes they traveled the six miles to Long Branch, the nearest real town, for canned food.

One night, Bradley and Baker went for a walk along the Atlantic.

"How about a bath?" Bradley suggested.

"No, no," Baker said.

"Remember, John, cleanliness is next to godliness."

With that, Bradley stripped off his clothes and walked naked to the surf. Baker waited farther back.

At the waterline, Bradley hesitated. He considered "the way bathers usually enjoy the surf, the waves crashing over their heads." But the vastness of the ocean, endless, unknowable, was too intimidating. Instead, Bradley lay in the soft sand and let the water rush past. He felt a strange kind of melancholy, even loneliness, as he surrendered to the ocean. It was perhaps more solitude than he had bargained for.

In fact he was not alone. John Baker had stripped off his own clothes and made his way to the water's edge. "He had plucked up courage by my example," Bradley wrote. Baker lay down in the sand next to his friend, and together they let the waves bathe them—two men brought by different forces to the same ocean, to be baptized side by side.

*

Bradley's dream of rejuvenation was not a dream he held just for Baker and himself. He envisioned a modern Methodist sanctuary arising from the scrub brush, sprouting from the sand. Where before there was nothing, now a town, a community, a resort—a haven for those who wished to flee the wantonness of secular society and be renewed, down to their weary souls, in the glow of the Savior. A new Eden.

Bradley's dream took root in Ocean Grove, which in 1870, when he first saw it, was merely a summer campground for Methodist groups and other denominational unions and gatherings. It was not a city or a town or anything. It was designed to be a seasonal retreat, absent of buildings and bustle, drainage or sewage. Ocean Grove was isolated from the nearest town, Long Branch, by Wesley Lake on its northern border, and beyond that by five hundred acres of uninhabitable wilderness, a stretch of windswept land so thick with brush and briars, wildflowers and marshmallow plants, that not a single soul had seen fit to make use of it in the century America had been a country.

Yet even the lake and the wilderness were not enough insulation for Ocean Grove's God-fearers, given the unsavory character of Long Branch.

The Branch, as it was known, was a drinking and gambling town. Operated by the portly stockbroker and robber baron James Fisk— Diamond Jim to most—it was known for its garish nightclubs and dance bands, prostitutes, and ample liquor. On July 4, 1870, around the time James Bradley first arrived in Ocean Grove, the 128-acre Monmouth Park racetrack opened three miles outside Long Branch, solidifying the resort's status as the premier gambling mecca on the East Coast. With its proud debauchery, Long Branch was the spiritual antithesis of Ocean Grove.

For that reason, the Methodist clergymen who established Ocean Grove considered buying the five hundred acres of wilderness between the two places, lest it fall into the hands of someone who didn't share their pure intents. But the land was too rough, and the price too high. So the parcel sat. On one of his visits to Ocean Grove, James Bradley, curious about the scrubland, asked a Methodist clergyman, Rev. William Osborne, to come with him on an expedition through the brush.

It was not an easy go. They had to hack through the thick briar and risk "having our clothes torn from our bodies," Bradley wrote. Once they made it through the half mile of sand and marsh and overgrowth, they encountered another lake, which seemed to Bradley to be "as beautiful a stretch of water as can be found anywhere." Maybe it was the hard journey through the woods that made the lake seem so heavenly to Bradley, as if the trek had been a kind of spiritual quest—which, of course, it had been, just as his entire New Jersey adventure was a quest. Or perhaps the water, which would come to be called Deal Lake, was truly as serene and shimmering that day as Bradley took it to be.

Either way, beating his way through the brush and gazing upon the pristine lake changed the course of Bradley's life even more than his purchases in Ocean Grove.

His lots there were raw and undeveloped, but they were part of something man-made. The five hundred acres of scrub brush, though— these were *truly* untouched. They were the blank canvas Bradley had been desperate for. "Not a foot of cultivated soil in the whole place," he marveled. After spending a few moments at Deal Lake, Bradley and Osborne walked back to Ocean Grove along the beach, and Bradley got to work setting up a company to buy the forsaken land. He joined with seven clergymen, who together pledged to raise the ninety thousand dollars (nearly two million dollars today) needed to purchase the acres.

Then the deal fell apart. The clergymen backed out. "When the cool nights of autumn came around, it chilled their enthusiasm," Bradley wrote. Yet even the winter freeze didn't lessen his own. He borrowed ninety thousand dollars against his brush business, and bought the five hundred acres by himself.

What followed was a feat of sheer audacity and will. Bradley paid to clear-cut the woods and level the unruly sand dunes. He paced the land with a measuring stick and blocked off where the streets and churches and parks would go. He planned for wide avenues and boulevards that would run parallel to the ocean and create pleasing open spaces. He dreamed of a vast public walkway along the water. He envisioned homes and hotels, small businesses and meeting halls, a library and a school. He created what he called "a perfect system of drainage," pushing the existing technology to fashion fifteen miles of pipelines carrying waste from every home. He hired the state geologist to build artesian wells connected to an aquifer, providing his future residents with the purest water.

Doggedly, Bradley dreamed his haven into existence, gouging it out of primal earth and christening it after the frontier missionary who helped bring Methodism to America—the eighteenth-century English bishop Francis Asbury. The bishop was a morbidly gloomy man who had nothing of Bradley's optimism but instead was "a prophet of evil tidings," as Asbury put it, firm in his belief that the only thing saving us from the absolute horrors of the world was "faith in a prayer-hearing, soul-converting, soul-sanctifying, soul-restoring, soul-comforting God."

So it was that on March 26, 1874, James Bradley, admiring of the bishop's reverent soul and pioneer spirit, incorporated his five hundred rough-hewn acres and called his new township Asbury Park.

CHAPTER 4

Blood Under a Black Skin

*

1874–1910
Asbury Park, New Jersey

W hat began as Bradley's pursuit of purity became, in just a short time, a one-man crusade against sin.

Around him, Asbury Park flourished in ways Bradley couldn't have dreamed. New railroad lines opened up the entire Jersey shore to New York City commuters seeking getaways by the sea. In 1877 Bradley laid the first planks of a narrow ocean walkway that by 1880 had been replaced by a wide and grand boardwalk. He built a pier and an orchestra pavilion, and provided generous financial assistance to interested entrepreneurs who further built up the town. Within ten years of its founding, Asbury Park was home to some two hundred hotels and boardinghouses, with rooms for many thousands of visitors. In 1888, it was reported that as many as six hundred thousand people spent time in Asbury Park.

In 1869, Bradley's land had been valued at a mere fifteen thousand dollars. By 1890, it was assessed at $2,500,000 (or nearly $50 million today).

What drove its remarkable growth—from wasteland to wildly popular resort in fifteen years—was the culture of escapism and wholesome entertainment that quickly took root.

An enterprising German immigrant, Ernest Schnitzler—modest and reserved except for a stocky mustache that connected to his even stockier sideburns—came to Asbury Park in 1888 with a vision of his own. He built a grand carousel, with dozens of ornate wooden horses and space for seventy-eight riders, inside a festive pavilion decorated with bright murals of the boardwalk. It was the first attraction in what would become Schnitzler's sprawling Pleasure Palace Amusements complex, which, among such complexes, was "the largest, most unique and most complete under one roof of all found on the Atlantic Coast," a local historian declared. Schnitzler created the Crystal Maze, a vast hall of funhouse mirrors that captivated visitors, and he sank many tens of thousands of dollars into pioneering electrical generators called dynamos, which brilliantly lit his arcade with two thousand thirty-candle-power lights.

Another unique attraction soon followed—a fifty-foot-high wooden wheel called a roundabout. Riders climbed into passenger cars that rose and fell as the big wheel slowly revolved. It was designed by William Somers, who was influenced by William Forrester's more basic epicycloidal wheel in Atlantic City. Somers's design earned him a U.S. patent and contracts to build the wheel in Atlantic City and Coney Island as well as Asbury Park. One of the ride's earliest passengers was George Ferris Jr., who, one year after experiencing it, built a similar wheel for Chicago's 1893 World's Fair. Somers sued for patent infringement, but the case was dismissed—and the ride, fairly or not, became known as the Ferris wheel.

Elegant hotels like the Plaza and the Marlborough came next. During the days, visitors enjoyed crabbing and sailing in leased yachts and bathing in the Atlantic salt water, and at night they flooded Schnitzler's Palace and other pleasure halls. Some enjoyed strolling or riding bicycles past the majestic, candy-colored Victorian homes that lined the ocean-bordering avenues. The effect of a day at Asbury Park was dizzying, almost sensual, given the many opportunities for indulgence and amusement. Not quite the placid nature retreat James Bradley had envisioned, Asbury Park became, by the turn of the century, America's most dynamic seaside resort.

And yet, nearly from the start, not all was well in Bradley's paradise. An 1880s editorial in the *Asbury Park Journal,* the local paper founded by Bradley, described evil, undermining forces at work.

"In this pleasant place," the paper stated, "Satan came in his worst form." That form was alcohol—something Bradley considered "the curse of America." He banned the sale of alcohol and crafted hundreds of property deeds containing anti-liquor clauses. And yet, in the shadows, or even out in the open, dozens of illegal saloons flourished. Drugstores and pharmacies peddled medicinal alcohol, while roving "beer arks" supplemented liquor sales. Even legitimate hotels and restaurants discreetly served alcohol to customers who knew to refer to lager beer as "sea foam," and whiskey as "cold tea."

Bradley gamely fought against them all, creating a Law and Order League of police officers and charging hotel owners with illegal sales. Often, he would chase beer wagons down a dark street himself. He also patrolled the streets and boardwalk at night, on the lookout not only for booze peddlers but also young couples engaging in what he called "summertime propinquity." He posted handwritten signs around the village, warning against "evil forces" and quoting his favorite scriptures. "Jesus Saves From Hell Praise Him," read one. He printed and distributed cards listing his rules of conduct for visitors, which included no peddling, profanity, or bathing suits "open to the suggestion of immodesty." Even "questionable poses" were outlawed.

Bradley pushed greatly for the innocent pursuits he preferred—spying sea lions and turtles on a whaling boat he anchored offshore, for instance—over the ones more naturally encouraged by the seductions of the sun and the sea. But that, in the end, would prove to be Bradley's greatest foe—the tide of human nature, with its slow and steady pull.

*

Another built-in fault line in Bradley's plan was race.

Just as the hedonistic instincts that drew people to Asbury Park ran counter to Bradley's puritanical urges, the very nature of what he was doing—creating, he hoped, "a white people's resort"—required a subclass to cater to the well-heeled visitors: waiters, carriage drivers, attendants, street sweepers.

It was black workers who filled nearly all these jobs.

Bradley understood this necessity, and by the mid-1880s there were some two thousand full-time black residents living in or near Asbury Park. They settled mainly in an unincorporated stretch of land adjacent to Asbury Park in Neptune Township, across the railroad tracks from the gilded part of the city, in an area known as West Park. Despite his friendship with the former slave John Baker, Bradley was, at heart, a fierce segregationist. As the unofficial mayor of Asbury Park, and owner of most of the land (he chose to lease out lots instead of selling them), Bradley made it his mission to keep the white and black populations of his bustling resort separate.

Bradley, however, could not control the flow of black tourists into Asbury Park, nor did he think to regulate, at least early on, the access black workers would have to his beach and boardwalk.

It was the opinion of many white observers that black workers were abusing their proximity to the resort's finer features, "intruding themselves," as the *New York Times* reported, "in places where common sense should tell them not to go." Black women, for instance, "flocked by the hundreds to Bradley's beach, jostled for room on the plank walk, and said impudent things to persons who resented any effort at familiarity." The most egregious example, the *Times* explained, was a blacks-only picnic hosted by vacationers from Newark, who "took possession of the [beach] and left it strewn with peanut shells."

The picnic was a final straw. It led Bradley's newspaper, the *Asbury Park Journal*—and possibly Bradley himself—to craft a blunt editorial titled "Too Many Colored People." They "are becoming a nuisance in Asbury Park," the paper declared. "We allow them to vote, to have full standing and protection in the law . . . but when it comes to social intermingling, then we object most seriously and emphatically."

It was not a toothless complaint—Bradley had already forbidden black people from using the boardwalk or pavilion between 7:00 a.m.

and 10:00 p.m., a near-total ban, and he could impose similar limits on access to the beach if he wished. The reluctance of most whites to mingle with blacks was a simple truism in the South, if not in the presumably more enlightened northern states, such as New Jersey. But Bradley's angry editorial, the *New York Post* observed, revealed that the reality of segregation "is also true to some extent in the North."

With the editorial, Bradley drew a stark color line in Asbury Park. It was as if, in his battle against all the evils that might befall his seaside idyll, what he deemed the "impudence" of blacks was just another evil for him to combat. Equal rights for all, Bradley believed, was a practical impossibility. As long as that was true, he would not allow Asbury Park to become an experiment in integration.

The *Journal* editorial, however, roused the black population. Its harshness "irritates every negro stepping in the borough," the *New York Times* reported three days later. "Every drop of blood under a black skin smarts with indignation." Rev. John Francis Robinson, pastor of the African Methodist Church in Asbury Park, said in a speech that "we colored people fought for our liberty some years ago, and we do not propose to be denied it at this later date. We will not be dictated to in this manner by Mr. Bradley or any other man." Rev. A. J. Chambers, pastor of the Bethel Methodist Church and a traveling minister, marched into the office of the *Asbury Park Journal* and declared the charges in the editorial "uncalled for, unwarranted, un-Christian-like and cruel."

In the end, Asbury Park in the 1880s *did* become a kind of test case in integration, in that it forced whites and blacks to find a way to coexist in relatively close quarters.

James Bradley, holder of all the legal power, won most of the battles, but not all of them. He eventually permitted black workers full access to their own stretch of beach—albeit the section nearest the pipe spewing sewage into the ocean. The editorials and sermons subsided, then flared up again. Ground was gained and lost. Bradley even came to call himself "a friend" of the black race, and explained away his segregationist efforts as necessary to protecting "the vast amounts of capital" invested in Asbury Park.

It was only in his later years that Bradley, in trying to shape the foundational myth of Asbury Park, began to share the story of his old friend, John Baker, who had long since left his employ and moved away from New Jersey. Though Baker's characterization of their relationship was never recorded, Bradley wrote fondly of their pivotal night in the cleansing surf—ironically, the very first full and peaceful integration of the sands on his hallowed property.

That the spirit of that moment had been so thoroughly lost in Asbury Park did not seem to dawn on Bradley, or at least not to trouble him. Perhaps he didn't realize that he could no more keep every evil out of his town than he could hope to calm the waves that frightened him.

*

Around the time Bradley was grappling with racial strife in his wonderland, an evil far worse than any he had ever encountered visited a small town just seven miles north of Asbury Park. It happened in Eatontown, a borough west of Long Branch, on March 5, 1886.

Earlier that day, a blond, twenty-two-year-old woman named Anna Herbert walked home by herself through the woods. Someone snuck up from behind and struck her with a club on the left side of her head. She struggled with her attacker, but he was bigger and choked her to unconsciousness. When she came to, she staggered to a neighbor's house and gave the name of the man who attacked her—a sixty-six-year-old black stable hand named Samuel Johnson, better known as Mingo Jack.

A constable was summoned, and Mingo Jack was arrested while eating dinner in the home he shared with his wife and twenty-two-year-old daughter, Angeline, in a marshland called Hog Swamp. Asked about Anna Herbert, Mingo Jack denied knowing anything about her. The constable took him in anyway, and put him in one of the two cells in a small brick prison house by the banks of a frozen pond, across from the Eaton Mill. Word of the assault spread quickly, and within an hour an angry crowd surrounded the prison. Police managed to disperse it, and at 10:00 p.m. the warden left Mingo Jack unattended in his locked cell, alone in the prison.

Sometime around midnight, the prisoner heard a gunshot and crashing glass. Someone had shot out the window above the wooden prison door. Then, more gunshots and more breaking glass, and the thudding sounds of a sledgehammer, stolen from a nearby marble cutter's shop, bashing the prison's brick wall. When the wall held, Mingo Jack heard the wrenching sound of a pickax prying open the double-thick wooden door. He knew full well what was happening. He knew he was trapped. He screamed out in the night:

"Murder! Murder!"

The door fell away. Men rushed in and pulled Mingo from his cell. He struggled hard, but the men beat him so badly they cracked his skull and gouged out one of his eyes. The floor was drenched with his blood.

The next morning, a young black boy on his way to trap muskrats saw the bullet-torn body hanging from a thick rope tied to the prison transom bar. The boy ran into town crying, "Mingo Jack is dead!"

At a coroner's inquest in the town's broad hall, witnesses sat on a piano stool and told what they knew. The final verdict was vague. "We find that Samuel Johnson was willfully murdered . . . by being beaten upon the head by clubs and by hanging by the neck," it read. "Said beating and hanging having been done by some person or persons to the jury unknown." Most in Eatontown knew the names of the men who had been at the jail that night: they were the fathers and brothers and sons who walked among them, some of them prominent men. But no one ever served any time for the lynching.

At the African Church in Eatontown, Rev. John Hammett read a sermon over the body of Mingo Jack. He chose a scripture from Matthew: "We must all die, and after this the Judgment." Mingo's body was buried in a pauper's plot in the South Eatontown Cemetery. Newspaper accounts called him a "bad character" and a "dangerous and desperate man." Many said the town was better off without him. At least two other men would, in later years, confess to the rape and beating of Anna Herbert. Most likely, Mingo Jack was innocent of the crime.

He was the first black man ever lynched in the northern state of New Jersey.

*

Just seven miles away, in Asbury Park, the lynching had little impact. James Bradley relentlessly kept up the façade of innocent splendor he wished so desperately for his city. There wasn't a dispute or distraction, he believed, or even a lynching, that couldn't be drowned out by the shrill jangle of some shiny new attraction.

No event in Asbury Park better reflected this philosophy than the lavish parade Bradley dreamed up and launched in 1890, four years after the Mingo Jack killing. He called it the Baby Parade.

It was a simple idea. Mothers pushed their infants and toddlers in decorated wagons and carriages single file along the boardwalk, led by a marching brass band. And that was it. Bradley saw it as a patriotic celebration of motherhood, as well as an emblem of the wholesomeness of Asbury Park. He persuaded two hundred mothers and nurses to participate in the first parade, held on a hot July afternoon. Some fifteen thousand people lined up to cheer them on.

Bradley's instinct paid off, and within a few years the Baby Parade was an extravaganza, drawing national coverage, hundreds of participants, and many tens of thousands of spectators. Judges awarded prizes to the most elaborately festooned floats and carriages, and the parade became part of a weeklong, family-focused carnival. In 1910, the twentieth anniversary of the parade, special trains from New York, Philadelphia, and Trenton brought in more than one hundred thousand spectators.

The 1910 Baby Parade, twice postponed by bad weather, still

became the biggest single event in the short history of Asbury Park. "Midget Marchers Present Magnificent Pageant," boasted the *Asbury Park Press*, which devoted several full broadsheets to their coverage. Public buildings were covered with flags and bunting; trolley cars and automobiles stalled in the heavy traffic. At 3:00 p.m., Arthur Pryor, dressed in white, led his band in their signature song, "Jersey Shore," to start the procession. All kinds of toddlers were on display: "fat babies and lean babies; babies with tow hair and red-headed tots; consummate little actresses, diminutive bosses," the *Press* described. A panel of dignitaries judged the costumes and carriages for originality and spectacle.

The top winner was two-year-old Ruth Klatenbach. In an exhibit her mother titled "Our Jewel," little Ruth was displayed as "the Tiffany setting of a huge diamond ring," according to the *Press*. "The ring was mounted in a huge box, with an open purple plush lid and white silk lining," while Ruth's small body "was squeezed within the pronged forks of the ring." The judges awarded her the grand Gold Trophy prize—five hundred dollars provided by the Eskay Food Company.

It would have been, by all accounts, the most successful Baby Parade ever—James Bradley's crowning achievement—had it not been for a shocking and gruesome incident that marred the proceeding.

That morning, a thin, sharp-jawed man, Dewitt Moore, traveled from Newark with a friend to watch the parade.

Moore and his friend pushed aggressively through the crowds, using profanity and subjecting women "to improper embraces," the *Press* reported. A bystander, Herald Smith—a young photographer who lived in town—was at the parade with his business partner, Earle Williamson, and his sister Mabel. As babies and children in floats rolled by, Smith and Williamson noticed the commotion and confronted the unruly men.

At first, there was only yelling and fist-waving. Then a roar went up from the crowd for an especially festive float. For just an instant, Herald Smith turned to see what the crowd was cheering for.

And in that instant, Dewitt Moore took out a small folding knife and pushed it into Smith's back just below the shoulder.

Before Smith could even turn around, Moore stabbed him again, sticking the knife just below his ear and dragging it downward. Smith cried out and was stabbed again, a vicious swipe to his left arm that tore open an artery. A fourth thrust nearly cut off two of Smith's fingers.

Before Moore was done, he had stabbed Smith seven times.

As Moore made his escape, Smith, dazed and bleeding, staggered out of the crowd and into the parade route, crying in pain and panic.

Some mothers saw the blood streaming from his head and spurting from his arm and he fell to the ground in full feint. Others pulled their babies out of their wagons and hurried away. Screaming children called out for their parents and ran blindly into the crowd to flee the bloodied creature stumbling toward them. The band stopped playing and the parade was halted as police officers scrambled through the throng.

Herald Smith was rushed to his nearby house and tended to by Dr. George Potts. He survived the attack. Dewitt Moore was stopped from escaping by a burly eighteen-year-old Native American named Clarence Tahamout, and quickly arrested. After a short break, the parade resumed, at least for those mothers and babies who were not too shaken to continue. The crowd trampled away most of the blood that remained.

There, in one grisly incident, lay the inexorable tension between James Bradley's dream and the reality of his playground—the battle between good and evil, between the wholesome and the carnal. The battle that never ends and cannot be won, only waged.

Bradley hoped for Asbury Park to be a promise of goodness and godliness. Instead, it became a promise of indulgence and satiation—a place where pure and impure instincts could not be separated.

Asbury Park, after all, was not a real city, so much as it was an illusion of community, forced and transparent, built on myth, and ultimately no more or less moral than any other human meeting ground.

Bradley had always been wrong to believe he could manage the behavior of his hordes with posted signs and printed rules—the sheer humanity that flocked to his shore was never his to control. So it was that his dream of purity became like the brass ring that hung forever out of reach of the gleeful riders on his glorious carousel.

"Oh, what people of God we ought to be!" Bradley's idol Francis Asbury once said, as if to Bradley himself. "And grace can make us so!"

But what grace was there to be found in the bloody boardwalk stabbing of an innocent, virtuous man, or, just two months later, the disappearance of the young schoolgirl Marie Smith?

CHAPTER 5

The Wanamassa

*

November 1910
Asbury Park, New Jersey

On the morning of November 12, uniformed soldiers from the New
Jersey National Guard—among them expert horsemen from the
elite cavalry Essex Troop—marched into Asbury Park.

By then, Marie Smith had been missing for three days. The Guardsmen re-canvassed the woods near Deal Lake, inching through the slog
alongside ten- and eleven-year-old boys recruited from the Bradley
School to beef up the ranks of the searchers. The boys quit the hunt at
nightfall. The Guardsmen kept going through daybreak.

"If the girl is anywhere within a twenty-mile radius of Asbury Park,"
a town official said, "she ought to be found within twenty-four hours."

Investigators had three theories of what might have happened—
kidnapping, accidental death, and murder. The first theory made little
sense. Marie's parents were far from wealthy. Who would believe they
could extract any significant amount of money from them? Beyond a
ransom, any other motive for a kidnapping was too heinous for authorities to publicly discuss.

The second theory, that Marie had been murdered, suffered from a
lack of any evidence of an attack or struggle. The same was true of an
accidental death. If Marie had been struck by a car, surely there would
have been some sign of it, a tire track, a spatter of blood. But there

wasn't. Nothing pointed to anything. The only early suspects were the wandering gypsies living in campgrounds in and around Asbury Park. They were European immigrants and nomads who set up temporary tent villages and isolated themselves from townspeople, resisting all assimilation and, often enough, surviving through theft and con games. The Guardsmen rooted through their camps and dug through tents looking for clues, but once again found nothing.

By the morning of Sunday, November 13—a full four days after Marie's disappearance—no evidence of any kind had turned up anywhere. In the stores and on the streets, the people of Asbury Park whispered the same sad question to each other.

"Has the girl been found?"

*

At noon that Sunday, William Stewart Benson walked into the Wanamassa woods.

A groundskeeper and landscaper, Benson, fifty-eight, owned a greenhouse and flower plant in Bradley Park, just north of Asbury Park. His fresh flower business was one of the best and most modern in New Jersey. Benson didn't look like the hard laborer he was—his narrow shoulders and small rimless glasses made him seem soft, and he had a guileless smile that hid his teeth. That morning, Benson delivered a flower arrangement to a client on Central Avenue in Asbury Park. After the delivery, he walked north on Central Avenue, turned left on Third Avenue, and headed to the woods.

He entered the Wanamassa on an unpaved drift road that ran through the forest—a shortcut to the stone bridge that would lead him back to his town. But Benson wasn't going home just yet.

He left the traverse road and walked among the trees for a reason. Benson was looking for something, and he knew that what he was looking for would not be found in the open. It would be hidden away.

He was after the two-hundred-dollar reward.

He chose a random direction and took one hundred fifty steps over a dense carpet of dead leaves and fallen branches. To his left he could see the deep gully that was used as a town dumping ground for cartloads of leaves, which just a week earlier had caught fire and been put out by the Enterprise Hose Company. The crackle of dry wood beneath his shoes and the croak of pond frogs may have been the only sounds he could hear. Benson was in a place now that was stripping itself of green, of life, leaving only the dark blacks and browns of dormancy.

Then—he saw it.

It was just a bundle of something.

"A huddled little heap of brown beneath a clump of leaf-stripped bushes," a newspaper later described.

Benson moved closer and the bundle took shape.

The heap of brown was a winter coat.

Benson saw a black shoe. A plaid skirt. The top of a face, the rest hidden by the coat.

Blood on the back of the head.

The florist ran from the woods. He hurried onto Third Avenue and looked for a policeman. He asked a passerby where the parents of Marie Smith lived, and after a few minutes he found the frame house on West Monroe Avenue. He knocked and went inside. Peter Smith was there, and his wife, Nora, and a police officer, William Truax. Benson swallowed hard and told them what he had come across in the Wanamassa.

"I found the child," he later said. "The hind parts were exposed, her skirts were pulled up, and the drawers were pulled down. I saw a wound on the back of the head."

Nora Smith staggered and nearly collapsed. Peter Smith ran from the house. Benson and Truax followed. After a sprint they came upon the child in the woods, just where Benson had found her. Peter Smith went to his daughter and knelt over her and pulled her dress down over her bare legs. It was a father's gesture. He stayed over her and let out a terrible moaning sound.

"Marie."

She was found on her right side, her arm pinned beneath her body, her right fist frozen in a clench. Her left hand was open, palm up, two inches off the ground. One leg was bent and her buttocks were exposed.

The gray skating cap that she wore when she left home four days earlier was wrapped around her throat. So was her blue satin hair ribbon.

Her skull had been caved in. She had also been sexually attacked.

Just a few inches from the child, a white handkerchief lay open on the dirt. Placed neatly on it, as if in ritual—the cheap, red plastic bracelet Marie slipped on her wrist the morning she disappeared.

Officer Truax called for a blanket to cover the girl. Word spread quickly, and townspeople melted into the woods and ringed the scene. Some, inexorably drawn to the morbid, tried to lift the blanket to better see the victim, but Officer Truax shooed them away. William Benson stood stiffly by and thought of his own children—one of them a daughter the same age as Marie.

The crowd parted as someone came through—a woman, too weak to walk on her own, held up by relatives. It was the girl's mother. Nora Smith had gone against all advice and insisted on being taken to the woods. She had to see for herself. The first thing she recognized was Marie's winter coat, and when she saw it, the person she had been dissolved, and what was left crumpled to the ground. She was led away, weeping, hysterical.

Not much later, Peter Smith finally got up from his daughter, and turned and walked through the ring of onlookers, slowly, as if in a trance, away from Marie and back to his wife, and whatever remained for them.

The unthinkable had happened. The worst fear was true. The world had taken something beautiful and broken it, horribly.

Marie Smith, the missing schoolgirl, had been murdered in the most godless way.

CHAPTER 6

Burn Scars

*

November 1910
Asbury Park, New Jersey

Special Officer William Truax, the first policeman at the scene, was no stranger to sin and vice in Asbury Park.

For years he'd done the dirty work of safeguarding its streets. He'd broken up gangs engaged in sneakthievery (shoplifting); wrestled a violent, demented landlady into a vegetable cart for a trip to the asylum; piloted a motorboat through the willow-shrouded coves of Deal Lake to root out "spooners"—young couples violating James Bradley's law against public shows of affection. William Truax trafficked along the rough underbelly of his town, and he knew it well. Still, he had never seen anything this disturbing before.

Truax had someone from the crowd of onlookers run into town to notify the Asbury Park chief of police, William H. Smith, of the grim discovery. He called for a blanket and covered the body. He stood sentry over it, trying to preserve some dignity for it.

At police headquarters on Mattison Avenue, one block from Main Street, Police Chief Smith called the town coroner, Robert M. Purdy, and ordered him to the woods. Smith then sped to the scene himself. He got there around the same time as Randolph Miller, Peter Smith's boss. Several more officers arrived and helped Smith and Truax keep the gawkers away from the body.

Coming up from the town of Manasquan, seven miles south, Robert Purdy made it to the scene around 2:00 p.m., two hours after Marie was found. The coroner knelt on the dirt, opened his satchel, and performed a quick examination of the body. It took only a few minutes. When he was done he signaled that he was ready to remove the body to the parlors of Fred E. Farry, the town funeral director, who worked out of an inelegant two-story building at 806 Main Street.

Within an hour, Marie's small body was laid on the cold cast-iron surface of Farry's long embalming table, above the big circular gears that managed the metal vacuum pumps.

*

At 4:00 p.m. two Asbury Park physicians, Joseph Ackerman and Earl Wagner—who offered coroner services for anywhere from fifteen to thirty-five dollars an exam—joined Purdy at Farry's parlor for the autopsy. Their task was to catalog the wounds and determine a cause of death. Forensically, it would not be complicated. They had seen all kinds of carnage. But this was a child on the table, still in school clothes. They might not want to see what had become of her, but it was their job to look. They had to know the next few minutes would change them.

The men got to work. They found a compound fracture at the back of the head roughly where the parietal and occipital bones articulate, slightly above the neck. The wound was three inches across and almost three inches deep, allowing blood and brain tissue to spill out. It suggested blunt force.

Marie "had been struck on the head probably with some heavy object," Ackerman later testified—possibly an ax or hatchet.

The forehead bulged above the left eye where blood had rushed and gathered while the body was on the ground.

Purdy had found a small pool of blood next to the body in the woods, an indication she had been murdered there. The child had bled, but she had not bled out. There were no injuries to her torso or limbs, beyond some scratches on the palms and wrists. The cause of death was apparent but not certain, in that there were *two* possible causes: the crushed skull, and the blue satin hair ribbon tied tightly around the neck—"tight enough," Ackerman said, "to cause strangulation."

Which came first, the blow or the strangling? The doctors couldn't say. The best they could do was conclude that the blow happened "just before or immediately after" strangulation. Both assaults were sufficient to have caused death. Ackerman would offer an opinion that Marie had died from strangulation. But he couldn't be certain.

The worst part of the autopsy remained. The doctors determined that the vagina was, in Ackerman's words, "standing open." On the embalming table, the doctors cut across Marie's stomach and opened the abdomen to look for a tear in the uterus or any other damage. They found none. They chose not to conduct a microscopic examination, because they didn't deem it necessary. That left a pressing question— what was the extent of the assault on Marie? Had she been raped?

"I wouldn't like to state that the girl had been raped," Ackerman later testified, "but the vagina had been entered."

A rape, the doctors concluded, would have caused more obvious damage. But there was no question that a sexual assault had occurred.

There was one small mercy, the doctors agreed. The sexual assault most likely took place after Marie was dead.

The examination also revealed two mysterious injuries—a dark discoloration on the bridge of Marie's nose, and another similar, smaller mark on the top of her left ear. The nearly black marks couldn't be removed or washed off. These, the doctors said, were burn scars.

Could they have been abrasions caused by dragging the child through the woods facedown? No, the doctors said. Friction alone wouldn't explain them. The scars were caused, Ackerman said, by "coming into contact with heat, direct heat." Not a flame, which would have singed the face and hair—some other heated body. What it was, they couldn't say.

The autopsy lasted thirty minutes. Ackerman and Wagner left the body to be sewn and dressed. At 4:30 p.m., Fred Farry arrived and took over for an assistant who had been reconstructing the skull. The assistant's work was sloppy, and Farry worked into the night preparing the corpse for her family.

CHAPTER 7

19½ Atkins Avenue

*

November 1910
Asbury Park, New Jersey

Tom Williams fell under suspicion almost from the start. Not by police, who had been on the case for only a few hours, but by a young reporter who got the jump on them: Alvin B. Cliver.

It happened that Cliver and his wife, Belva, lived across the street from the Bradley School, in a home at 1203 Third Avenue that Cliver built himself. Early on Thursday, November 10, Belva looked out her window and saw a desperate Nora Smith searching the faces of children in front of the school. Later that morning, she asked Nora to come in for hot coffee, and she listened to the story of Marie's disappearance. Alvin Cliver heard it, too, and set out to investigate.

Most of his life, Cliver had been more than he seemed. He was small and slender, just five feet and 115 pounds, yet he had strength and speed. Nicknamed "the Bantam," he ran for two touchdowns against a team of U.S. Marines playing his Oreo Athletic Club. He was good at basketball and tennis, too. As a cub reporter at the *Asbury Park Press* in 1901, covering the arrival of notables at hotels and summer homes, he became the first reporter in the paper's history to turn in typewritten copy, using a new, open-faced Munson typewriter with nickel-plated parts and a rubber striker that belonged to the publisher, J. Lyle Kinmonth, and that scared off the older beat writers.

That Thursday morning, after hearing Nora's story, Cliver walked the streets and roads of Asbury Park, asking people if they had seen the girl. One of the first men he talked to, at 8:30 a.m., was Tom Williams. He found him chopping wood at the house of Delia Jackson, Marie Smith's aunt.

Where were you yesterday morning? Cliver asked him.

Williams, according to Cliver, did not seem anxious to talk. But he gave his whereabouts anyway: he had been at the barroom at Griffin's in the morning, before leaving to finish painting a house in nearby Oakhurst. After that, he walked to Delia Jackson's Asbury Avenue home to resume chopping up a tree for her.

When did you get to Delia Jackson's house? Cliver asked.

Williams said he got there at quarter to noon.

What about the rest of the day?

Williams said he spent most of the day sitting on the front porch of Jackson's next-door neighbor, Mollie Williams, talking politics, and chopping the tree next door.

Cliver didn't believe him. Something about Black Diamond's story didn't seem right. He set out to do more digging.

*

Tom Williams knew the Smith family, and he knew Marie Smith.

After the Smiths were evicted from a home in Whitesville for not paying rent, they temporarily moved in with Delia Jackson in her home on Asbury Avenue. At that time, Tom Williams and another contractor, James Wright, were doing repair work on Jackson's home. Most days, Delia and Nora's children ran and frolicked outside the house as Williams did his work. "Marie was running around all the time, the same as my children were," Delia would say. This is how Williams came to know her.

Marie's mother, Nora, confirmed that her family was acquainted with Williams. "I would know him when he came into the yard," she said. "He would say, 'Good morning,' and I would answer back." Her three children came to be familiar with Williams, too. "They were friendly," Nora said. "Marie knew him."

In fact, Nora Smith was friendly enough with Williams to ask him to buy beer for her, which, apparently, he did. When Peter Smith found out about it, he sternly let Williams know not to do it again. That, in the eyes of some, amounted to a history between Williams and the Smiths. And the fact that Marie knew Williams suggested he could have more easily coaxed her to go with him than a stranger could have. Alvin Cliver had learned of this connection, and his suspicions about Williams were growing.

Yet Marie's parents had no reason to believe Williams was involved. On Friday, November 11—with Marie missing for two days now—Peter Smith ran into Williams on the street and asked for his help searching a dumping ground off Springwood Avenue that evening. Williams agreed to go. Just a few hours later, Peter Smith got a tip that Marie had been spotted near the lake not far from Griffin's barroom. He found Williams and changed their plan.

"Diamond, I ain't going with you, can you go alone?" he said.

"All right," Williams said, "I'll go alone."

The Ayers tip turned out to be nothing. The next morning, Friday November 11, Peter Smith went looking for Williams to learn about his search of the dumping ground. He couldn't find him. Neither could Alvin Cliver, who had more questions for him. Cliver went to the police with his suspicions, and Chief Smith put an officer on Williams's trail. The officer couldn't find him, either. Police asked Peter Smith if he knew where Williams lived. He said he didn't. No one did. Williams just came and went, and it hadn't matter to anyone where he went when he left.

Now, it mattered.

While the search for Marie Smith continued, nearly three full days after she vanished, a new search, for Tom Williams, began.

That no one could find him only increased suspicions about him. Word spread that he was missing, and that brought out two new witnesses. They were John C. Conover and William Taylor, who told police they were sitting on an embankment on Ridge Avenue the morning of November 9. They remembered seeing Tom Williams leave Griffin's barroom at about 10:30 a.m., and head in a direction that could have taken him to the very street corner where Marie Smith was spotted by Emma Davison, the last known person to see Marie alive.

Conover and Taylor put Williams in the area of Marie's disappearance, at precisely the time she disappeared.

Now it was imperative for police to find him. Friday, November 11, passed with no sighting of Williams, and the next day was no different. Black Diamond hadn't been seen in more than two days.

One day later, on Sunday, William Benson made his awful discovery in the woods.

That same evening, it was Alvin Cliver who finally tracked down Williams.

Cliver didn't reveal how he found him; instead, he decided to bring Williams in himself. The reporter in him wouldn't allow for turning the tip over to police and losing the scoop. Cliver telephoned a detective he knew, David Hankinson, and Hankinson called Randolph Miller, who owned the Flavel rendering plant where Marie's father, Peter, worked. Miller agreed to drive them to the location.

Randolph Miller was playing a large role in the Marie Smith case. Fit and trim and tireless, he was one of the most influential businessmen in town. Besides owning the Flavel plant, he was a director of the Seacoast National Bank, the most important financial institution in Asbury Park. When Marie disappeared, Miller immediately gave Peter Smith time off with pay, and spent countless hours personally searching for her and making phone calls to neighboring police departments, asking for reinforcements and search dogs.

"I have a little girl of my own, about the same age as little Marie," he later explained. "I am eager to bring the guilty man to justice."

With Cliver's tip, here was his chance.

*

On Sunday night, Cliver and Hankinson climbed into Miller's sleek gray Packard. They picked up Peter Smith, who insisted on going along. The four men drove into the part of town known as "the colored colony," on the western outskirts of Asbury Park. Cliver steered them to an address—a boardinghouse at 19½ Atkins Avenue. Miller pulled the Packard in front of a house that looked to be coming apart at the hinges. Peter Smith waited by the car while the other men headed into the home.

Inside, it was dark. There was no one in the front, no sign anyone was there at all. In a back room, they saw a man—a black man. When he stood up, they could tell it wasn't Tom Williams. His name was William Wynn, and he was much older than Williams. The old man pointed down the hall, toward the rear of the home. The men made their way into the deepest part of the house.

Finally, they came to another small room. A man lay on an old couch in the dark, half dressed, half asleep. He saw the men and grumbled about the pain in his back. Here was Tom Williams.

The detective got him up, handcuffed him, and marched him out of the house. When Williams spotted Peter Smith out front, he said, incongruously, "Hey, Pete, how's your health?"

"Hello, Diamond," Smith said. "What are you doing here?"

Before they took Williams to police headquarters, the men searched the dilapidated house. Inside a barrel, near where they got Williams, they found a shirt, underdrawers, and a pair of overalls.

The shirt had stains on it that looked like blood.

They also found a towel and a blanket stuffed inside the barrel. These items, too, appeared to be stained with blood.

Evidence.

Then the short drive across town to the police station on Mattison Avenue, Tom Williams in his handcuffs, Peter Smith still numb with shock, Alvin Cliver already crafting a dispatch in his head, and the rough wheels turning, the process of justice begun.

CHAPTER 8

Came the Men

*

November 1910
Asbury Park, New Jersey

The Asbury Park Police Department had its headquarters in a two-story building, topped by a striking bell tower, on Mattison Avenue, just east of the railroad depot, and it shared space with the Independence Hook and Ladder Company. There were jail cells on the second floor, and another lockup in the basement.

Detective Hankinson brought Tom Williams in on the night of Sunday, November 13, and turned him over to William Smith, the chief of police. Smith took Williams to the second floor and put him in a cell isolated from the others. There Williams was informally arraigned and ordered held without bail. Smith asked him to give up his suspenders, and Williams balked. He promised he wouldn't use them to hang himself in the cell. Smith took them anyway, and left Williams with a small coil of rope to wrap around his waist to keep his pants up.

There were stains on the suspenders, too; they would have to be tested for blood.

By then Chief Smith had been running law enforcement in Asbury Park for several years, and he was controversial. He cut a modest figure, with clipped eyebrows dwarfed by a deep mustache, and big ears that made him seem boyish. He often wore a Gendarmerie-style, box-topped police hat and a silver-finished, solid copper police badge with an eagle sentry on it. Smith took pride in the low number of arrests made by his department, which he took as a sign that his enhanced police tactics were working. In 1903, there were a record-low ninety-nine arrests in Asbury Park, and the next year, only 102—including nineteen for drunkenness, seven for grand larceny, two for fast driving, and two for "peeping." One year, Smith boasted of not having had to arrest a single burglar or pickpocket.

In fact, many wondered if Smith had grown too close to the criminal element. In 1905, he was accused of running protection for bookmakers and partaking in gambling himself. He was known to play poker in the back of Doc McBride's drugstore, and a slip with his name on it proved he'd laid bets with a bookie named George Vunck. The six-member City Council convened a vote and debated for hours, into the night, before deadlocking on Smith's fate. It wasn't the majority acquittal he was hoping for, but at least it meant he got to keep his job.

Now, Police Chief Smith would be the first law officer to formally interrogate Tom Williams. He began by creating a timeline.

"On Wednesday morning, what time did you get up?" Smith asked.

"About six-thirty o'clock," Williams said.

"After you got up, what did you do?"

"I went out to Bill Brower's place."

"And after that?" Smith asked.

"I went to Bill Griffin's about seven-thirty o'clock."

"Who did you see at Griffin's?"

"Well, I saw the bartender, who they call John the Cripple."

"How many drinks did you have?"

"Well, I don't just remember how many I had."

Smith kept pushing, and Williams admitted to having four or five shots of whiskey and gin.

"How long did you stay at Griffin's?"

"I stayed there until about eight-thirty o'clock."

Williams offered this further account of his morning—at 9:00 a.m. he left Griffin's barroom and went downtown to buy a newspaper at the railroad depot. He got back to Griffin's about 9:30 a.m. He said he stayed at Griffin's until roughly 11:45 a.m., when he left and walked over the bridge near Griffin's to Brickyard Road, in search of an old jug he had seen in the woods on an earlier scavenge. He wanted the jug to fill up with oil for his house-painting job in Oakhurst. He took the jug to Mollie Williams's home, next door to Delia Jackson.

"I was there from about twelve o'clock to nearly sundown and I didn't leave the place during that time," he told Smith. "When I left, it was getting dark."

After that, Williams said, he stopped by Stolze's butcher shop and bought hamburger steak and hog liver, and then to a grocery for a loaf of bread. He went to the house of 19½ Atkins Avenue and sent William Wynn to buy them six bottles of beer. And that, he swore, was his day.

Smith asked Williams if he had seen anyone on his walk from Griffin's to Mollie Williams's house.

"Yes, I saw two men setting on the south side of the bridge," he said. "I spoke to one of them and I said, 'Well, are you taking a sun bath?' And they said yes, and we sort of laughed, and I went on."

These were the two men, Conover and Taylor, who told police they remembered seeing Williams leave the barroom at 10:30 a.m. and not around noon, as Williams claimed.

That was crucial. Marie Smith was last seen at 10:30 a.m., and police believed she was taken sometime between then and 12:30 p.m. If Conover and Taylor were to be believed, Williams was lying about when he left Griffin's—which meant there was a ninety-minute gap in his timeline. A gap corresponding to the time of Marie's disappearance.

Smith pushed Williams on one other point. On November 8, 1910, the day before Marie disappeared, there was an election for governor of New Jersey. The Democrat, Woodrow Wilson, defeated Republican Vivian Lewis by roughly 50,000 votes out of more than 433,000 votes cast. Williams admitted to Chief Smith that he spent much of the following day discussing the election with patrons at Griffin's and with Mollie Williams. Smith asked Williams if he himself had voted.

"No, I didn't," Williams said.

"Are you a registered voter?"

"No, sir."

By then, Chief Smith knew that Williams had boasted to Mollie Williams of voting in the election. As a felon, Williams was flatly prohibited from voting. Here was a discrepancy, perhaps a lie, and possibly a criminal offense. Smith concluded his interview without once bringing up the murder of Marie Smith. He knew there would be many further interrogations, and plenty of time to grill Williams about it.

*

Chief Smith sent an officer to Delia Jackson's home to find the ax Tom Williams used to chop up her tree for kindling. The coroners said an ax might have been used to kill Marie Smith, and if Williams was guilty, the ax could be the murder weapon. Police found it on the ground outside Delia's home, but she insisted she had used it twice the Wednesday morning in question, first to cut wood chips for a fire, then to split a board. Williams didn't arrive at her home until after noon that day. The ax couldn't be the murder weapon.

Still, there were problems with Williams's statement. Police tracked down John F. Carlton—John the Cripple, the bartender who had seen Williams at Griffin's Wednesday morning. Carlton confirmed that Williams was there early, and left to buy newspapers. But, Carlton said, "Williams returned with two papers shortly after 10:00 a.m. and immediately left, going out the back door." That bolstered the testimony of Conover and Taylor, who saw Williams leave Griffin's sometime between 10:00 a.m. and 10:30 a.m. that morning. Williams's assertion that he was at Griffin's until 11:45 a.m. was, police believed, simply false.

Early on Monday, November 14, 1910, the morning after Williams's arrest, Alvin Cliver—who had good sources in the police department—

forcefully stated the case against Williams in his article in the *Asbury Park Press*, starting with the large-type headline.

NEGRO IS PLACED AT SCENE
AT THE TIME OF BRUTAL MURDER

"Strong evidence is hourly being produced to show that Williams is the man who committed the crime, one of the most brutal and dastardly ever committed in the state," Cliver wrote. He referenced Williams's interview with Chief Smith and concluded, "the Police and a press reporter have found it to be radically incorrect in many instances." He stressed that Williams knew Marie, and she knew him: "Naturally, if the negro had beckoned to her she would have gone to him. Possibly she would have followed him into the woods without suspecting anything wrong."

Now the people of Asbury Park, riled by the crime and demanding information, had themselves a suspect, and a good one. It was there in black and white in the *Press*. What's more, they knew where they could find him. He was among them. He was right there in the jail.

That night it began to rain, a cold rain, and soon it turned into sleet and snow. Word of Williams's arrest spread all through Asbury Park, and through surrounding towns—Long Branch, Ocean Grove, Eatontown.

From these places came the men.

Many were fathers who brought along their eldest sons. Some were grandfathers, too old for this sort of business but not about to miss it.

Some of the men took their longest ropes and fixed them in coils around their belts.

Another group gathered in Whitesville, the area just west of Asbury Park where Marie Smith had lived. Around 9:00 p.m., they marched in the direction of the ocean. On the way, they passed the store of R. E. K. Rothfritz, a stonemason who dealt coal, wood, lime, and cement. One of the marchers, William Davison, broke open the front door and led the others inside. They came out with an arsenal—a twenty-pound sledgehammer, a long pinch bar, a steel crowbar, an ax, an iron roller.

The men took their tools and merged with the other marchers on Mattison Avenue, beneath the bell tower. There were hundreds of them now, packing into the narrow street, drenched by the rain and sleet. They made no secret of their purpose.

"Diamond will never leave this town alive!" yelled one.

"Lynch him!"

"Mingo Jack! Mingo Jack!"

This was a reference to the 1886 lynching of the black stable hand accused of attacking a white woman in Eatontown, seven miles north—still the only lynching in the state at that time. Some of the men on Mattison Avenue bragged of having been there, in Eatontown, among the hangmen, more than a quarter century earlier.

Now, here they were again.

A few of the men dragged logs and fence posts across the roads leading out of Asbury Park, then waited in the woods with rifles, in case police tried to spirit Tom Williams away. Outside the police station, the mob grew and stirred and tightened. Chants echoed—"Shoot him, lynch him, let us at him," loud enough for the prisoner to hear.

Iron bars, hatchets, files, guns, waving in the night.

Now a surge, and the latticed wood door leading to the police station tearing away.

Now a push, and the men flooding into the jail, bound by determination to reach Tom Williams's cell.

CHAPTER 9

The Cry of Humanity

*

September 1883
Memphis, Tennessee

A thousand miles southwest of Asbury Park—and long before Tom Williams ever lived there—a child was born a slave, and born in war.

The infant was given the sweet-sounding name Ida Bell Wells, and through history's long unfolding she would one day play a role in the case of Tom Williams—as well as in the shaping of her country and its ideals. In the words of preeminent Wells scholar and biographer Paula J. Giddings, Ida Wells would become "the reformer whose . . . progressive ideas became the foundation of the modern civil rights and women's rights movements."

Her life was a life of conflict. She was born in the northern Mississippi city of Holly Springs, on July 16, 1862, eighteen months after the start of the Civil War. Just five months later, Major General Ulysses S. Grant stationed thousands of Union troops in Wells's hometown, and filled a large depot there with more than a million dollars' worth of medical equipment, clothing, ordnance, and other crucial supplies. In the middle of the night on December 19, 1862, one of Grant's colonels, Robert C. Murphy, largely ignored a report from a black citizen of Holly Springs who swore he spotted Rebel forces in the area. Instead of rising to battle, the Union troops slept.

The next day, in a surprise attack, Confederate major general Earl Van Dorn and his troops stormed Holly Springs. They captured fifteen hundred unprepared Union soldiers, destroyed the supply depot, and laid waste to the town. Train tracks were uprooted, stores looted and razed. A new two-thousand-bed hospital and several other buildings were torched and burned to the ground. Holly Springs was left largely in ruins.

Two weeks later, on New Year's Day, 1863, President Abraham Lincoln put into effect an executive order—Proclamation 95—decreeing that some three and a half million African American slaves in the United States "shall be then, thenceforward and forever free."

One of the emancipated was the infant Ida Wells, who, technically, had been born enslaved. Her father, Jim, was a slave, and the son of a slave named Peggy. Jim's father was Morgan Wells, the white plantation owner in Tippah County, Mississippi, who owned his mother, Peggy.

Ida Wells's mother, Lizzie, was the teenaged slave of Spires Boling, a white home builder in Holly Springs. Lizzie prepared meals for Boling and became, in Ida's words, "a famous cook." Jim and Lizzie met when Jim—who'd been taught carpentry, and would become a master mason—was sent by his owner to Holly Springs to help build a new house there. They married first in bondage, and, after Lincoln's proclamation, married again, in 1869, as free persons.

Ida Wells was the first of their eight children (one of her brothers, Eddie, died not long after birth). A child of the deepest South, Wells grew up in a state, Mississippi, that lagged behind only South Carolina in seceding from the Union. A state that proclaimed, in its Declaration of Secession, "Our position is thoroughly identified with the institution of slavery—the greatest material interest of the world."

The concept of black people as property was so integral to the cotton-rich economy of Mississippi that its population included more black people than white people, making it one of only two states in the Union with a majority made up of the enslaved.

Yet Wells was also born in a time of new hope for black people in the South. The end of the Civil War created new paths to education, land ownership, and voting rights for them; indeed, Ida's father, Jim, bought his own plot of land for $130 in 1870, and built a three-room frame house on it for his growing family. The Freedmen's Aid Society, founded by a collection of churches in the North, helped build dozens of new schools in the South, including one in Holly Springs, on the very land where General Grant's men had camped a few years earlier. Ida Wells was schooled there, and her job as a youngster, she and her siblings were told, "was to learn all we could."

To be sure, some of the classes Ida and the forty other girls in her school were forced to take dealt with cooking, cleaning, and laundering. But Ida focused more on reading, and consumed books at a pace that impressed the adults around her. In the evenings she would read the newspapers aloud to her father and "an admiring group of his friends," she later wrote. She read them articles about the nascent Ku Klux Klan, not understanding who they were, only that there was "something fearful" about them.

In this way the Wells family struggled, grew, survived, and thrived in the new landscape of the South. Ida's mother, who had been severely whipped and beaten by her owners, was now learning to read alongside her children at school. Ida's father became a leader in the community, advocating for political awareness among his fellow blacks. The family worshipped at the new Asbury Baptist Church in Holly Springs, and listened to sermons on the spiritual value of piety and mercy.

This was all before the arrival of the terrible scourge.

*

In 1878, a steamboat deckhand, William Warren, arrived in Memphis from New Orleans on the steamer *Golden Crown*. Warren was sick but did not know it. As was custom, the steamer was temporarily quarantined to ensure no one on board was carrying a tropical disease that might have come up the Mississippi River from some southern port. But Warren broke the rules, snuck off the boat, and went into town.

In Memphis, at 212 Front Street, Kate Bionda and her husband owned a snack house where they cleaned and cooked fish and meats and served them to patrons in a back room. The eatery was popular among rivermen, and William Warren chose to go there. Not long after his visit, Warren began showing signs of a serious ailment—coughing, sweating, high fever, jaundiced skin. He was sent to a quarantine facility on President's Island, twelve miles away.

Within thirty hours, Warren was dead.

On the mainland, Kate Bionda fell ill, too. Her symptoms were similar to Warren's. Dr. E. Miles Willet examined her, and gave his grim diagnosis—Bionda had yellow fever, the dreaded, mosquito-borne virus that originated in West Africa and made its way to America aboard slave ships. Yellow fever was highly contagious, and often fatal. The Memphis health officer, Dr. John Erskine, ordered the closing of Bionda's restaurant and sealed off the area around it with fencing and rails. Men in face masks fumigated the building with carbonic acid and hydrated ferrous sulfate. They did the same to every neighboring building on Front Street. Police officers manned stations along the block to keep people away.

It was all too late.

Two days after Warren's visit, Kate Bionda, mother of two young children, died at 11:00 a.m. She was hastily buried at 4:00 p.m. the same day. She was the first known victim of yellow fever—or "Yellow Jack," as it was called—in Memphis that year. She would not be the last. The virus quickly spread through the city. Newspapers called it the Saffron Scourge.

Memphis had suffered earlier epidemics, and its residents knew the hell that was coming. If they could afford to flee, they did, hundreds a day, by wagon, carriage, cart, and trains "packed to suffocation," according to one account. Out of the city's 47,000 residents, more than 25,000 left in a frenzied exodus. Most of those who remained fell ill—17,000 out of 19,000.

Around them, their city ceased to function. Everywhere, the disease—retching, convulsions, delirium. Black vomit, so named because of digested blood. Faces warily searching faces for traces of imminent death. Schools and courthouses, suddenly infirmaries. Priests and nuns dying while tending to the sick; policemen collapsing on their posts. Fathers, mothers, friends, one by one, swallowed into comas.

As it happened, Ida Wells was not in Holly Springs that summer. Her parents had sent her for a long visit to the home of her grandmother Peggy in Tippah County, forty miles away. Wells was sixteen and stayed with Peggy on her farm, most likely helping with chores, for most of the run of the epidemic. Through word of mouth, she heard about the outbreak in her hometown, and she assumed her family had also left Holly Springs to stay with an aunt in the country, out of harm's way.

She was wrong. Ida's parents remained in Holly Springs with the rest of their children. For most, fear was greater than pity, but not for Ida's father, Jim Wells. He stayed behind and busied himself with helping the least fortunate, bringing food to the dying and building coffins for the dead. For Jim and a small band of other young men who chose to stay, "the cry of humanity was like a bugle call to action," one eyewitness, Mrs. John M. Craig, later wrote. Jim Wells surely knew that, historically, yellow fever was far more deadly for white people than for blacks, for reasons not yet known. Some even believed black people were immune to it. Indeed, through the first weeks of the epidemic, no one in the Wells family fell ill.

Even so, it was a highly perilous time. The hometown that only sixteen years earlier had been nearly obliterated by Confederate troops was now utterly ravaged by disease and death, with bodies by the dozens being dragged out of homes and tumbled into shallow graves, and their clothing and bedding burned in great bonfires on the streets. "There were no sounds of lamentation, for grief was beyond expression in voice or tears," the eyewitness Mrs. Craig wrote. "No tolling bells announced the lonely, unattended funerals, and a settled gloom seemed to have fallen upon every heart."

One September day in Tippah County, two months into the outbreak, Ida Wells felt the rumble of approaching horses outside her grandmother's farmhouse. She ran to the door and recognized the three men dismounting their rides—they were her family's next-door neighbors in Holly Springs.

Excitedly, she led them in and asked if they had any news about her town. She was homesick and hadn't seen her family in weeks. One of the men said he did, and handed Ida a long letter.

She sat down to read the letter, but never got past the first page.

The letter contained news of the epidemic. It included the names of victims. One passage stopped Ida cold.

"Jim and Lizzie Wells have both died of the fever," it read. "They died within twenty-four hours of each other."

CHAPTER 10

Gather My Race in My Arms

*

September 1883
Memphis, Tennessee

The news that her parents were dead, delivered so starkly, had profound consequences for Ida Wells. Out of necessity, the orphaned Wells children would have to be separated, divided up among whoever might take them—one here, two there, however pity determined. Her family would be dissolved and scattered. Wells wanted to return to Holly Springs immediately to be with her siblings, but she was told the risk was too great—more than five thousand of those who remained in Memphis died of the scourge, along with fifteen thousand more victims across eight states. It was safer and smarter, Wells was told, to send a letter instead.

But as she prepared the letter, "the conviction grew within me that I ought to be with them," Wells later wrote. Ignoring the warnings, Wells boarded the next train out of Tippah County, and to Holly Springs.

Passenger cars were no longer running in or out of infected cities, so Wells rode in the caboose of a freight train. The interior of the car was draped in black bunting in honor of two conductors who had just died of yellow fever. On board the train, the replacement conductor saw the teenaged Wells—his only passenger—and told her she was foolish to be returning to Holly Springs, where her infection and death were all but assured. Wells asked him why he was operating the same train that had seen two prior conductors felled.

"Somebody has to do it," he replied.

"That's exactly why I'm going home," Wells said. "I am the oldest of seven children. There's nobody but me to look after them now. Don't you think I should do my duty, too?"

The conductor shrugged and walked away.

In Holly Springs, Wells found six siblings, not seven. The baby, Stanley, had caught the fever and died. Within a few days, members of the Masonic brotherhood, to which her father had belonged, assembled in the Wells home to divide the children.

Two Masons laid a claim to each of Wells's brothers, James and George, believing they could be trained into master carpenters like their father. Wells's sisters, five-year-old Annie and two-year-old Lily, would go to the wives of Masons who desired little girls to raise.

Wells's other sister, Eugenia, who was crippled and bent at the waist, went unclaimed, dooming her to the poorhouse. "The unanimous decision among the Masonic brothers," Wells would write, "was that I was old enough to fend for myself."

According to Wells's telling of the story, as this clinical dividing of her family took place, she sat in a corner of the room and stayed perfectly silent. But as soon as it was over, she rose from her chair.

"I calmly announced that they were not going to put any of the children anywhere," she wrote.

Instead, Wells declared, she would keep the children with her.

The Masons scoffed—how could a sixteen-year-old possibly raise a family of six by herself? Wells, however, had a plan. The house belonged outright to her and her siblings, and their father, Jim, had left them three hundred dollars in the care of a friend—enough to survive until Wells found a way to support the family herself. They would be just fine, Wells assured the Masons, so long as someone could help her find work.

A Masonic brother advised her to take the test to be a schoolteacher, which she promptly did. She found a teaching job at a school six miles away, for twenty-five dollars a month. She got there by mule and stayed the week in a rented room near the school while one of her mother's old friends minded the children in Holly Springs. On weekends, Wells came home to do the cooking, cleaning, and laundering.

What was left of the Wells family stayed a family, and got by.

*

After one term at the country school, Wells found a better-paying teaching position across the border in Tennessee, in the Shelby County town of Woodstock. Getting to her new public school meant a trip aboard a Chesapeake, Ohio & Southwestern train along an old Appalachian coal-hauling route.

One summer day in 1883, when Wells was just twenty-one, she arrived at the Poplar Street Train Depot in Memphis, Tennessee. Wearing a linen duster coat and carrying a parasol, Wells passed thirty cents through a window to the station teller. The teller handed her a first-class ticket printed: *One Continuous Trip, Memphis to Woodstock*. Wells boarded the train and found a seat in the last of three passenger cars. She was the only black person in the car.

She had just started working at her new job in Woodstock, ten miles north of Memphis. The position paid her thirty dollars a month, at a time when most black women in the South earned far less working as maids and helpers. Her previous teaching job had been at a small country schoolhouse outside her hometown of Holly Springs, Mississippi, near the Tennessee border, and the only way for her to get to the schoolhouse was to climb on a mule and ride six miles each way over barely passable roads. Her first-class train ride to Woodstock would be a big step up.

Wells was a short woman with high cheekbones and sharp, pretty features. "She is rather girlish-looking in physique," one colleague would later write, "with penetrating eyes, firm set lips and a sweet voice." Her expression, however, tended to be severe. Those who knew her knew she could be rough-edged, and in photographs she rarely seemed to make much effort to smile. That had not always been the case—when she was young she'd been a "happy, light-hearted schoolgirl," Wells would later write. But that had changed. Events had hardened her.

Just after 4:00 p.m., the steam whistle sounded and the Covington train jolted backward, then forward. The conductor, William Murray, began his walk down the aisles, collecting tickets. The first station stop, in the town of Frazier, was only a short distance away, and the train slowed down to give Murray enough time to finish taking fares.

The train was idling on a 1,200-foot-long trestle bridge over the Wolf River, just outside Frazier, when Murray reached Ida Wells. He looked at her, and at her first-class ticket. He saw that she was a black woman sitting in a car reserved for whites.

"I cannot accept this in this car," he told her.

Murray left to collect other tickets, and Wells went back to reading the newspaper she had bought at the Polar Street station. A few minutes later, as the train pulled into Frazier, Murray was back.

"You're in the wrong car," he told Wells. "You'll have to go to the coach in front."

"I have a seat and I intend to keep it," Wells said.

"I will treat you like a lady, but you have to go to the front car."

"If you wish to treat me like a lady, you will leave me alone."

Murray grabbed the satchel, travel bag, and parasol Wells had placed in the seat next to hers and walked them into the front car. Then he returned for her. He told her he had a seat waiting for her in the front, and once again asked her to come with him.

"I am in the ladies' car, and I propose to stay here," Wells replied.

That was it. Murray put his hands on Wells. "I took hold of her and tried to lift and carry her," he explained.

He was met with surprising strength and resolve, summoned from a place far deeper than he could have known. Wells held tightly to her seat, and braced her feet beneath the seat in front of her. Murray kept pulling, but Wells would not be lifted.

It was then, she later said, that "I fastened my teeth in the back of his hand."

Murray was bleeding now. Two white passengers in the seats in front of Wells stood up and pulled their seatbacks forward, so Wells could no longer hold on to them. Two more white passengers helped Murray wrestle Wells out of her seat. Together they lifted Wells in the air and carried her out of the train car as she thrashed and resisted. The sleeve of her linen coat ripped and nearly tore away. Some passengers cheered.

"I used no more force than necessary and I got the worst of it," Murray later insisted.

The men finally set Wells down on a platform in between train cars. Still, Wells refused to go where they wanted her to go. Rather than ride in the forward car—where, she claimed, men were drinking and smoking—Wells took her bags and got off the train in Frazier. She stood at the station and watched the train rattle away down the tracks.

It was the end of the incident, but not the end of the story. In the days that followed, Wells hired Thomas Cassels, a black attorney, and filed a lawsuit against the Chesapeake, Ohio & Southwestern Railroad. She asked for one thousand dollars in damages. Her case reached the highest court in the state of Tennessee.

Barely out of her teens, Ida Bell Wells was about to take on an American industry.

*

Wells's lawyer, Thomas Cassels, a Shelby County assemblyman, filed the suit in November 1883, two months after Wells was dragged from the train. On November 30, the Shelby County sheriff, W. D. Cannon, served a summons on J. W. Graham, the railway's senior representative in the county. Depositions in the case were heard in January 1884.

That November, the trial was held in the Shelby County Court House, an ornate three-story former hotel that during the Civil War had served as a Confederate hospital. The Chesapeake Ohio, with no financial constraints, hired Holmes Cummins, a prominent West Tennessee attorney and an expert on parliamentary tactics, as their lead counsel.

It was a nonjury trial. The assigned judge, James O. Pierce, was a former Union infantryman from Wisconsin with a reputation for being fair and well read. On its face, the case seemed simple—Wells alleged that Chesapeake Ohio failed to give her what she paid for: transport aboard a first-class car. The ticket "entitled her to a seat in a first class coach of her own choosing," read her complaint. "It contained no stipulation or provisions reserving to said defendant or its agents the right to direct into what coach or car she should go, and did, after that she had taken her seat in a first class coach car."

Instead of honoring her ticket, Wells's lawyer claimed, Chesapeake Ohio "by its agents did unlawfully and forcefully lay violent hands on her and beat and mistreat and misuse her."

Holmes Cummins argued that the railway "offered Wells seating in another first class car equal in every way to the one she was in." As for Wells's forcible ejection, the railway disavowed its own conductor, William Murray, and claimed it "could not be liable for such unlawful acts of persons who chance to be in its employ."

The case, therefore, hinged not on Wells's skin color, but on whether or not Chesapeake Ohio had offered her an alternate first-class coach car in which to travel. Technically, the trial was not about race.

And yet, like so much in postbellum America, it was.

Since the end of the Civil War, the process of securing civil rights for the millions of freed slaves had been haphazard. For every victory for black Americans, there was a setback or two, like rungs on a ladder being added and giving way. In 1875, Congress passed a Civil Rights Bill that awarded blacks the right to sue for discrimination in public accommodations, such as trains—a provision that opened the door for Wells's lawsuit. That same year, however, in response to the Civil Rights Bill, Tennessee legislators passed House Bill No. 527, which granted proprietors the right to refuse business to anyone "for any reason whatever"—a provision that included railroad companies. Another statute in 1881 required the railways to furnish separate but equal train cars "for colored passengers who pay first-class rates," establishing a legal basis for segregation.

And in October 1883, four months after Wells was pulled from the Chesapeake Ohio coach car, the U.S. Supreme Court, in an eight-to-one ruling, repealed the 1875 Civil Rights Bill, finding that Congress had no authority over private individuals or organizations. Exactly how black Americans were to be transported by white-owned railroad companies was, after years of legislative battles, still largely undecided. Wells was the first black person to have a case against the railroads heard *after* the 1883 repeal of the Civil Rights Bill, which raised the stakes even higher. "The success of my case," Wells wrote, would "set a precedent which others would doubtless have followed."

Wells sat in the Shelby County Court House, waiting her turn to testify, as her lawyer, Thomas Cassels, questioned a series of witnesses who were aboard the same train as Wells that day in September 1883. Two of them, G. H. Clovers and G. W. Maseley, were black ministers; a third, Silas Kearney, was a black man who lived in Frazier, the first stop on the train line. All three testified that Chesapeake Ohio's claim of having provided two identical first-class train cars was false. The rear car, from which Wells had been ejected, was indeed a first-class car—which, in essence, meant that it was reserved for white passengers.

But the forward car—which the railway argued was an identical first-class accommodation—was, the witnesses said, simply not. "There were drunken persons in there and some smoking," Silas Kearney testified. "It was not a fit place for a lady to be." When it was Wells's turn to testify, her argument was the same—the forward car could not be considered a first-class car because it had not been properly reserved for respectable black passengers, as mandated by the separate-but-equal statute.

Holmes Cummins's chief witness was the conductor, William Murray, who by then had quit his railroad job and was operating a saloon. Murray explained the Chesapeake Ohio rule that "the rear coach should be reserved for white ladies and gentlemen, and colored passengers should ride in the forward coach." He insisted the rear and forward cars "were alike in every respect, built, equipped and furnished alike," and that he was zealous about policing the front car. "I am sure that I saw no smoking in the forward coach that afternoon," he testified. "I saw no drunken or rowdy behavior there."

With many key facts in dispute, the trial came down to believability. If Judge Pierce accepted that Chesapeake Ohio had provided Wells with an adequate first-class seat, she would lose her case. If Pierce believed Wells's claim that she had been denied the same accommodations afforded white first-class passengers, she would set an important precedent in a time of great racial upheaval, and strike a blow for the civil rights of all black Americans.

In the end, Judge James O. Pierce believed Ida Wells.

"The allowance of smoking and drunkenness in [the forward] car reduced it to below the grade of first class," Pierce decided, citing the separate-but-equal provision of the 1881 law. "The plaintiff," he went on, "is a person of ladylike appearance and comportment, a school teacher, and one who might be expected to object to traveling in the company of rough or boisterous men, smokers or drunkards.

"Judgment," Pierce declared, "for the plaintiff."

*

Pierce awarded Wells five hundred dollars—half of what she asked for—but still, her victory was all but complete. The *Memphis Appeal Avalanche* ran a story headlined "A Darky Damsel Obtains a Verdict Against the Chesapeake and Ohio Railroad—What It Cost to Put a Colored School Teacher in a Smoking Car." The consensus was that Wells had won a major success, and paved the way for more such lawsuits. Many, however, were convinced Wells was a scammer. She "is making a good thing out of the Chesapeake and Ohio Railroad," read one Mississippi newspaper editorial. "She buys first-class tickets, attempts to ride in the ladies car, gets put out and brings suit for damages."

What mattered to Wells was that she had won the case, and in the process proven the power of a lone voice against the might of industry.

Yet even then, even in victory, she had underestimated that might.

Holmes Cummins immediately appealed Judge Pierce's decision, and Chesapeake Ohio was granted a second trial.

In 1887, the Supreme Court of Tennessee upended the first trial's findings. "We know of no rule that requires railroad companies to yield to the disposition of passengers to arbitrarily determine as to the coach in which they take passage," the court decided. "Having offered, as the statute provides, 'accommodations equal in all respects in comfort and convenience to the first-class cars on the train' . . . the company had done all that could rightfully be demanded."

As for Ida Wells, the ruling went on, "we think it is evident that the purpose of the defendant was to harass with a view to this suit, and that her persistence was not in good faith to obtain a comfortable seat for the short ride. Judgment reversed, and judgment here for the plaintiff."

The court ordered Wells to pay $200 in court costs.

*

The reversal left Wells shattered. She believed the appeal had been decided not on the merits, but on the basis of her race, and the inconvenience of her complaint to such a huge, white-owned business. Her new attorney on the appeal, James Greer, argued that the "personal prejudices" of the Tennessee Supreme Court justices had led to a blatantly unjust verdict. The irony for Wells was that, in the months before the first trial got under way, Chesapeake Ohio had repeatedly tried to get her to settle the case for money. "I indignantly refused," she later wrote. Had she settled, "I would have been a few hundred dollars to the good instead of having to pay out over two hundred dollars."

As hard as the reversal was on Wells financially, the sting of injustice was far worse. She felt "utterly discouraged," she wrote. "I have firmly believed all along that the law was on our side and would, when we appealed to it, give us justice. I have been shorn of the belief." She felt aggrieved not only for herself, but for all blacks.

"If it were possible," she lamented, "I would gather my race in my arms and fly far away with them."

Wells understood that all the legislative upheaval regarding America's color line had, in the two decades since the Civil War's end, not secured anything resembling actual equality for America's black population. "The South wanted the Civil Rights Bill repealed," she concluded, "but did not want or intend to give justice to the Negro after robbing him of all sources from which to secure it."

Just as the death of her parents had hardened Wells, her loss in court would transform her again. The quality that the Tennessee Supreme Court had chosen to disparage as inauthentic and not in good faith—Wells's "persistence"—would become, going forward, her calling card, her greatest strength. "The characteristic of heroism is its persistency," Ralph Waldo Emerson wrote right after the Civil War. "All men have wandering impulses, fits and starts of generosity. But when you have chosen your part, abide by it, and do not weakly try to reconcile yourself with the world. The heroic cannot be the common, nor the common the heroic."

Despite the loss in court, the case gave Wells something that was systematically denied black men and women in the post–Civil War South—it gave her a voice. The case made her someone to listen to.

Still young and unsure and wounded enough to lament, "Oh God, is there no redress, no peace, no justice in this land for us?" Wells would soon find her full voice, and use it to fight the most extreme and violent injustice of all, a horror that blocked out the sun—the extrajudicial lynching of black Americans by the thousands.

It would be her persistence in this fight, over the years and decades, that would one day connect her to Tom Williams.

CHAPTER 11

A Negro's Crime

*

November 1910
Asbury Park, New Jersey

Up in his cell in the Asbury Park jail, Tom Williams heard the men clamoring on the street below, calling for his blood. He listened as they crashed through the outer door and barreled into the station. He could not have expected Police Chief Smith and his officers, who made no secret of their belief in his guilt, to protect him from the coming mob. More likely, he must have thought they would let the men pass and stand by as they dragged Williams to his death, as so many sheriffs and law officers had routinely done throughout the South for years.

Earlier that day, before the full mob had assembled, Williams underwent hours of interrogation. The original plan had been to transport Williams from Asbury Park to the jail in the town of Freehold, the seat of Monmouth County, some seventeen miles west, and have him officially questioned there. That was the order received from County Sheriff Clarence E. F. Hetrick. But with rumors of a forming mob going around town—and small groups of men already gathering outside the police station by midday—Hetrick revised his order and instructed that Williams not be moved until later, when it was deemed safe. In the meantime, the suspect would be questioned in Asbury Park.

Sheriff Hetrick gave the job of lead interrogator to County Detective Elwood Minugh.

A lean, handsome man with black hair and a wide curled mustache, Minugh was the county's enforcer. He took the hardest assignments and handled the trickiest arrests. He chased after horse thieves and men who deserted their wives and so-called midnight marauders—crooks who broke into stores late at night. Minugh was the one who would not only impound an illegal slot machine but also break it open at the station to get at the change inside. In 1908, he was sent to the Fireman's Hall in Highlands, a town north of Asbury Park, to follow up a tip about an illegal boxing match. Minugh, working undercover, watched the fight for one round before climbing into the ring and arresting both boxers, nearly causing a riot among the three hundred mostly drunken fans in the hall.

Beyond his fearlessness, Minugh was known for wrangling confessions and leads out of suspects. He famously sweated two twelve-year-old black suspects, Fred Hohman and Irving Reeves, and got what he needed to solve a series of robberies in Red Bank in 1908. A local paper wrote that Minugh extracted his information through "the administering of the celebrated third-degree"—a reference to a relatively new investigative practice involving physical force and psychological browbeating. "The Sweat Box Method" was another term for it.

On Monday, November 14, Minugh arrived at police headquarters in Asbury Park and waited for the latest suspect to be brought to him.

*

Police Chief Smith took Williams out of his cell and brought him to his office for the questioning. Detective Minugh was already there. Minugh began with some basic questions—where Williams was born, details about his family—before zeroing in.

"You quite a drinker?" he asked.

"Well, I do drink sometimes," Williams said.

"Did you ever do anything under the influence of liquor that you didn't know about?"

"No."

"If you should have committed a crime while under the influence of liquor, who would have done it?"

"It would be Tom Williams."

"It would not have been the liquor that would have done it?"

"No, it would be me."

"Was any of your family ever insane?"

"No they were not."

"Last Wednesday there was a little girl named Marie Smith missed. She was found in the woods on Sunday. She had been murdered and foully treated, and I believe you are the man who committed the crime."

"Well, you accuse me very wrong," Williams said, his tone suddenly defiant. "I swear before God and man that I am innocent."

"You know this girl Marie Smith very well?"

"Yes."

"Did you ever speak to her?"

"No, I never did. I never had occasion to."

The line of questioning, tight and repetitive, went on for two hours. Williams did not crack. Three other detectives, Thomas Broderick, Edward Hankinson, and William Ireton, took their turns with Williams, too. As the questioning went on, the crowd on the street below grew larger and louder.

Meanwhile, the town undertaker, Fred E. Farry, made his way through the mob and headed to the police station.

A funeral director and licensed embalmer who had lost his own infant son to disease, Farry worked out of a modest parlor on Main Street, next to a barbershop. He handled funeral services for the wealthiest families in town, and also buried the indigent for a twenty-five-dollar fee paid by the county. He had opened his parlor for an autopsy of Marie Smith's body the afternoon she was found. Now Farry took the two-block walk from his parlor to the police station, carrying something in his outstretched arms that was covered with a black blanket. The steady sleet iced the top of Farry's bowler hat and the blanket. Once inside the station, he was led down to the basement.

Not long after Farry's arrival, Detective Minugh took Tom Williams by the arm and led him out of Chief Smith's office, down past the Wesley Company fire engines that shared space in the building.

Minugh brought Williams to a room just off the basement jail cell. The other detectives were already there. The room was bare except for a table. The lights were off and the room was pitch black when Minugh walked Williams inside.

Someone switched on an electric lantern and aimed the bright beam at the table.

There in the shaft of light was the small body of Marie Smith.

She resembled a child in size and shape only; otherwise, she was ghostly. Her round face was pale and sunken, discolored by her injuries—purple bruises, lacerations, a black burn mark. Minugh took hold of Tom Williams and walked him closer to the table, until Williams was no more than a foot from the cold body.

"Swear that you did not murder this child," Minugh demanded.

Williams did not hesitate.

"I swear to God I didn't touch the girl," he said. "I had nothing to do with it."

Minugh took Williams's head and pushed it toward the body.

"Get down and look into her face!" he yelled.

Williams was inches away from Marie. Minugh held his head down and waited for a reaction. Williams, forced to look into the child's lifeless eyes, stayed silent for a moment. Then, unprompted, he placed his hand gently on Marie's face, as if blessing her.

Slowly, he said, "I thank God I can say I didn't do it. I am sorry for her and for her family, but I didn't do it, so help me God."

Minugh kept Williams by the body for thirty minutes, but the suspect did not break. Finally, the interrogation ended. Minugh took Williams to the basement cell and locked the metal bars. Fred Farry covered Marie's body with his black blanket and carried her back to his parlor.

*

At the same time, in a municipal chamber just above the jail, town officials held a meeting to determine the amount of a reward for information that would help convict Marie Smith's killer. They settled on five hundred dollars.

Outside the station, as the sleet turned to snow, more men gathered. A little earlier, a train from Freehold had delivered a black prisoner, escorted by four police officers, to the Asbury Park train depot, one block west of the police station. Some of the men in the crowd saw the black prisoner and ran toward him, believing he was Tom Williams. In an instant, a crowd surrounded the depot. The officers desperately yelled, "This isn't him! This isn't the man!" In fact, the prisoner was James Hickson, arrested for purse snatching.

Somehow the officers convinced the men to let them pass. But there was no mistaking the situation now. The purpose and passion of the horde was clear. This was a lynch mob.

By then, Police Chief Smith knew this was the case. He could see the crowd on the street below steadily growing until the entire block was filled with angry men. Smith ordered his entire police department, every last officer, to report immediately to the station. Calls were made and all across town off-duty officers got in their uniforms, got out their nightsticks, and hurried to Mattison Avenue.

They were not fast enough. Around 9:00 p.m., the crowd around the police station surged forward. Led by the men from the Whitesville section—who had broken into a mason's store and armed themselves with picks and sledgehammers—the mob tore away the latticed gate guarding the front door of the police station, and pushed through the entrance and down the stairs, headed to Williams's basement cell.

This was it. The crowd numbered some six hundred men, and the police officers were badly outnumbered.

Still, somehow, the officers held their ground.

In the stairwell, rather than let the men pass, a handful of officers pushed back at them with the hard points of their nightsticks. More officers arrived, and joined in the push and pull, and the police forced the charging men back up the stairs and out of the station.

"The officers emerged from the jail entrance and, spreading out in fan fashion, made a determined attack on the crowd," reported the *Asbury Park Press*. "How they stopped the mob without bloodshed, the police themselves never knew."

Chief Smith's small force—no more than twenty men—managed to push the mob two blocks back from the station, before cordoning off all of Mattison Avenue. Many men gave up and went home, and the cold and snow further thinned the crowd, but there were still many dozens of men in place as midnight passed. Chief Smith couldn't be sure the mob would not reassemble. He saw the bad weather and the late hour as his best chance to end the standoff, and he devised a plan.

Chief Smith came out of the police station and stood on a box placed in front of the remaining men. He said he had an announcement, and the crowd quieted down. Then Smith told a lie in the service of good. Tom Williams, he said, had produced a credible alibi. Now it was up to the coroner's jury to determine if he was guilty or innocent. No justice would be administered at this hour or in this place. It was time for the men to go back home to their families.

"Let no one be able to say that the citizens of Asbury Park have no respect for law and order," Smith preached in his midnight speech. "Let the law take its course. I appeal to you not to be hasty but to return home and to help us preserve order. You may rest assured that we shall do all in our power to bring the slayer of the child to justice."

While the police chief addressed the crowd in front of the station, an unmarked car pulled up behind it.

The driver stopped at the station's back door, but kept the engine running. Detective Minugh came out of the station, holding tight to Tom Williams. He rushed Williams to the car and pushed him down on the floor in the back, and climbed in behind him. The driver gunned the engine and with a loud screech the car tore away at top speed.

Once the car was out of town, Minugh sat Williams up in the backseat. The driver took a circuitous route, staying off the main roads. Williams was worried about running into a lynch mob, and asked Minugh for a smoke to calm his nerves. Minugh told him he had no tobacco.

Sometime after 2:00 a.m., the car arrived in Freehold. There were two hundred men waiting at the Freehold train station—they'd gotten word of the transfer and believed Williams would arrive by train. But there were no men outside the Monmouth County jail, and Minugh walked Williams inside without incident. For the moment, he was safe.

Yet he was still the main suspect in the murder of Marie Smith, and his ordeal was just beginning. There was no reason for anyone to believe his story, and any new evidence, most were convinced, only further suggested his guilt. Alvin Cliver made sure that the reports of how strongly Williams had maintained his innocence were interpreted as proof of how evil he was. "A man who could gaze upon the mutilated body of a child . . . and swear that he was innocent without a tremor in his voice," Cliver wrote, "could be capable of almost any crime."

Even Chief Smith, who had saved Williams's life by holding off the mob, was heard to call the murder "a negro's crime," and say "there is no doubt in my mind but that Black Diamond is the guilty man."

The police chief also had one especially disturbing bit of evidence.

It was a story related by Martha Coleman, who lived on Springfield Avenue in Asbury Park. Coleman knew Tom Williams and had spent time in his company. When police questioned her, she said she'd heard Williams make a startling claim a few days before the murder, and she swore others heard him say it, too.

Williams, she said, had told her there was a little white girl in town he planned "to get next to."

CHAPTER 12

The Secret Plan

*

November 1910
Asbury Park, New Jersey

A day after Fred Farry carried the body of Marie Smith to police headquarters, the undertaker moved her again, this time to the home of her grieving parents on West Monroe Avenue.

It was the first time Peter Smith and his wife, Nora, had been reunited with their daughter in their home since she walked out the door and set off for school six days earlier.

There would be no service or memorial for Marie in Asbury Park, just a small wake, for friends and family only, in the Smiths' home. Father Thomas A. Roche, of the Catholic Church of the Holy Spirit, presided over the wake. Nora Smith remained in a terrible state, barely eating or sleeping, but somehow she made it through the speeches and prayers. Afterward, she collapsed. A doctor examined her and said she was in "a precarious condition from shock." He expressed a fear she might die.

The next day, Peter Smith got on a train and accompanied his daughter's body from Asbury Park to New York City. He chose the 7:17 a.m. train to avoid crowds at the station. His wife did not make the trip.

In New York City, Smith went to a brief 10:00 a.m. requiem mass in St. Patrick's Catholic Church in the Hamilton section of Brooklyn, where the Smiths lived before moving to Asbury Park. Smith's father and mother were there. The next day, the Smith family crossed under the arched stone gates of the Holy Cross Cemetery in Flatbush. They stood in a line and watched as caretakers lowered Marie into Plot 23 in row D, off to the side of a small white chapel on the western edge of the cemetery, not far from the section where the city's paupers were buried in graves dug hastily three feet down.

Marie's casket was set atop the small casket that already occupied the plot. That casket held the remains of Marie's brother John, dead at eighteen months from poisoning. The caretakers shoveled dirt over both wooden boxes, and the simple ceremony was done.

The Smiths were too poor to afford any kind of marker or stone, so Plot 23 remained a bare patch of earth.

*

The mood in Asbury Park, among police, merchants, and families, was anxious and grim. It was a town on edge. Just three weeks before Marie disappeared, the area had seen another terrifying crime involving a young girl—the kidnapping of four-year-old Mamie Patillo, snatched from the front porch of her family's home in Red Bank, just north of Asbury Park. Elwood Minugh, Tom Williams's interrogator, was the lead detective on the Patillo case as well, but her disappearance remained unsolved for two months, until the day she mysteriously reappeared on the same porch from which she was taken, with a broken front tooth and no information about her abductors.

In just one month, two local girls taken and no one made to pay. Townspeople locked their doors and windows for the first time. Mothers walked their children to and from school. The pressure was on the authorities to catch the killer, and an editorial in the *Press* sought "Swift Justice" for Marie Smith: "This case is one that calls aloud for vengeance. The honor of Asbury Park is at stake, and the public safety demands that the murderer be brought to justice."

The task of swiftly bringing such justice fell mainly to a team of four—Police Chief William Smith; Robert Purdy, the coroner; John S.

Applegate Jr., the Monmouth County prosecutor; and the clean-cut, genial county sheriff, Clarence E. F. Hetrick.

Hetrick grew up in Asbury Park and played right halfback on the town's football squad. He looked sturdy and stalwart, like a sheriff should, but by nature he was a politician. He'd been elected and appointed up the career ladder, and in 1908, at the age of thirty-five, he won the office of county sheriff. Many considered him a crass opportunist. As sheriff, he was accused of plotting to charge the state thirty-five cents for every prisoner housed in city jails, rather than the customary ten cents. He escaped prosecution only because the plan fell through.

The county prosecutor, John S. Applegate Jr., had his own scandals. His father, John Applegate Sr., had held several state and county offices, and John Jr., with his neatly trimmed dark hair, unsmiling mouth, and serious stare, looked every bit the part of his father's political heir. Then, in 1906, on the day of an election for Red Bank assemblyman, a witness claimed to see Applegate Jr. hand a thick wad of bills to the Republican candidate, Frank J. Manson, who in turn handed it to an associate, who then handed it out to voters. Applegate Jr. survived the accusation, and two years later assumed the office of county prosecutor.

Clarence Hetrick and John Applegate Jr. knew each other, having served together on the Red Bank Republican County Convention Committee. They were insiders, career men, and together managed law enforcement in all of Monmouth County, which covered the Jersey shore towns of Red Bank, Long Branch, and Asbury Park. Early on in the Marie Smith investigation, they both believed—as did Chief Smith—that Tom Williams was guilty. But five days into the case, newspapers began criticizing them for not having any other suspects besides Williams.

"Police Lack Conclusive Evidence Directly Linking Williams With Crime," read an *Asbury Park Press* headline, likely written by Alvin Cliver. "Facts in possession of the coroner and police are now reported to be insufficient to warrant the continued holding of the negro suspect."

In fact, the evidence against Tom Williams was entirely circumstantial. Williams couldn't account for his whereabouts at the time of the crime, but neither had anyone spotted him near Third Avenue, where Marie Smith was last seen. The stains on the towel found where he was staying, and on his suspenders, had not yet been proven to be blood. There was no murder weapon, and no motive. Even Peter Smith could not bring himself to suspect Williams. Smith "had no quarrel with Williams at any time, and could conceive of no reason why he should do such a thing," the *Press* reported. Even after police told Smith the murder was a crime of assault, not revenge, he didn't believe Williams had done it.

There were also the bloody leaves found by Peter Smith and his boss, Randolph Miller, on one of their many searches of the woods. They said they picked up a trail of bloodstained leaves leading to the murder site, and the physician and part-time coroner Joseph Ackerman confirmed the blood on the leaves was human. That opened up the possibility that Marie Smith had been murdered elsewhere and dragged into the woods.

As a theory, this made more sense than the accepted thinking that Marie was killed where she was found, considering that teams of police officers and schoolboys had scoured that very spot more than once before the body was discovered. And if Marie had been killed elsewhere, that meant she had to have been hidden away for three full days, most likely in a house or barn or shed. If that were true, then Tom Williams, known to be itinerant, was less likely to be the murderer.

Finally, there was the suspect himself, who in several harsh interrogations had never wavered in declaring his innocence.

"His repeated assertions and the way he has borne up strengthen the conviction that he is guiltless," the *New York Tribune* declared. The *Camden Courier-Post* wrote "Williams has told his story over and over again and been contradicted only on one material point"—whether he left Griffin's bar at noon, as he insisted, or closer to 10:30 a.m., as two witnesses claimed. "Everything else he told us," Police Chief Smith was quoted as saying, "has been substantiated."

While there were no other official suspects, there were other leads and theories and people worth looking at. Some suspected Henry Litman, who owned the home in Whitesville where the Smith family had lived before he put them out for not paying rent. Witnesses had seen Litman and Peter Smith quarreling more than once, suggesting some kind of feud, but police learned Litman had a good alibi—he was carting ashes from the Hotel Ormond in Ocean Grove at the time Marie went missing.

Two other possible suspects were Max Kruschka and Frank Heidemann, who lived in the house at the corner of Third and Asbury Avenues—the spot where Marie Smith was last seen. Kruschka was a florist who had several greenhouses on his property, and Heidemann was the young assistant he hired just a month before Marie disappeared.

The men, both German-born, had different reasons for falling under suspicion. Heidemann lived on the second floor of Kruschka's house, and had been on the property at the time of Marie's disappearance. And Kruschka, fifty-one, was a known drinker with a history of violence. In 1904 he was jailed for chasing his wife from her bedroom while she was "in scant attire and barefooted at the point of a revolver," reported the *Asbury Park Press*. The day after his arrest, Kruschka's twenty-year-old daughter, Adelaide, told police her father had tried to rape her.

Police questioned both men and accepted that neither knew anything of the crime.

The biggest problem for Hetrick and Applegate was the lack of physical evidence implicating anyone. They needed to start over and re-canvass Asbury Park. Somewhere, something was waiting to be found. But Police Chief Smith simply lacked the manpower to conduct a more thorough investigation. Like most small-town police forces, Smith's handful of officers was already overburdened by other crimes and duties. They often received help from county detectives like Elwood Minugh, but now, under increasing pressure, they would need even more help.

Five days after Marie was found, the team agreed that the prosecutor's office would hire two detectives from outside the county. Applegate turned to the Greater New York Detective Agency, headquartered in Greenwich Village in downtown New York City.

The field of detective work was roughly one hundred years old, dating back to a French ex-convict, Eugène Vidocq, who started the first detective agency, the Brigade de la Sûreté, in Paris in 1811. The Greater New York Detective Agency, founded in 1900 by a secretive figure named John E. McKenna, was one of only fifteen detective agencies licensed by the state of New York. One classified ad described their services this way: "Reliable, daily habits of suspected persons ascertained; private matters confidentially conducted; operatives sent to all points; terms reasonable." The agency also offered bodyguards, and ran ads looking for "Big Men."

Most famously, the coal and railroad baron Harry Thaw, who suspected his chorus girl wife, Evelyn Nesbit, of having an affair with the famed architect Stanford White, hired the agency to provide twenty-four-hour surveillance of White for more than two years. White figured out he was being tailed and spent $6,000 to hire detectives of his own to follow the detectives hounding him. In the end, McKenna's operatives found nothing to implicate White—which didn't stop Thaw from shooting and killing White in the Madison Square Roof Garden restaurant in 1906.

Prosecutor John Applegate Jr. arranged for two Greater New York detectives—B. F. Johnson and George W. Cunningham—to come to Asbury Park at an eventual cost to the county of $1,289.48. The men arrived in town at 2:20 p.m. on Tuesday, November 15, six days after Marie disappeared. They met with Police Chief Smith and Detective Minugh for a briefing, then visited the woods where Marie's body was found, and later the boardinghouse where Tom Williams was arrested. They reinterviewed Max Kruschka and Frank Heidemann but found nothing new. Kruschka had an alibi: he was away in New York City the morning Marie disappeared. As for Heidemann, one paper said, the detectives "have failed to pick any flaws in his story."

Johnson and Cunningham also interrogated Tom Williams in his cell, waking him at 2:00 a.m. and lying that someone had implicated him. Williams told them what he told Police Chief Smith and his men.

"I swear by all my hope for the future that I did not kill this poor little girl," Williams pleaded in his cell. "I knew her and liked her. I am only a poor black man that earned my living by chopping wood and doing odd work. My past record don't show that I could be guilty of this crime."

The detectives didn't buy it. Just a few days into their stay in Asbury Park, one of them made it clear who he believed killed Marie. "Just so positive am I that the negro Thomas Williams is the murderer of Marie Smith," he told a reporter, "that if he declared in the gallows that he was innocent of this crime, I would still believe him guilty."

The detectives devoted the bulk of their time to searching the woods and the area around Griffin's roadhouse, looking for the one thing they felt they needed to pin the crime on Williams—the murder weapon. "We have enough circumstantial evidence against the negro 'D.W.,'" they wrote in a report, "but must get some weapon, or someone who actually saw him in company with the girl."

Were the detectives merely parroting the suspicions of the men who hired them—in effect, working backward from the assumption that Williams was guilty? There is no evidence they developed any other serious suspect in their time in Asbury Park. This focus on Williams did not sit well with at least one prominent person in Asbury Park.

Randolph Miller, owner of the rendering plant where Marie's father, Peter, worked, had thrown himself into finding Marie's killer as heartily as anyone else on the case. He spent hours personally searching the woods, and, after Marie's body was found, hours going over all the evidence. He'd given Peter Smith time off with pay, and provided other comforts to the family. What bothered Miller most was that—despite some pushback in the press about police having no other suspects—the case against Williams continued to fall neatly into place. It all seemed too easy, too pat. Was he to accept that Williams was the killer simply because, as Police Chief Smith put it, Marie's murder was "a Negro's crime," or because Williams had a bad reputation?

One bit of evidence, in particular, gnawed away at Miller—the mysterious burn marks on Marie's nose and left ear.

What had caused them? Who had caused them? Could they simply be ignored as evidence? After studying the scars, the coroner, Robert Purdy, described "corrugation marks on the burn on the left ear, faint as the threads in a bank note. These marks correspond to the tracery on asbestos materials covering boilers and pipes."

This convinced Miller that the burn marks on Marie's nose and ear were a key piece of evidence. "It seems to me that these corrugation marks on the ear indicate that the body was placed for a time at least near a boiler or steam heating apparatus," Miller told the *Camden Courier-Post*. "This would make it appear that the body was kept for a time in the basement of a factory or in a private house."

It was more than a hunch, but less than a lead. Even so, Miller was determined to follow it. To do that, he knew he couldn't rely on just Police Chief Smith and his men, or even on the two detectives from New York City. He had to bring in someone new.

Miller asked for a meeting with Smith, Purdy, and Hetrick. The prosecutor, John Applegate—who among all the men on the case was most convinced of Tom Williams's guilt—was kept out of the meeting.

Miller made his case and said he would put up three thousand dollars of his own money to hire another detective. But, he insisted, this detective had to be independent. He had to be free to follow the evidence without any guidance from interested parties. Miller was persuasive. Under pressure to solve the case, Smith, Purdy, and Hetrick accepted Miller's offer, and Hetrick even promised to contribute funds of his own. They agreed to keep the plan secret, both from the press and the prosecutor. No one but them would know about the new investigator.

Two days later, a slender, well-dressed detective named Raymond Schindler arrived in Asbury Park. He was twenty-eight, and he had never worked a murder case before.

CHAPTER 13

A Guilty Mind

*

April 18, 1906
San Francisco, California

Raymond Schindler arrived in the modern city of San Francisco
one day after the earth cracked open.

Starting out at the northern edge of the city, he walked into a surreal
shower of white ash. He saw, in the distance, horrific thick looming
pillars of black smoke. He felt heat, deep heat, like a wall. He smelled
fire and death. This was, as sure as any place could be, hell itself.

Still, Schindler slipped through the safety lines sealing off the city,
skirted the fleeing survivors, and walked headlong into the worst of it.

The day before, miles and miles of tectonic plates along the northern part of the San Andreas Fault on the California coastline began
to shift and rupture at 5:12 a.m., causing a massive shuddering that
lasted one minute. San Francisco, then the ninth-largest city in the
United States, lay in the doomed heart of the shuddering, and endured
a primary tremor rated at a 7.9 magnitude, and more than twenty-five
lesser tremors that same day. In the city, cobblestone streets were broken
in two, and jagged, mile-long cracks exposed subterranean streams,
bottomless chasms, the planet itself. In the aftermath, on the buckled
streets, there were five-foot piles of clothing, salvaged, then abandoned;
large black rats, alive and dead, by the thousands; shocked, shuffling
people in nightgowns and bare feet lugging family portraits, ironing

boards, birds in cages. Enormous brick buildings toppled, shorn in half, leaning at drunken angles; whole houses sunk violently into their basements. The great James Flood Mansion atop Nob Hill, reduced to a single standing wall.

When the earthquake hit, most people were asleep. More than half the city's four hundred thousand residents lost their homes. Twenty thousand survivors had to be rescued by the USS *Chicago* in one of the largest sea evacuations in history. As many as three thousand perished.

The earthquake caused significant damage, but the voracious, city-wide fire that followed, fed by broken gas lines and shattered water mains that made containment impossible, raged for four days and flattened hundreds and hundreds of city blocks. Everywhere, there was despair. "Mothers searching madly for their children who strayed, little ones wailing for their protectors," one witness recalled. "Strong men bellowing like babies in their furor." Said another: "The city is ablaze. We will all be burned. This must be the end of this wicked world."

For a long time, the calamity would be called the Fire. Only later would it be known as the Great San Francisco Earthquake of 1906.

Ray Schindler came from elsewhere and randomly chose San Francisco as his destination. He was twenty-four, a high school graduate who skipped college, and he was at the tail end of a long, westward journey to discover his destiny. Seeing the smoldering bones of the stricken city, he could have, probably should have, fled to somewhere safer, somewhere more opportune. Instead, he decided to stay.

Quickly, he found a job wheeling a small refreshment stand into the ruins of Market Street and selling water to emergency workers and stranded survivors. It was the latest of several odd jobs he'd held. In his life, he had tried to be many things, but none had worked out. Something was waiting for him somewhere, this he knew, but he couldn't have hoped to find it there, in the ashes of cataclysm. And yet . . .

There were no operating newspapers in San Francisco, and the news arrived in scattered leaflets. One day, while on duty at his stand, Schindler picked up a leaflet printed with the latest updates on the fires.

He read through the wanted advertisements. There was an ad placed by the G. Franklin McMackin Society seeking "historians" to help "record the greatest catastrophe that ever occurred on this continent." The ad said college graduates only, but Schindler ignored that part. He figured he could talk his way around it. The ad also said "Good Salary." That was all the motivation Schindler needed. Happy for the chance at a new adventure, he applied for the position, and he was hired.

What he didn't yet know was that the McMackin Society did not have the slightest interest in hiring a historian.

What the society desperately needed was a detective.

*

Investigative work was not a calling for Raymond Campbell Schindler. If anything, he was raised to be a preacher. His father, John Franklin Schindler—born in the same log cabin in Ohio his own father was born in—attended the Theological School at St. Lawrence University in Canton, New York, and studied subjects like Hagenbach's History of Doctrines and Ware's Hints on Extemporaneous Preaching. His Christianity was stern but redemptive. "When people sincerely believe in a benevolent God," he wrote, "they try to act honestly and uprightly." Young Raymond grew up hearing of punishment and salvation.

John Schindler's work as a minister for the Universalist Church took him to Ohio, then Iowa, then Stillwater, Minnesota. In 1880 he married Isabella Campbell, and they had six children. Raymond, born in the upstate New York town of Mexico, was their second child and eldest son. From his father, Raymond learned to be moral, patient, and serious. But it was his kind, giving mother, Belle, who first exposed Raymond to the criminal element.

Belle Schindler volunteered at the Minnesota State Prison in Stillwater. Since it opened in 1853, it was known as a truly bleak place. Among its inmates when Belle worked there were the infamous Younger Boys, a trio of brothers who robbed banks with Jesse James and finally got caught after a botched bank job in 1876, and sentenced to twenty-five years. Many new prisoners at Stillwater—called "fresh fish" by inmates—"had been known to break down completely after spending their first night in a cell, with its iron bed, whitewashed walls, scant furnishings, iron floor and the dimensions of only five by seven feet."

Inmates had exactly nineteen temporary possessions—a Bible, two cups, a small mirror, a cuspidor, one spoon, one face towel, one dish towel, one piece of soap, one comb, one blanket, one sheet, one pillowcase, a mattress, a bedstead, a wooden chair, an earthen water jar with cover, an electric light, and one small shelf. Belle Schindler saw to it that they had one more privilege—a library catalog.

Belle founded the prison library and worked there without pay, dispensing thousands of books to inmates who for the first time had something to read besides the Bible. The library was hugely popular and endured for the life of the prison. Belle also held Sunday school classes for the inmates, and it was through her efforts that Ray Schindler "acquired his first realization that criminals are human, the prey of their own natures and environments," the biographer Rupert Hughes wrote. Both of Ray's parents, then, encouraged him to see the humanity behind the horror, to reach for that part of every man, even the crooked and the seemingly lost, that still yearned to be honest and upright.

In 1895 Raymond's father left the ministry and hired on as a sales agent for the Northwestern Mutual Life Insurance Company in Milwaukee. He brought Raymond into the business with him. By then Raymond had shown a solid work ethic, starting as a boy delivering newspapers for twenty-five cents a day, then as a theater usher who dabbled in acting, and also as a nighttime hotel clerk. When Ray was eighteen, his father sent him out to sign his first insurance client, a music store in Alliance, Ohio. Ray sold them a policy and earned an eighteen-dollar commission. But he was so taken with the solicitation part of the business—making contacts, sizing people up, getting along with different types—that he spent most of his time helping his music store clients hold contests, sign bands, and increase sales. He never signed a second client, and his father ended Ray's insurance career right then.

Next, John Schindler steered his son toward a job selling typewriters. After two years, Ray managed to save $2,400 in commissions. That was enough to launch him on his next adventure—an investment in a gold-mining property in Sierra County in northern California. The property was called "Sky High." A half century after the Gold Rush, Ray and a friend set out on their own quest for fortune, buying cheap tickets for the long train ride out west. Their money ran out before they reached Colorado. For five dollars, a brakeman let them ride in the refrigerator car of a freight train, as long as they stayed out of view by crouching high on the crossbeams. Unluckily, there was a blizzard that dropped temperatures well below freezing, which, coupled with the great blocks of ice in the train car, nearly ended their adventure, and their lives.

They survived the trip, and for the last leg of the train journey they bribed another brakeman to smuggle them onto the platform between the first baggage car and the billowing engine, a bit of transport known as "riding blind baggage." After a few hours they were covered in soot and frozen snow, and choked by heavy smoke. A train staffer saved them from possible death by bringing them inside and finding a way for them to warm up—shoveling coal into the engine boiler for the next ten hours.

Ray finally arrived in California in a winter storm, and reached his mountain property atop a horse outfitted with snowshoes. He stayed in a home he could leave and enter only through a second-floor window, so high were the snowdrifts. He helped excavators with the backbreaking work of tunneling into the mountain, working ninety hours a week.

But by springtime, the funds ran out and the mine was abandoned.

Instead of crippling him, the dismal failure only "trebled the young man's enthusiasm," Alva Johnston wrote in a *New Yorker* profile of Schindler many years later. "He became a gold-fever Typhoid Mary, infecting his father and friends with the craze, [and together] they raised $80,000 for a hydraulic-mining venture" on a mountain near Scales,

California. Between 1854 and 1884, hydraulic mining had unearthed more than $100 million in gold, and this time, with an army of three hundred Chinese workers, the outlook for Ray seemed much more promising. Until the federal government banned all hydraulic mining, and the Schindler mine was shuttered.

Ray Schindler was twenty-four and broke. But he was not defeated. Something was waiting for him somewhere, this he knew. He left Scales with no money and no plan, and he made his way nearly two hundred miles south to the booming, modern city of San Francisco.

*

The G. Franklin McMackin Society wasn't a society at all. McMackin was a person—a detective from New York City. He'd been hired by insurance companies to evaluate the damage in San Francisco with an eye toward lightening the companies' enormous financial liabilities. The 1906 earthquake was, for the insurance industry, a near apocalypse. The destruction of thousands of buildings—including the city's famed, gilded playhouses, the Majestic, the Columbia, the Orpheum, the Grand Operahouse—would eventually total $235 million in losses, or, in modern dollars, more than $6 billion. At least twelve insurance companies in the United States went out of business because of the earthquake. Many insurers offered claimants "six-bit" coverage (a small percentage of what policyholders were owed) or simply denied them any payment at all.

The soundest loophole for insurers was that most policies at the time included a falling-building clause, but no coverage for earthquake damage. Earthquakes were an act of God. But in San Francisco, only an estimated 2 percent of the ruined buildings were destroyed by the quake. The other 98 percent were destroyed by fire. Thus, insurers were desperate for proof that a building had already been destroyed *before* it ever caught fire. In one case, an insurer paid fifteen thousand dollars for a photograph of a collapsed building that only later burned to the ground.

McMackin was hired to survey damaged buildings and find proof the earthquake had wrecked them. He brought in forty-two men, including Ray Schindler, and told them they were historians documenting the catastrophe. As historians, they could question homeowners and expect more candor than an insurance agent could ever hope to get. This subterfuge was key to their success. In effect, they were going undercover to glean information that would ultimately hurt the people they extracted it from.

Ray Schindler did not catch on right away. The work appealed to him for the same reasons he enjoyed his brief time as an actual insurance agent—he found he was good at earning people's trust and getting them to share important details about themselves. That he was producing the information for good, historical reasons also appealed to him.

Two weeks in, though, Schindler realized there was nothing scholarly about his job. He was, he discovered, working for a detective, and thus essentially a detective himself. There were no actual requirements to become a detective—no test to pass or license to earn. Ray was a detective because he was doing a detective's work, and he was doing it well. Without knowing it, he had stumbled into his destiny.

Schindler kept working for McMackin for several weeks, until he felt confident enough to continue as a freelancer. He would assess a damaged building top to bottom—reports, photographs, affidavits— for four hundred dollars. His thoroughness, and his patient pursuit of a sound conclusion, stood out among McMackin's forty-two hirees. When McMackin was called back to New York City for another job, he recommended that Schindler take his place. Schindler stayed on the job in San Francisco for eighteen months.

Yet even his skills at reconnaissance and documentation proved useless to the insurance industry. In the end, state judges found in case after case that insurers were responsible for the fire damage that destroyed hundreds of buildings after the earthquake. In 1907, Schindler quit the McMackin Society and took a job with a San Francisco lawyer, Hiram Johnson, who knew of his work and hired him to do research on a small blackmail case. This was Schindler's first real case as a detective.

When the case was done, Johnson asked Schindler to submit a bill. Schindler turned in an invoice for fifty dollars. Johnson wasn't happy, but not because Schindler asked for too much. He had watched Schindler charge another man just ten dollars for services Johnson believed deserved ten times as much. Now Schindler was undercharging again.

Johnson taught his protégé a good lesson by giving him a check for five hundred dollars and a warning to stop undervaluing himself.

Johnson wasn't done with Schindler. He saw a role for him in the ongoing legal battle against the notoriously corrupt political system in San Francisco—which, after the earthquake, became only more corrupt. In 1907, the president of the United States, Theodore Roosevelt, sent an assistant U.S. district attorney, Francis J. Heney, and one of his Secret Service officers, William J. Burns, to San Francisco to prosecute the city's corrupt element. Hiram Johnson, then highly prominent in legal circles, recommended Ray Schindler for a spot on the investigative team assembled by Heney and Burns.

Schindler spent the next three years caught up in the thicket of San Francisco politics. It was hard, painstaking work. The city was under the control of a brazen operative named Abe Ruef, a lawyer who arranged for a naïve musician, Eugene Schmitz, to be elected San Francisco mayor, allowing Ruef—known as Curly Boss for his stylish mustache—to collect illegal fees from nearly every important transaction in the city. President Roosevelt sent Heney and Burns to take down the powerful Ruef and his puppet Schmitz in court. Burns assembled a team of investigators led by Schindler, who hired sixteen of his former McMackin "historians."

Schindler's task was to assemble thorough histories of the principals in the case, and to profile the hundreds of men being considered as jurors for the trial. The prosecutor's biggest fear was that Ruef would somehow flip a man or men on the jury, and throw it in his favor. Burns charged Schindler with identifying those prospective jurors most likely to be vulnerable to Ruef's advances. To get the intimate information he needed, Schindler had to work undercover, this time willingly posing as a historian researching the corruption case for posterity. He got many prospective jurors and their families to tell their life stories by describing how their histories and opinions would one day be immortalized in books found in libraries around the globe.

Schindler's work nearly came to nothing when a Ruef-Schmitz operative paid William Burns's secretary fifteen hundred dollars for copies of Schindler's precious biographies. Schindler investigated the theft and learned the president of a streetcar company had the files in his office safe. Schindler got a search warrant and hired a safecracker. But before he could leave the president's office with his files, dozens of men charged in and cornered him. He was going to lose the files a second time.

So Schindler ran to a window, flung it open, and threw the documents in the air. He was arrested for burglary, but not before one of his fellow detectives on the street below scooped up the stolen files.

The clean jury that Schindler helped assemble led Abe Ruef to cut a deal that earned him a fourteen-year sentence in San Quentin. The jury also found Mayor Eugene Schmitz guilty of corruption, and had him removed from office and sent to jail.

*

The case was Ray Schindler's initiation into the world of big-time law enforcement, and of all the colorful figures he had met, he was most taken with the Secret Service agent, William John Burns.

Burns, a Maryland native, was handsome and brash, and he owned "a nasturtium-colored mustache, which he did up nightly in curlpapers," a *New Yorker* profile reported. He wore a deerstalker cap like the great fictional detective Sherlock Holmes. Schindler was impressed with Burns's creativity and devotion to detail, which he saw firsthand in the San Francisco corruption case. At one point, Burns set up a phony oil company, with one of his operatives posing as the head of the company.

The operative, Schindler learned, was known as a "roper"—someone used to rope in unsuspecting criminals. Burns's deceptions and setups were elaborate and complex, and they were risky. His oil company roper embedded himself in San Francisco's corrupt waterfront, and eventually cut a deal with the head of the Board of Supervisors, Big Jim Gallagher, to illegally smuggle his oil through the docks. Gallagher's price was $150,000. Burns's men were so convincing they earned invitations into the homes of the supervisors and left no doubt in Gallagher's mind that they were, like him, criminals.

Instead, after getting Gallagher to accept a down payment of fifteen thousand dollars in bills marked by tiny needle punctures, Burns's detectives arrested Gallagher, and Burns himself sweated a thirty-six-hour confession out of him. So thorough was Burns's demolishment of the powerful Gallagher that several other corrupt operatives quickly lined up to make their own confessions and cut their own hopefully lenient deals.

The Gallagher trap, to Schindler, was a marvel of cunning and engineering. Its many moving parts, its meticulous attention to detail, its demand for sureness and bravery in action, all struck Schindler as a new and daring type of detective work. It required an ability to psychologically assess targets and, in effect, get them to incriminate themselves.

Just as impressive was Burns's marathon interrogation of Jim Gallagher, whose nearly uninterrupted confession amounted to an epic exorcising of his criminal self. For Schindler, it had echoes of his father's teachings—that even the most incorrigible sinners have a need to unburden themselves of their transgressions, either by bathing in the redemption of God's loving embrace, or, in the case of Big Jim Gallagher, by accepting the salvation offered him by his own omniscient adjudicator, Williams J. Burns.

Thanks to Burns, Ray Schindler had found his calling.

"He had imagination," Schindler would say of his mentor. "It was his training, particularly in the art of setting up a pretext that was foolproof, that caused me to make this my life's work. The challenge to outsmart, to analyze the workings of a guilty mind and cause that person to assist you in obtaining evidence against him, is fascinating."

After his success in the San Francisco case, William J. Burns left the Secret Service and started his own detective agency. In 1909, he went to New York City to open a headquarters there, in the twenty-nine-story, granite and limestone Park Row Building in lower Manhattan—one of the world's first skyscrapers. Burns brought Ray Schindler with him as his first hire, and named him office manager and lead detective.

The following year, in November 1910, Burns got a call from a County sheriff in New Jersey, Clarence Hetrick, who asked for help with a disturbing and puzzling murder case. Burns opened a file—Investigation No. 149—and handed the assignment to his new top man, Ray Schindler.

CHAPTER 14

Grace Foster

*

November 1910
Asbury Park, New Jersey

Ray Schindler dressed formally and did not carry a gun. He could have passed for a buttoned-up accountant or lawyer. He was five foot nine with dark hair cut short and swept in a neat line across his forehead. He had a long face with a rounded chin, bushy eyebrows, and a wide mouth set in a natural half smile. He favored three-piece suits with a lapel pin and a pocket square, and white dress shirts with club collars, and decorative tie tacks just above his tightly buttoned vest. In the summers he'd wear white suits with bow ties and sporty boater hats, but for the most part he dressed in black, topped off by a slick fedora.

The most striking thing about him was his eyes.

Deep-set and blue-gray, they were uncommonly round and wide, like owl eyes, and they made him seem perpetually alert, or extremely curious. His gaze was hard and fixed, and if it fell on you, you knew you were being observed. Schindler's eyes gave him the eerie intensity of a magician, and it was not hard to imagine that he wasn't simply looking at you but somehow *into* you.

At 9:30 a.m. on November 19, 1910, Ray Schindler had a visitor in his office at the Park Row Building in lower Manhattan. It was Robert Purdy, the Asbury Park coroner who was technically in charge of the inquest into the cause of Marie Smith's death, and who had come to New York to escort Schindler back to New Jersey.

In Schindler's office, Purdy laid out the details of the case, starting with Marie's disappearance and ending with the arrest and interrogation of Thomas Williams. Schindler asked if there were any photographs of the wounds on Marie's body. Purdy told him no. What about fingerprint impressions on the body? Those had not been searched for, Purdy said. The technology was too new. Around 10:30 a.m., the men left Schindler's office to make the 11:00 a.m. train to Asbury Park. They arrived at the shore at 1:19 p.m. and went straight to Sheriff Hetrick's office in the Seacoast Bank Building on the corner of Mattison Avenue. Randolph Miller, Peter Smith's boss, was there, too.

Hetrick explained that, besides Tom Williams, his men had made no headway on other suspects. The investigation was at a standstill. Hetrick told Schindler "the community at large were greatly worked up over the conditions and feel that it is not safe to have children at large until the perpetrator of the crime is apprehended," Schindler later wrote in his daily report. "There is a great deal of feeling on the matter and it is obvious that some results must be obtained."

After the briefing, Purdy and Miller took Schindler into the Wanamassa woods, to the spot where William Benson found Marie's body. They walked the path Marie was thought to have taken when she left the Bradley School the morning she vanished, and from there went to the home of her parents, where Schindler interviewed Peter Smith and his wife. He asked them to focus on any enemies they might have made, but Peter—despite a history of agitation—gave Schindler no useful information. Schindler met with Hetrick one last time in his office before leaving Asbury Park around 5:30 p.m. and heading back to Manhattan.

Two days later, Schindler was back in Asbury Park, this time with the lead detective on his team, Charles Scholl, one of several Burns detectives who would work the case with him. Once again, they met with Sheriff Hetrick and Robert Purdy in Hetrick's office.

At Schindler's request, Purdy summoned Joseph Ackerman and

Earl Wagner, the local physicians who had performed the autopsy on Marie Smith. Schindler had studied the autopsy report, and now grilled the doctors on the precise nature of the wounds, and on the kinds of instruments that might have made them. The main injury to Marie's head, a clean four-inch by two-inch gash, was likely made with the edge of an ax or a shovel, the doctors told Schindler.

Could it also have been made by a mason's tool? Schindler asked. A trowel, for instance? They allowed that it could have. In other words, no one had much confidence in what the murder weapon had been. All they knew for sure was that it had been something sharp. Schindler was frustrated by how little the autopsy had revealed. Too many knowable things were still not known.

Schindler asked more questions. He learned about the mysterious burns on Marie's nose and ear. He heard about the small cluster of maggots that had been found on the ground in the woods near Marie's face, but which had not yet eaten into her skin. He absorbed all the technical information, then asked a different kind of question.

What was Marie's expression like?

"Peaceful," one of the doctors replied.

The detail didn't have much apparent value or relevance to the investigation. But it was important enough for Schindler to include it in his daily notes.

*

Schindler and Scholl spent the next few hours getting familiar with other characters and locations—scouring the murder site again, visiting the boardinghouse where Tom Williams had been arrested. By early evening they were back in Schindler's Park Row office, and they stayed there until 9:30 p.m. reading every newspaper clipping about the case and making a list of anyone who could possibly have seen Marie Smith the morning she disappeared. The list stretched to thirteen names, and it became the first true list of potential suspects in the case.

Very quickly, Schindler narrowed it down to seven names. One of the seven, of course, was Tom Williams. Another was a psychic named Adeline Dey, who had boasted around town of knowing what happened to Marie. The florist Max Kruschka and his apprentice, Frank Heidemann, were also on the list, because they lived in the house near where Marie was last seen.

The following day, November 22, Schindler sent Charles Scholl back to Asbury Park on his own. Scholl booked a room for several days at the elegant Marlborough Hotel on Grand Avenue, and lined up interviews with some of the people who had already been questioned by police—Miss Emery, Marie's principal at the Bradley School; Albert Foster, a young classmate who saw Marie the morning she vanished; Emma Davison, the last known person to see Marie alive.

Scholl also interviewed a local life insurance agent named Francis J. Clancy, who told Scholl that he and some other volunteers had searched the exact patch of woods where Marie's body was found the night before it was discovered. "He declared that no one with fair eyesight could be shut out from view of an object as large as a child," Scholl wrote, "and therefore he believes that the body of Marie Smith was placed where it was found at a time after his visit to the spot on Saturday, Nov. 12."

Because of that, Clancy told Scholl he strongly suspected Max Kruschka, who had been involved in a sex-related crime some years earlier, and who, unlike other suspects in the case, had cellar space beneath his greenhouses, where he could have hidden Marie's body for three days before it was discovered.

Schindler did not want Scholl to interview Max Kruschka yet. Kruschka had already been interviewed and cleared by Asbury Park police, but he was still a viable suspect, and Schindler wanted his team to have as much information as possible from other sources before they approached him. Instead, Charles Scholl continued his tour of the streets and houses near where Marie was last seen.

One of those houses, a few dozen yards past Max Kruschka's property, belonged to Seymore Foster, an electrical engineer at the Asbury

Park electric light plant. Foster's eight-year-old son, Albert, was the classmate who left school after morning recess about the same time as Marie the day she disappeared.

Albert had told his story to police—he had last seen Marie heading toward Max Kruschka's home—and he told the same story to Charles Scholl when he visited. On his second day in Asbury Park, Scholl returned to the Fosters' home to go through Albert's testimony again.

Scholl knocked on the front door in the early afternoon and Seymore's wife answered. Her husband was at work and would be home that evening, she explained. She sat with Scholl and discussed her son's testimony, but it was clear something else was on her mind. She told Scholl she'd just remembered an incident that he might find relevant to the case. It didn't involve her son, Albert.

It involved her seven-year-old daughter, Grace.

Mrs. Foster explained that several days earlier, Grace—whom she described as sweet but rugged—had gone with her brothers Albert and Norman to play with a neighbor's young son in the neighbor's front yard.

When Grace came home that day, she told her mother an odd story. While she and her brothers were playing, a man approached her and asked her to come back to the yard the next day, so he could give her some candy. He asked her to come alone, without her brothers.

Mrs. Foster warned her daughter to never accept anything from strangers. Then she forgot about the incident. But the next day, her son Norman came home from playing in the same front yard, and handed his mother a nickel.

What's this? she asked.

It was from the same man who spoke to Grace the day before, the boy said. The man told Norman he'd promised Grace candy, and since she hadn't shown up, he wanted Norman to give her five cents so she could buy candy on her own.

Mrs. Foster took the nickel from her son and put it on a shelf. She warned him, too, not to accept anything from strangers. That Sunday, she brought the nickel to the First Congregation Church and dropped it in the collection plate. And again, she forgot all about it.

Three days later, Marie Smith disappeared.

Scholl scribbled down his notes and asked if he could talk to Grace himself. She was at school, so Scholl arranged to return that evening, when both Grace and her father would be home.

Later that day, Scholl knocked on the Fosters' front door again, and this time Seymore Foster answered. Seymore knew the story of Grace and the man and the nickel. His wife had told him about it when it happened, but, like her, he hadn't been overly troubled by it. He knew the man in question, but did not consider him threatening. The Fosters had not considered, as Scholl later noted, "the underlying motive and possible criminal intent" of the man who approached Grace.

But now, in light of Marie Smith's murder, everything was different. The events carried much more weight. When Seymore Foster talked about Grace's story now, Scholl wrote, "he was incensed."

Grace was in bed when Scholl arrived. Her mother went to wake her and brought her to the sitting room. Grace stood in front of Scholl and told her story again, clearly and without hesitation. The man had promised to buy her candy if she came back the following day by herself.

As Scholl listened to Grace talk, he noticed her father becoming enraged. Without a word, Seymore stood up, went to the front door, and put on his winter coat. Scholl caught him at the door.

We have to bide our time, Scholl told him. *That will further our chances of uncovering the perpetrator of Marie Smith's murder, who could be this very man.*

Scholl got Seymore to calm down and take off his coat. He thanked young Grace and thanked her parents and told them he would be in touch soon. Back at the Marlborough Hotel, Scholl hastily transcribed his notes. This new evidence, he concluded, pointed strongly toward the man in Grace's story "as being somehow seriously connected with this case."

Scholl wrote down the name—Frank Heidemann.

CHAPTER 15

My Besetting Sin

*

March 2, 1892
Memphis, Tennessee

I t began with two boys shooting marbles on an unusually warm
spring day following a nearly snowless winter. They were laughing
and teasing in the front yard of the home of Cornelius Hurst Sr., the
father of one of the boys, Cornelius Jr. The Hursts, a white family,
lived in a mixed-race neighborhood just outside of Memphis known as
"the Curve," named for the sharp bend of the streetcar tracks around
Mississippi Boulevard. Hurst was a shotgun messenger, or express
messenger—a guard hired to protect safes and strongboxes being
shipped by train. That day, his son was playing with his friend, Armour
Harris, a black boy who also lived in the Curve.

Something went wrong with their game of marbles, and they argued.
Then they fought. It was likely a well-matched fight, and nothing too
serious, but the Nashville *Tennessean* would later describe it as a "half-
grown Negro lad [striking] a little son of Cornelius Hurst."

What followed was a tragic chain reaction.

The elder Hurst ran out to the lawn and punched young Armour
Harris. The black boy's father, W. H. Harris, either saw or heard about
what happened and rushed to the Hursts' yard. He brought along two
black men, Will Stewart and Calvin McDowell, who worked in the
Negro-owned People's Grocery near the Hursts' home. They confronted

the elder Hurst and, as the *Tennessean* reported, "abused him in the vilest terms." Hurst "sallied forth and gave Harris a clubbing," too.

Soon a team of police officers arrived. Then citizens by the dozens, white and black, filled the streets. There was more fighting, and in the melee a white man named William Barrett was clubbed. He identified his attacker as Will Stewart, the black clerk at the People's Grocery.

Police stopped the fighting, and the crowd thinned away. The next day, an officer went with William Barrett to the People's Grocery, in search of Will Stewart. Calvin McDowell stopped them and told them no one matching Stewart's description was there.

Barrett, unhappy with that answer, pulled out a revolver and struck McDowell in the face with it, knocking him to the floor. In the process Barrett dropped his gun, and McDowell picked it up and shot at him. McDowell missed, but even so, his fate was sealed.

The two sides retrenched. There were newspaper reports of black citizens banding together and vowing to rid the Curve of "white trash," and reports of whites enlisting town officials to break up "a nest of turbulent and unruly negroes." A judge issued a warrant for the arrest of Calvin McDowell, and another for the arrest of the young boy, Armour Harris, for allegedly striking his white friend. Several white men were quickly sworn in as assistant deputies.

The following day, March 3, a group of armed white men made their way to the People's Grocery. They would claim their only aim was to enforce the warrants. But there was a wrinkle to the story—William Barrett, the man whose accusation against Will Stewart led to the arrest warrants, was the owner of a rival market not far from the People's Grocery. His market had been losing business to the new store. The Curve's black residents believed the true aim of law enforcement was to shutter the People's Grocery and reestablish William Barrett's monopoly.

The encounter at the store was disastrous. The black men were waiting and armed, and shots were fired. Three deputies and two black men were injured. Press reports called it an ambush, but the pastors of Memphis's black churches insisted the white men who surrounded the grocery gave no indication they were deputized sheriffs, and looked like part of an advancing white mob. After the shooting, more than one hundred white citizens were hastily deputized, and some forty black men and women were arrested and taken to jail.

Armour Harris, the boy shooting marbles, was among them, as were Will Stewart, Calvin McDowell, and the president of the People's Grocery, Thomas Moss.

The arrests prevented what might have become a full-blown race riot. There was outrage in the neighborhood, on both sides, as black lawyers tried to free the prisoners and white-owned newspapers exaggerated the injuries of the deputies who'd been shot. The Curve's black citizens assembled a small militia to watch over the Shelby County Jail, lest Will Stewart or anyone else meet the fate of the many dozens of unlucky men who'd been lynched by white mobs in Tennessee since the end of the Civil War.

For three days, all was quiet at the jail. The tension in the town began to give way. Surely Memphis had come too far to permit another atrocious lynching in such a high-profile case. Surely the modernizing city, where economic opportunity blossomed for both whites and blacks, would not take such a drastic step backward. No doubt "there was serious apprehension of further violence, especially a lynching," the black pastors would later write in their description of the events. But there was also, it seemed, some faint hope for a fair and bloodless resolution to it all, and on the third night, the black militia disbanded and no longer kept an overnight watch at the jail.

They were too optimistic.

One night later, on March 9, 1892, at 2:30 a.m., some seventy-five white men in black masks and hoods gathered on Front Street, near the Shelby County Jail. They were quiet in the night. "No one saw them assemble, no officer of the law noticed their passage," one newspaper reported. Inside the jail, a night watchman named O'Donnell chatted with a friend called Seat. A loud ring sounded—someone was at the front gate.

"Who's there?" O'Donnell called out.

"Hugh Williams of White Haven. I have a prisoner."

O'Donnell said, "All right" and opened the gate.

Three masked men pushed in. O'Donnell reached for his pistol and asked, "What does this mean?" Before he could draw it, he was tackled and pushed hard against a wall. Then he heard a terrible sound, a deep rumble, thundering, insistent. More men were coming. All the watchman could do was meekly ask an unnecessary question—"What do you want?"

"The keys to the cells where the Negroes are," was the reply.

*

In 1892, the year of the trouble at the Curve, Ida Wells was twenty-nine years old. Five years earlier, in 1887, the Tennessee Supreme Court overturned her surprise legal victory over the Chesapeake, Ohio & Southwestern Railway, and Wells went back to teaching—this time in rural Memphis—to pay off the debts from the trial and the verdict. It was a difficult time financially for Wells, who was still caring for part of her family. But while she had lost the case, Wells had gained things of value—a reputation, and a voice.

As the biographer Paula J. Giddings put it in her definitive biography of Wells, *A Sword Among Lions*, Wells became "certainly the most famous teacher in the Memphis school system." She taught first grade in two different rural Memphis schools, and earned an impressive fifty dollars a month. She built a reputation that was only partly based on her activism and persistence in the black cause. She also became known for her uncommon literary mind.

In an era when more than half of all blacks were illiterate, Wells was steeped in books—"a voracious reader," as she put it. She consumed every bit of fiction she could find in her local libraries, and discovered a sort of romance to losing herself in literature. "In the country schools where I had taught many times there was no oil for lamps and there were no candles to spare," Wells wrote in her autobiography, *Crusade for Justice.* "I used to sit by the blazing wood fire with a book in my lap during the long winter evenings and read by firelight. My only diversion was reading, and I could forget my troubles in no other way."

She read Charles Dickens and Louisa May Alcott, Charlotte Brontë and Walter Scott. She knew the Bible cover to cover (it was the only book her parents allowed her to read on Sundays), and by one account Wells read every work of both Dickens and Shakespeare before she turned twenty.

In Memphis, while teaching first grade, Wells joined other local teachers in a group called the Memphis Lyceum, part of a national movement of gatherings devoted to literary and scholarly activities—speeches, readings, debates, lectures. Wells's lyceum met every Friday afternoon in the Vance Street Christian Church, and she was one of its stars. She was a confident public speaker, and she was picked to read essays and news articles to the group. She acted in staged plays and began writing small items—notes, poems, ideas, criticisms—for the Memphis Lyceum's modest publication, the *Evening Star.*

The Lyceum, Wells wrote, "was a breath of life to me."

And it was at the Lyceum that Wells's truest talent emerged—not teaching, as it turned out, but rather *reporting.*

Wells was surprised when, after the *Evening Star*'s unpaid editor, Virginia Broughton, gave up the position, the members of the Memphis Lyceum elected her to be the new editor. She was humble about it—"I tried to make my offering as acceptable as [Broughton's] had been," she wrote. But she was also delighted. "Before long," she would write, "I found that I liked the work."

When she was a teacher, Wells understood the job to include serving as a counselor to those in need of guidance, not unlike the job of pastor. A teacher should be a resource for the community beyond his or her work in the classroom. A teacher, Wells wrote, was supposed to be "a leader." In her early years in the profession, Wells shied away from that side of the job, because she believed she was too young: "As a green girl in my teens, I was no help to the people outside of the schoolroom."

Yet even before she developed the confidence she needed to step into the role, Wells had grown dismayed with the perceived leaders in her community—the pastors and preachers. While attending the A.M.E. Church in Memphis, Wells listened to sermons and wondered why "the preachers did not give the people practical talks. I had already found that people needed guidance in everyday life, and that the leaders, the preachers, were not giving them this help." Instead, Wells wrote, people "would come to me with their problems" because she was a teacher.

Wells recognized this void in leadership—this absence of material guidance in combating real, day-to-day problems—and made it one of the core themes that eventually defined her career. She simply believed that leaders needed to do *more* to help their followers. First through the Lyceum, and then through her encounters as editor of the *Evening Star*, Wells found the means—and the nerve—to try to fill that void.

With no training as a writer or journalist or editor, Wells transformed the *Evening Star*. She wrote stories and essays and news items about current events and concerns, and she grew the following of both the paper and the Memphis Lyceum. She felt she had few "literary gifts and graces," yet she was confident in her observational skills. "I had thought much about conditions as I had seen them in the country schools and churches," she wrote, "and I had an instinctive feeling that the people who had little or no school training should have something coming into their homes weekly which dealt with their problems in a simple, helpful way." Her style of writing, therefore, was "plain and common sense."

One visitor to the Memphis Lyceum, where the *Evening Star* was read aloud, was Robert Countee, a Baptist pastor. Countee published a weekly paper of his own called the *Living Way*. He asked Wells to write for it, and for her first assignment he asked her to cover a local lawsuit. The article, one critic wrote, revealed Wells to be "a writer of superb ability, and demands for her services began to come in."

Over the next three years, Wells wrote more articles and columns for an array of outlets—the *Living Way*; the New York *Age*; the Detroit *Plaindealer*; the Indianapolis *World*; the Little Rock *Sun*; the Chattanooga *Justice*; the Memphis *Watchman*, among others. She wrote under the pen name Iola, which may have referred to a misspelling of Ida. Most likely the name was a way to create an identity separate from her role as a teacher, so that her opinions as a columnist might not endanger her job.

"Iola" wrote dispatches from her travels to different cities and landmarks, as well as thinly fictionalized stories that reflected her life. Many of her pieces dealt with the same subject—the failure of leaders, both white and black, to do enough for those in need of their help and guidance. She named and called out black politicians, shop owners, and pastors, and she developed a pointed and stinging style of criticism. "Ida was not the only journalist who wrote such acerbic prose," according to her biographer Paula Giddings, "but in a period when most female journalists wrote more mundane 'women's columns,' she was the only woman to do so with such intensity and sarcasm."

Incredibly, none of her work as a journalist had been paid. That changed when William J. Simmons, president of the National Colored Press Association and publisher of the *American Baptist* newspaper, tracked Wells down and asked her to join the *Baptist* as a weekly correspondent, with pay. "He offered me the lavish sum of one dollar weekly," Wells wrote. "It was the first time anyone had offered to pay me for work I enjoyed doing."

The boldness glimpsed in Wells's landmark case against the railroads in 1883 was gaining dimension. Wells, not yet thirty years old, was emerging in her community and across the country as a distinctive and audacious writer, and more—an influential journalist, a provocative critic, a conveyer of ideas, a motivator to action. "She has become famous as one of the few of our women who handle our goose quill with diamond point as easily as any man in newspaper work," wrote T. Thomas Fortune, the owner of the popular black newspaper the *New*

York Age. "She has plenty of nerve and is as sharp as a steel trap, and she has no sympathy for humbug."

And yet Wells had still to find her full, authentic voice. She was still young, and she questioned her writing skills, especially the "dreary sameness" and "monotonous" style of her articles. She complained in her diary about "a paucity of ideas." She also wrestled with the side of her that first emerged after her parents' deaths—the fierceness of her spirit and her ready sense of indignation. She thought of her anger as "my besetting sin," as if the rage she felt about perceived injustices was something that needed to be tempered, or even snuffed out.

But her thinking would change—her moment would come. Events would demand more and more of her. Some furies and indignations, the times would teach her, were not sins at all.

*

These were the existential questions that all prominent black thinkers had to address in the decades after the Civil War—what is the right response to the continuing suppression of black people in America? To the systemic repression of black businesses? To Jim Crow laws and all-white juries? To violent resistance to integration? To the rise of vigilante groups like the Ku Klux Klan? To the bedrock principle of white supremacy that permeated the South?

To the very notion that the grand, healing experiment known as Reconstruction had, in the quarter century after Abraham Lincoln's murder, not healed the country's wounds at all, and perhaps even made them worse, at least for black Americans?

Most urgently: What was the right response to the most horrific and damaging method of suppressing the black race of all—the terroristic and inhuman practice of lynching?

Lynching—a term thought to derive from a Revolutionary era Virginian named Charles Lynch, a local court manager who aggressively jailed British supporters without proper jurisdiction—came to refer to any extrajudicial killing of an individual by a group, usually in public. In the United States many lynchings were hangings, but victims were also shot, burned, beaten, and dragged through streets. Racial lynchings existed throughout the history of slavery in America, but they intensified after slavery was abolished and blacks were given the right to vote. By one estimate, the KKK alone was involved in four hundred lynchings in the United States between 1868 and 1871. The majority of all lynching victims were black.

The matter of how to confront lynching was tied to the larger question of how to assert the place of black people in American society. Was the answer retribution and aggression, or a philosophy of dialogue and alliance-making? The most prominent black leader of the nineteenth century, the former slave and brilliant orator Frederick Douglass, believed in a mix of resistance and integration—"an egalitarian ethos of inclusion and a robust conception of mutual responsibility," as one historian phrased it. He saw the place of blacks in society as equal to and interdependent on the white race—a dual emphasis on blacks becoming self-reliant, and whites becoming acclimated, through moral suasion, to the concept of social justice.

Other black leaders, however, believed in compulsion over suasion. One such thinker was T. Thomas Fortune, whose newspaper, the *New York Age*, was likely the country's most influential black-owned newspaper in the 1880s. Born into slavery, Fortune was self-taught and never took a class until he enrolled in college. There he considered studying law but switched to journalism, and quickly rose to prominence because of his confrontational style. Fortune laid out his core philosophy in a heralded 1883 essay, "The Virtue of Agitation."

"There is no half way ground between right and wrong," he wrote. "The one or the other must obtain, and prevail. Mental inertia is death. Indifferent acquiescence in wrong is death. Tame submission to outrage is death. Agitation, constant protesting, always standing up to be counted, to be heard, or to be knocked down—this spirit breeds respect and dulls the edge of tyranny."

More pointedly: "If others use the weapon of violence to combat our peaceful argument, it is not for us to run away from violence. A man's a man, and what is worth having is worth fighting for."

There it was, the choice—peaceful, deliberate mutual integration, or aggression and agitation in pursuit of equality?

Ida Wells, in her early years as a journalist, did not come down forcefully on either side. By her own admission, she had a narrow view of the causes and dynamics of lynching, believing that they were primarily brought about by white women accusing black men of rape. "Like many another person who had read of lynching in the South," Wells wrote, "I had accepted the idea meant to be conveyed—that although lynching was irregular and contrary to law and order, unreasoning anger over the terrible crime of rape led to the lynching; that perhaps the brute deserved death anyhow and the mob was justified in taking his life."

But of course, not all lynching had to do with rape. The notorious 1886 massacre of thirteen black men by a white mob in a courtroom in Carrollton, Mississippi—after the men became witnesses for black defendants accused of attacking a white lawyer—was as shocking a crime as had occurred in the South since the Civil War, and led to mass protests across the country. Still, these terroristic and horrific murders, which happened just 125 miles south of Memphis, did not inspire Wells to produce any article or column or opinion about them, other than to write in her diary, "O God, when will these massacres stop?"

In 1889, two partners of the *Memphis Free Speech & Headlight*, a newspaper published in the basement of the Beale Street Church in Memphis, invited Wells to join the paper as an editor. Wells agreed, but only if she was made an equal partner with the two men, Taylor Nightingale and J. L. Fleming. Less than a year later, T. Thomas Fortune was one of the first people to commend Wells on her work for the paper—which, thanks to Wells's tireless travels through the South promoting the *Free Speech* at church conventions and lodge gatherings, had seen its circulation rise from fifteen hundred to four thousand.

Fortune admired Wells and followed her career. Wells did the same. She was certainly aware of his radical ideas, and considered Fortune a mentor. He would become one of two men to have a profound and dynamic influence on Wells's views on racial strife in America—and particularly on lynchings—in the years after the *Free Speech* gave Wells her biggest public platform yet.

The other man who changed Wells forever was her friend Thomas Moss, one of the black men arrested after the trouble at the Curve.

CHAPTER 16

Turn Our Faces to the West

*

March 9, 1892
Memphis, Tennessee

Just about every black resident in the Curve knew and liked Thomas Moss. He was a postal carrier and he made regular stops in most homes and stores, and if there was any news in town—a tussle, a romance—Tommie Moss knew it before most people, and he didn't mind sharing it along his route.

Moss was diligent and enterprising. He opened a bank account at thirteen, apprenticed as a barber, and later passed a civil servants exam to work as a mail carrier. He saved enough money to buy his own home, and to join ten other black investors in a new collective, the People's Grocery. The store was designed to cater to the growing black population in Memphis, and to compete against the only other grocery store in the Curve—the one owned by William Barrett. The men chose Tommie Moss to be the store's president.

One of Moss's best friends in Memphis was Ida Wells. They met while he was delivering mail to her *Free Speech* office on Beale Street, not far from where he worked nights at the People's Grocery. They grew so close that Moss asked Wells to be godmother to Maurine, his young daughter with his wife, Betty. "A finer, cleaner man," Wells wrote, "never walked the streets of Memphis."

Wells was away in Natchez, Mississippi, promoting the *Free Speech*, when violence broke out at the Curve on March 2, 1892. She would have to read and hear about what happened after Moss was arrested, and several men in black hoods quietly pushed their way into the Shelby County Jail, where twenty-seven black men were locked up, around 2:00 a.m. on March 9. As the newspapers reported it, the night watchman, O'Donnell, told the masked men he didn't have the keys to the jail cells, and a rough search proved that he didn't. Two of the intruders bound O'Donnell's hands and stayed watch over him, while two others invaded the main jail office and found the keys on a table.

Then the men went to the cells and searched in darkness for their three main targets—Will Stewart, Calvin McDowell, and Thomas Moss.

Finally, they found the cell they were looking for. A key went into a lock. Thomas Moss was pulled from his cell, a hand over his mouth, and he was bound and gagged with rope. Stewart and McDowell were next. The three were rushed out of the jail and marched down Auction Street, toward the Mississippi River. The mob reached the tracks of the Chesapeake & Ohio Railroad—the very railroad Ida Wells sued—and headed north along the tracks, into the pitch-blackness of a moonless night.

They stopped in an empty and desolate brickyard near Wolf River.

The men in hoods ungagged the men, and Thomas Moss was first to speak. By one account he begged to be spared and pleaded on behalf of his daughter and unborn son, Thomas Jr. By another, he was defiant.

"If you're going to kill us," Moss was quoted as saying, "turn our faces to the west."

As if to say, *There is no justice for us here, in the South. Let us at least gaze upon our future as free men, someplace else.*

The sharp crack of a revolver. The bullet piercing Thomas Moss's cheek. A cascade of shots, deafening. "A terrible volley was poured in among the shivering negroes, who instantly fell dead in their tracks," reported the *Indianapolis Journal.* "The bodies presented a horrible sight."

Calvin McDowell's jaw was shot clean off, leaving him with a massive hole in the back of his head. Because he grabbed the hot muzzle of a shotgun in self-defense, his right hand had been blasted off. An eyeball hung from its socket. Will Stewart was shot in the mouth and the back of his head, "and his body was riddled with buckshot," the *Journal* wrote. Thomas Moss had an ear shot off and a row of bullet holes in his forehead. Twenty-five shots were fired in just three seconds' time.

One newspaper called it a "Wholesale Lynching." Another: "The Curse of the Southland." By all accounts, the lynchings were orderly and efficient, with no hollering or celebrations, the vengeance workmanlike. An inquest determined the black men "were shot to death by parties unknown to the jury." White looters ransacked the People's Grocery, stripping its shelves and forcing its shuttering and bankruptcy. The store's remaining stock was sold to William Barrett, the rival grocer, for less than eighteen cents on the dollar.

Just a few weeks later, Thomas Moss Jr. was born fatherless.

*

The gruesome slaughter of her friend affected Ida Wells like no other lynching. "The shock to the colored people who knew and loved [the three men] was beyond description," she wrote of the murders, citing William Barrett as the main instigator. "With the aid of the city and county authorities, and the daily papers, that white grocer had indeed put an end to his rival Negro grocer as well as to his business."

That the white mob ended not only the lives of three black men but also their thriving business clarified for Wells the driving force behind the insidious evil of lynching—not accusations of rape, or any crime at all, but the need to keep her race economically subjugated.

"Thomas Moss, Calvin McDowell, and Will Stewart had been lynched in Memphis, one of the leading cities of the South, in which no lynching had taken place before, with just as much brutality as other victims of the mob; and they had committed no crime against white women," Wells wrote. "This is what opened my eyes to what lynching really was: an excuse to get rid of Negroes who were acquiring wealth and property and thus keep the race terrorized, and 'keep the nigger down.'"

The calls by T. Thomas Fortune to meet violence with action, and the unavenged murder of her friend Tommie Moss, transformed Wells from a critic to an activist. Finally, she used the weapons of her voice and platform to articulate a decisive response to the issue that had once seemed too big for her. Now, like Fortune, she would issue a call to action—not violent retribution, not a race riot, but action, strong and impactful. Her advice to the black community in Memphis was based on Thomas Moss's poignant last words—"turn our faces to the west."

"The City of Memphis has demonstrated that neither character nor standing avails the Negro if he dares to protect himself against the white man or become his rival," Wells wrote in her first editorial in the *Free Speech* following the killings. "There is nothing we can do about the lynching now, as we are outnumbered and without arms. The white mob could help itself to ammunition without delay, but the order was rigidly enforced against the selling of guns to Negroes. There is therefore only one thing left that we can do—save our money and leave a town which will neither protect our lives and property, nor give us a fair trial in the courts, but takes us out and murders us in cold blood."

Hers was not the first call for blacks to leave the South and look for prosperity elsewhere. There had been other emigrations—black citizens by the thousands fleeing southern states and heading north. Now Memphis would see its own exodus. Pastors like Rev. R. N. Countee, who helped start Wells's writing career, left the city and took their entire congregations with them, heading to Oklahoma, where great swaths of land were being opened and sold. Those who couldn't afford train tickets packed wagons and left that way. A group of three hundred blacks set out on ferries across the Mississippi, bid good-bye and good luck by hundreds of black citizens on the shore. "The last person to go aboard the ferry boat was a horny-handed son of toil who led a yellow hound,"

Wells reported. "As he started up the gangplank the dog pulled back. His master, seeing that he had the center stage for a moment, yelled, 'Come on here—what you want to stay back there for, want the white folks to lynch you, too?'"

Wells also recounted how the treasurer of the City Railway Company asked her to use her influence to persuade black people in Memphis to start riding the streetcars again—evidence that the exodus would have a major impact on the white economy.

"So your own job then depends on Negro patronage?" Wells asked.

The treasurer, according to Wells, had no good response.

In the months and years after the lynching of Thomas Moss, Calvin McDowell, and Lee Stewart, an estimated six thousand black people fled the city of Memphis.

Ida Wells was preparing to be one of them. She understood she could be in danger if she stayed. One line in her *Free Speech* editorial—that "nobody in this section of the country believes the old thread-bare lie that negro men rape white women"—was particularly controversial. The white-owned *Memphis Daily Commercial* ran its own editorial in response, decrying and even threatening Wells. "The fact that a black scoundrel is allowed to live and utter such loathsome and repulsive calumnies is a volume of evidence as to the wonderful patience of Southern whites," the paper declared. "But we have had enough of it . . . the negroes may as well understand that there is no mercy for the negro rapist, and little patience with his defenders."

The call for retaliation against any black person who dared challenge the lynch law system was clear and urgent. Ida Wells was not surprised. She had heard rumors that she would be lynched as soon as she returned to Memphis, and she believed them.

"I had been warned repeatedly by my own people that something would happen," Wells wrote. "I expected some cowardly retaliation from the lynchers."

Soon after the murders in the Curve, Wells bought a pistol, and vowed "to sell my life as dearly as possible if attacked."

Still, leaving Memphis and taking the operations of the *Free Speech* to another city made sense. Wells was prepared to do it, but before she could, she received another shock.

She was away from Memphis, visiting her friend T. Thomas Fortune in Jersey City, New Jersey, when it happened. It was Fortune who broke the news to her.

"Haven't you seen the morning paper?" he asked her one day in May 1892, two months after the lynchings.

Wells hadn't. Fortune gave her a copy of the *New York Sun*.

A group of white men had broken into the Beale Street office of the *Free Speech*, and pistol-whipped one of its managing partners, J. L. Fleming. Later, Wells would learn the same men returned to the *Free Speech* office and destroyed the furniture and typesetting machines. They left a note warning that anyone who tried to publish the paper again would be punished by death. The note mentioned Ida Wells by name.

Now her newspaper was no more, and Memphis was no longer hers. Wells had no choice but to follow her own advice and leave. She had been cruelly exiled, and she chose to leave the South altogether.

T. Thomas Fortune offered her a job writing for his paper, the *New York Age*, and Wells accepted. She moved one thousand miles away from Memphis and found a place to live in Brooklyn. Once before she had seen her world crumble, her foundation stripped away, destroyed by the yellow fever epidemic. Once before she had been forced into a wholesale transformation. And, as before, Wells saw her exile from Memphis as an invitation to be bolder, braver.

Thanks to Fortune's "splendid help," Wells wrote, "I was given an opportunity to tell the world for the first time the true story of Negro lynchings." This, she realized, was her calling; this was how she would answer the existential question of lynching, of the place and fate of blacks in America. With all her prodigious reading of Dickens and Shakespeare and countless other classics, Wells had not, to her sadness and frustration, read anything that reflected the reality of life for men and women of her race. "There is in literature no true type of the Negro as he is today," she would say. "The press is in control of the whites, and the attacks upon us are colored to suit themselves."

Starting in 1892, Ida Wells set out to change that. She would tell the true story. She would spare no detail. She would go into the darkest places and bring the horrors to light. America needed to know.

CHAPTER 17

A Balance of Goodness and Evil

*

November 25, 1910
Asbury Park, New Jersey

The hunt for Marie Smith's killer now had its first legitimate suspect other than Tom Williams—the mysterious Frank Heidemann.

Heidemann, twenty-seven, was fairly new to Asbury Park, and no one knew much about him. He wasn't physically big—five foot five inches and 135 pounds, at most—but he was lean and wiry. He kept his dark black hair cut short, and he had high, sharp cheekbones that made his clean-shaven face look angular and intense, giving him a slightly feral appearance. His eyes had a tendency to widen and appear too big for his face. Even so, he was considered good looking. He was German-born, but he could have passed for Italian or Slavic. There was nothing brash or boisterous about him. Max Kruschka, his employer, called him "sober and industrious." In Asbury Park, Heidemann hadn't made much of an impression on anyone.

All that was really known about Heidemann was that he worked for Max Kruschka in his flower business, and that he lived in a small, second-floor bedroom in Kruschka's home on the corner of Whitesville Road and West Asbury Avenue—the exact spot where Marie Smith was last seen before she disappeared. Heidemann's offer of candy to Grace Foster happened in the front yard of Kruschka's property, which was right against the sidewalk that Marie Smith used to get to school and back.

In New York City, Investigator Raymond Schindler spoke with Charles Scholl and agreed that Grace's story about Heidemann made him their leading suspect. It was more circumstantial evidence, but it was compelling.

What was frustrating was that both Asbury Park investigators and the first set of detectives hired by Sheriff Hetrick had questioned Heidemann, and quickly discounted him as a suspect. Schindler learned the Greater New York Agency detectives had even allowed Heidemann to wash the clothes he wore the day Marie vanished, after merely inspecting them, rather than having them tested. The spotlight had never been fixed on Heidemann, and in the nearly three weeks since Marie's body had been found, he would have been free to lose or destroy all kinds of evidence. Schindler and his men had a lot of catching up to do.

The day after Thanksgiving, November 25, 1910, Schindler took the train back to Asbury Park, and Charles Scholl met him at the station on Main Street at 1:19 p.m. Schindler brought along Charles Severance, another Burns Agency detective assigned to the case. Schindler and Scholl went to the Sea Coast Bank building on Mattison Avenue and met with Sheriff Hetrick in his office. They shared the details of Scholl's interview with Grace Foster, and named Frank Heidemann their new top suspect. The talk turned to how they could get a confession out of Heidemann.

Schindler had an idea: he wanted to run a phony news article about the Marie Smith case. The story would announce an incredible break—the appearance of clear fingerprints on Marie's body, extracted by a fingerprint specialist using new technology. This fresh evidence, the story would say, meant new suspects and more interviews. "It is expected that someone will flinch upon reading this shortly before their summons," Charles Severance wrote in his report that day, "and this will aid in establishing their guilt." The intended "someone" was Frank Heidemann.

Schindler and Hetrick agreed to run the article on Monday, November 28—and to bring Heidemann in for an interrogation that same day, once he'd had the chance to digest the morning news.

After the meeting in Hetrick's office, Scholl returned to the Marlborough Hotel, where he was staying, to rent a horse and buggy. He steered it back to Main Street and picked up Schindler and Severance, waiting for him outside the Sea Coast Building. Scholl led the buggy to Asbury Avenue, where Max Kruschka and Heidemann lived, and through the surrounding streets, so the men could figure out where to best place detectives to keep an eye on and, if needed, arrest Frank Heidemann, should he try to flee Asbury Park.

After the tour of the area around the crime scene, Scholl brought the buggy back to Main Street so Schindler and Severance could board a 4:00 p.m. train back to New York City. Schindler would return on a date closer to the Heidemann interrogation.

That evening, Charles Scholl went to his room at the Marlborough and called Sheriff Hetrick around 6:00 p.m. Hetrick didn't answer, but just a few minutes later, the sheriff returned the call, and he had bad news. He'd been speaking with Coroner Purdy, and Purdy told him Frank Heidemann had left town earlier that day, headed for New York City. From what Purdy heard, it was doubtful Heidemann was ever coming back to Asbury Park.

*

Scholl quickly called Schindler with the news, and later that night Schindler and two operatives took the 8:50 p.m. train to Asbury Park. They arrived at Sheriff Hetrick's office a little after 10:00 p.m. Hetrick had been trying to confirm if Heidemann had returned from New York City, but hadn't been able to do so. No one could say for sure where Heidemann was, and it was possible he was gone for good. Schindler decided to give Heidemann a little more time to return, but if he didn't, they would need to get into Max Kruschka's home to confirm that he was gone.

Schindler and Hetrick sent lookouts to the Asbury Park and North Asbury train stations. The lookouts waited until the black traction engine and dark steel cars of the 1:45 a.m. locomotive pulled out of each station, on its way farther south. Heidemann was nowhere to be seen.

Next, Schindler and his men drove to a spot across Asbury Avenue from Max Kruschka's house. They parked behind some trees so they could not be so easily seen. They needed to get into Kruschka's home, but without revealing that Heidemann was their surveillance target. They needed another ruse.

The plan was this—the coroner, Robert Purdy, would knock on Kruschka's front door under the pretense of questioning him about a piece of evidence. The fake evidence, they decided, would be a cheap hand ax. The oddness of rousing Kruschka from sleep to show him evidence in the middle of the night was unavoidable, and Schindler decided they wouldn't even try to explain it away. They would simply find out if Heidemann was there, and, if he wasn't, find out where he was.

Sometime around 2:00 a.m., with Schindler and Scholl watching from their car, Purdy walked across Asbury Avenue and through Max Kruschka's front yard. He knocked on the door and waited with the cheap ax in his hand. After a while, the front door opened. Max Kruschka, sleepy and unhappy, stood and stared at his visitors in disbelief.

Behind him—Frank Heidemann.

So he had returned after all. Purdy went through with the ruse, apologizing to Kruschka for the late hour and asking him about the ax. The interview lasted just minutes. Purdy returned to the cars across Asbury Avenue, and Schindler instructed two operatives to watch Kruschka's house overnight. He and Scholl, now certain Heidemann was in their sights, went to the Marlborough for a few hours' sleep.

The next morning, the ruse to locate Heidemann had somehow become front-page news in the *Asbury Park Press*, under the blaring headline "New Arrest Likely in Murder Mystery." Alvin Cliver had learned about Purdy's late-night visit to Kruschka, and used it to announce a new development in the investigation—the imminent arrest of a "young white man believed to know more than he has yet told." The *Press* didn't name the mystery man, but the same article quickly pivoted to Purdy's visit to Kruschka, drawing a clear inference that the man was Frank Heidemann. That was certainly the conclusion an angry Kruschka came to, according to his many complaints to the *Press*.

"Why don't the police arrest others who know anything about the case and hold them as witnesses instead of sneaking around and standing on my corner?" Kruschka was quoted as saying. "I have done everything in my power to help the police in their search for the murderer. I have fed those detectives, allowed them to use my phone and thrown my place open to searchers. They didn't find a thing and yet they will get me out of bed after midnight and ask me all kinds of questions about an axe they found. I have given my time and my business has suffered."

Kruschka also distanced himself from the man he assumed was the target of all the attention—his boarder, Frank Heidemann. "If the police have any suspicion of him, why don't they arrest him?" Kruschka asked. "Tonight, I will pay him off. I am through with him if the police believe he is implicated in any way. If they want him, they should take him."

There it was. Not only had Kruschka essentially disclosed Heidemann to be the new suspect, but he'd also vowed to turn him loose. Heidemann now had a valid reason to leave town. Schindler had to act faster than he'd planned, so he moved his interrogation up one day, from Monday to Sunday. The phony article about fingerprints would also run a day earlier. That gave Schindler just one day, Saturday, to prepare for his formal questioning of Heidemann. He knew it would likely be his best chance to knock Heidemann off balance and, if he was indeed guilty of the crime, squeeze a confession out of him. Schindler had no evidence linking Heidemann to Marie's murder, and nothing to confront him with. It would come down to the incisiveness of his interrogation.

What the men who hired Ray Schindler did not know was that Frank Heidemann would be the first murder suspect Schindler had ever confronted face-to-face.

*

Schindler was fairly new to the business of murder and criminal concealment, but he had already come to believe one thing—that men wore their lies as surely as they wore their hats and shoes.

An uttered lie, Schindler believed, was not necessarily an ephemeral, uncapturable thing. It could be seized and dissected by the trained mind. The thoughts and emotions behind deception were measurable. Humans betrayed their lies because they simply couldn't help themselves. To Schindler, this wasn't speculation, it was science. A new science known as emotional inscription.

Earlier in 1910, Schindler began reading the works of Hugo Münsterberg, a German-American, Harvard-educated psychologist pioneering the controversial discipline of applied psychology. Formal and narrow-eyed, with a jutting jaw, bald head, and sprouting mustache beneath a prominent nose, Münsterberg believed that physiological changes such as a spike in blood pressure or a simple muscle contraction correlated to mental and emotional states like anger, relief, fear, and guilt.

Just as letters could be inscribed on a block of granite, emotions were inscribed on our minds and bodies.

"The physician needs his magnifier to find out whether there are tubercles in the sputum," Münsterberg wrote in one of his many papers on the topic. "The legal psychologist may, in the future, use his mental microscope to find out whether there are lies in the mind of a suspect."

Some of these emotional inscriptions, Münsterberg believed, were so subtle they could be detected only with the use of machinery.

Münsterberg loved his machines. He worked with a primitive chronoscope—a device for measuring very brief intervals of time—to evaluate a subject's reactions to provocative words and images. He used an early version of a sphygmomanometer—a clunky metal contraption mounted on the wrist like a medieval torture device—to measure changes in blood pressure. He had a pneumograph that recorded interruptions in respiration, and an automatograph that charted muscle contractions.

Münsterberg believed so firmly in mechanized lie detection that he pushed hard in essays and speeches for the integration of science and psychology—and he took plenty of ridicule for it. When he was hired to help create mental testing booths for the 1893 Chicago World's Fair, his laboratories filled with bizarre instruments and mental testing devices were likened to carnival sideshows—"a Münsterbergian circus," as one critic put it. Lawyers and judges were particularly dismissive of his work, to his great frustration.

"The psychology of the witness is treated in no way exhaustively," Münsterberg lamented in a 1908 study. "My only purpose is to turn the attention of serious men to an absurdly neglected field."

Ray Schindler was fascinated by Münsterberg's machines, but he was particularly intrigued by the intuitive dimension of his work—the idea that investigators could be trained to reliably detect deception *without* instruments. Like Münsterberg, Schindler was a fan of literature, and both were particular fans of Shakespeare, whose characters constantly spoke and acted in ways that revealed underlying states of mind. Long before applied psychology caught on, dramatists were the true pioneers of uncovering the hidden scaffolding of human behavior.

Why, Schindler wondered, couldn't detectives be at least as adept as playwrights at understanding and documenting deception?

There was something else in Münsterberg's thinking that deeply impressed Schindler—a notion that echoed his mother's compassionate conviction that the inmates who came through her prison library were not monsters, but rather broken men.

Münsterberg argued that criminals were, on a human level, no different from law-abiders. The villain, same as the fine citizen, had a balance of goodness and evil intent within him, and had simply encountered "the cruelty of misfortune, which once in a hasty hour destroyed that balance," Münsterberg wrote. A wise investigator would recognize this and approach his suspect as a man, not a demon, because "to make them feel that they are recognized as equals is to win them back over to decency." The most powerful expression of this thinking, Münsterberg believed, was the confession.

An investigator's true goal was to elicit a full confession from his suspect, not through violence or oppression, but rather through psychological trickery. The thinking was that criminals want—*need*—to confess. "The man who confesses puts himself again on an equal ground with the honest majority," Münsterberg stated. "He gives up his identity with the criminal and eliminates the crime like a foreign body from his life. A true confession wins the bedrock of life again."

In 1910, Münsterberg's machines were not quite ready for the mainstream—though he certainly cleared the path for the modern lie detector that would appear in a few decades' time.

But his faith in an investigator's intuitive prowess, and his view of the full and cathartic confession as the ultimate goal of both suspect and interrogator, were robust enough in 1910 to reach into Raymond Schindler's mind and transform him as a detective.

That year, Schindler was given his first murder case to handle as a lead investigator—the Marie Smith case. He felt confident enough about Hugo Münsterberg's ideas to put them immediately into practice. When Schindler arrived in Asbury Park in late 1910, he was already thinking of criminal intent as an internal imbalance that needed to be corrected—not something monstrous that needed to be destroyed. And he understood that the most imbalanced of souls, the most unfathomable of crimes, would require the deepest penetrations into the darkness of a mind.

*

Just after 10:00 a.m. on Sunday, November 27, 1910, Ray Schindler, along with Charles Scholl, arrived at the stately Seacoast Bank Building on Mattison Avenue, just off Main Street in Asbury Park.

The three-story building sat diagonally across from police headquarters and was built of red brick, stone, and terra-cotta. The Seacoast Bank kept $100,000 worth of capital and $1,200,000 in deposits, and the building housed a massive electrical roll press that churned out long sheets of blue-seal American banknotes—$372,250 worth of notes in its fourteen years of printing currency. The building was the thriving financial center of Asbury Park.

It was also where Sheriff Clarence Hetrick kept a second-floor office for his side business in real estate. Hetrick and Schindler agreed the best place to interrogate Frank Heidemann was in this office, which bore much of the weighty authority of the top lawman in the county.

The previous two days had been eventful. First, the false alarm about Heidemann skipping town. Then the article in the *Asbury Park Press* about how Max Kruschka was going to fire Heidemann, freeing him to leave for good. After the article, Schindler ordered round-the-clock surveillance of Frank Heidemann. At 6:40 the following morning, with the dark of night just lifting, two of Schindler's men watching Kruschka's home saw the front door open, and saw Frank Heidemann walk out.

He had something in his hands. A sign board. They watched as Heidemann set the sign on the front lawn and hammered it into the cold ground, before turning and going back inside. One of the detectives snuck forward for a better look at the sign. It read: NO TRESPASSING.

Right around that time, early on Sunday, November 27, Ray Schindler awoke early and checked the newspapers. He read through the fake article touting new fingerprint evidence in the Marie Smith case. The article declared "a certain man who lives near the scene of the crime has been under surveillance for some time. Impressions of his fingers have been obtained and these were compared with the prints that were found on some of the garments worn by the little victim." The two sets of prints, Schindler read, "are said to bear a close resemblance."

At 8:30, Schindler met with Charles Scholl, and together they left the Marlborough Hotel and headed to Max Kruschka's house. There they spoke with the detective who had kept watch overnight, and confirmed Heidemann was inside. Schindler had Scholl knock on the front door to officially summon Heidemann to an interview that morning at

10:00 a.m. Max Kruschka answered and said he would personally drive Heidemann to the sheriff's office for the interview.

Exactly at ten, Kruschka pulled his sedan up to the Seacoast Building and dropped off Heidemann. Scholl went down to the front of the building and walked Heidemann up to Hetrick's office. Ray Schindler was waiting for him there. Schindler watched as Heidemann marched grimly into the office and took a seat without a word. He got his first good look at his suspect. Heidemann's eyes were cast downward and his sharp jaw and sunken cheeks made him appear sickly. He wore a stubbly mustache. When he finally spoke, Schindler could tell his English was good, though occasionally it broke in the middle of a sentence.

Schindler knew Heidemann was already on the record about Marie Smith's murder. He claimed he never met Marie and certainly had not seen her the day she vanished—even though she walked past the house where he lived. He said he first heard of her disappearance one day later, when a schoolboy knocked on his door and told him about it.

Schindler found that hard to believe, considering all the commotion near the Kruschkas' home on the day Marie vanished.

The questioning began. Scholl and Hetrick sat to the side while Schindler faced Heidemann.

"What is your name?" Schindler asked.

"Frank E. Heidemann."

"Where were you born?"

"In Dortmund in Westphalia. Germany."

"What is your age?"

"Twenty-seven."

"Where are your parents?"

"My father died in 1901. My mother died in 1909."

Scholl later noted, "He answered all questions reluctantly and not in detail." But Heidemann did not squirm or shift in his seat. At times, Schindler observed, "he even became rather buoyant."

For the next two hours, Schindler and Scholl had Heidemann build a complete personal history up to the present day. His time in a boarding school as a child. His first job at eleven, as an assistant florist in a cemetery. His trip to America on the *Crown Prince Wilhelm* in January 1910. His arrival in New York City with four hundred dollars in his pocket, and his position as the night telephone operator in a German hospital on 77th Street and Park Avenue, for twenty dollars a month. Answering a help-wanted ad in the German newspaper *Staats Zeitung* and being hired by Max Kruschka in Asbury Park, just months before Marie Smith's murder.

Did he make any friends along the way? Schindler asked him. Did he have any female acquaintances? Heidemann answered no to both. He had no interest in women, he said.

Schindler asked Heidemann about his recent day trip to New York City. Heidemann provided the details with total assurance. "He was able to recite his movements rapidly, giving each move that he made, the time, etc.," Schindler noticed. "It was apparent he had rehearsed the story."

"You sound rather conversant with the streets of New York considering the fact that you were only there for such a short time," Schindler pressed Heidemann.

"I spent a great deal of time walking around. I knew my way very well."

Schindler deliberately asked the same questions over and over. Where did you go next? How long were you there? He took Heidemann through the events of the day three separate times.

After an hour of repetitive questioning, Heidemann finally showed a flash of agitation.

"I've already recounted all of these circumstances and I don't care to repeat them," he abruptly announced, flatly refusing to answer any more questions about his day in New York.

Schindler felt that he had him off balance now.

Schindler turned the focus to the events of November 9, the day Marie disappeared. He asked Heidemann where he was that morning. Heidemann said he was sweeping up ashes on Max Kruschka's property.

"Did you see Marie Smith that morning?"

"No."

Schindler brought up the testimony of Mrs. Emma Davison, who lived one town over from Asbury Park and was walking along Ridge Avenue, near Max Kruschka's house, at 10:30 a.m. on November 10. Davison was the last known person to see Marie Smith alive. According to a transcript of her testimony, which Scholl read to Heidemann, Davison told a prosecutor that she also saw Frank Heidemann, standing in his front yard just a short distance away from Marie.

"He stood in the path with nothing but the hedge fence between them," Davison recalled. "He spoke to the dog when the dog was barking at the little girl, and the little girl and the dog was closer to him than I was, and he couldn't help but see the dog through that fence, and he certainly would have seen the little girl."

"The girl was within eight or ten feet of him?" Davison was asked.

"No, she was not *three* feet."

Someone had placed Frank Heidemann *within three feet* of Marie Smith the morning she disappeared.

Scholl read the testimony to Heidemann while Schindler studied the suspect's face. When Scholl was done, Schindler asked Heidemann to give his version of events. Heidemann hesitated. His demeanor was changing. The buoyancy was gone. Heidemann resisted giving any details about that morning.

But what about Mrs. Davison's testimony? Schindler persisted. *You must answer this question.* Schindler got up from his chair and moved around the office as he spoke, asking questions one after the other, firing them "in rapid succession," he said, in an effort "to get Heidemann riled up."

Schindler saw that it was working. He kept circling, kept firing.

"Okay," Heidemann finally said, "if Mrs. Davison says she saw me with Marie Smith and that only the hedge divided us and that therefore I must have seen Marie, I say she is a liar."

The denial was not as important to Schindler as the way in which it was delivered. Heidemann, he noted, "appeared very dejected, as meek as a lamb." The fight was going out of him. It was time for more pressure.

First, Schindler brought in a bundle of clothes—the clothes in which Marie Smith was murdered. Schindler handed Heidemann the brown winter coat and the green Scotch plaid dress, both caked with dirt and blood. He watched for a response. Heidemann looked over the clothing and said he had never seen them before. He remained calm.

Schindler had one more surprise. A very big surprise. He backed up from Heidemann and spoke to Scholl.

"Okay," Schindler said, "bring in the girl."

CHAPTER 18

The Greenhouse

*

November 27, 1910
Asbury Park, New Jersey

There was a hard silence in Hetrick's office. Schindler kept his eyes on Heidemann. He believed he knew what Heidemann was thinking.

The "girl," Heidemann surely presumed, referred to the body of Marie Smith. What other girl was there? He had been handed her clothing, and now he was going to be made to look at her.

Schindler studied Heidemann's face and saw "his lower lip begin to quiver." He watched Heidemann slump down in his seat and look pleadingly up at his interrogator.

In a low, soft voice, Heidemann said, "I wish you were through questioning me."

At Schindler's order, Charles Scholl left the office, and within a minute returned with the "girl."

It was Grace Foster.

On their way to Sheriff Hetrick's office that morning, Schindler and Scholl stopped at the Fosters' home on Pine Street, and escorted the seven-year-old to the Seacoast Building. Grace waited in a side room with her mother while the Heidemann interview progressed and finally arrived at her part. Scholl walked Grace Foster into Hetrick's office, but kept her several feet away from Heidemann.

Grace, tell us what happened the day you were over at Max Kruschka's house, Schindler asked her.

Grace told her story again. "Frank Heidemann asked me to come over to the house tomorrow when the boys are not there," she said. "He told me he had some candy he wanted to give me."

Schindler turned to Heidemann, who was defiant.

"I will not say that she lies," he said, "nor will I say that she speaks the truth."

Schindler pressed him for more. Again, Heidemann got angry.

"I do not like children particularly," he said. "If they are around me too much, I get annoyed."

That was all he would say about Grace Foster.

Scholl led the girl out of the room. Heidemann withdrew quietly into himself. Schindler hadn't expected Heidemann to buckle in Grace's presence. He didn't believe the tactic would lead directly to a confession. It was all part of chipping away at the façade. Heidemann's discomfort in her presence, he believed, was a marker of deception. His reaction to possibly having to face the dead body of Marie Smith revealed raw emotions. Guilt? Remorse? Fear? Something was there. Something had caused a flinch.

Schindler also knew Heidemann's ordeal wasn't nearly done. The questioning would go on for several more hours. There would be other opportunities for Heidemann to slip up and contradict himself, get caught in a lie. More chances to see him flinch.

Yet Schindler wouldn't be there for much of it. Bringing Heidemann in for an interview had a secondary purpose, unknown to the suspect— to get Heidemann out of Max Kruschka's house, and give Schindler a clean shot at searching Heidemann's bedroom.

Not long after Grace's appearance, Schindler and Sheriff Hetrick left the Seacoast Building, handing Heidemann over to Scholl. Hetrick drove Schindler to Max Kruschka's home, and asked Kruschka to allow Schindler to search the property. Reluctantly, Kruschka agreed, and Hetrick left Schindler there by himself.

Kruschka's fenced-in corner lot was spacious. Besides the main two-story home, there were several outbuildings, including a handful of greenhouses. There was a big barn, and, back in a small courtyard, a doghouse. Schindler went straight to the largest greenhouse behind the main home. Just a few minutes into his search, he heard a noise at the entrance. The shuffle of boots. It was a police officer and the two Greater New York detectives. Max Kruschka, who had summoned the men, came bounding in after them. He yelled at Schindler to leave and "stormed about like a madman," Schindler later said. The officer escorted Schindler off the property.

The Greater New York detectives did not know about the hiring of Ray Schindler, and treated him like an invader. For Schindler, it was evidence of how chummy they'd become with Kruschka, whom they had cleared but who remained on Schindler's list of suspects. With one call to Sheriff Hetrick, Schindler straightened out the confusion, and was soon back on Kruschka's property. This time, Kruschka—still angry but now silent—led Schindler to the room Heidemann was renting, a room on the second floor of the main house, just above the kitchen.

It was nearly dusk, and the small bedroom was dark. Schindler asked Kruschka for an oil lamp. Once it was lit, he went back in the room. It was spare—a bed, a chair, a desk, and a window facing the back of the house. Schindler went to the desk. He lowered his lamp, and it lit up a small vial on the desk. Schindler picked up the vial. It was morphine. Next to it was another small bottle of morphine tablets.

Schindler moved his lamp across the wall behind the desk. Four black-and-white postcards were tacked to the wall. They were postcards of young, pretty women in their early twenties, holding a telephone and smiling. "Gee, I hate to wait," read one caption. Another: "Stop your kidding." The postcards were not pornographic, but they were suggestive. Earlier, Heidemann had insisted to Schindler that he had no real interest in women. These postcards proved that wasn't true.

Back on the desk, Schindler found a sheet of paper with a series of details written on it. It was a list of all of Heidemann's movements during his recent day trip to New York City. Schindler was right. Heidemann had rehearsed his answers.

Night was falling. Schindler left the house and went to the green-houses. Kruschka had a successful florist business, with several busy greenhouses operating at once. Schindler went into the largest one first. He knew he didn't have very much time to search them.

Inside the greenhouse, it was dark and damp. The last of the sunlight was passing through large glass panes and over rows of fragrant plants and flowers. The space felt moist and alive but eerie.

Just off the entrance, at the northern end of the greenhouse, there was a large, circular wooden platform. Four steps led to the top of the platform. A walk up the steps, and onto the platform, and you could see what was there.

The platform encircled a deep, dark pit.

The pit was oblong, five feet by ten feet across. It dropped nine feet down, and its sides and floor were made of concrete. A spindly three-rung ladder hung on to the edge of the platform and led down into the pit.

Down there, at the bottom, there was a massive coal furnace at one end—an imposing black iron machine that rose nearly to the top of the pit. Just in front of the furnace, a large pile of coal. And that was it. The pit was for making heat. Someone worked there, shoveling coal into the furnace. Someone spent hours there, shoveling, grunting, sweating, thinking, no sense of day or night. Alone except for the nearly human rumble and hiss of the hungry furnace. Frank Heidemann had to know this pit. He had to know every inch of it.

That night, the furnace was silent. It hadn't been fed in a while. But it was not cold to the touch. It was hot. Not burning hot, but still hot. Even the coals on the ground were warm from being next to it. Imagine how hellishly hot the furnace would be during operation.

Could it be that Marie Smith had been lured into this greenhouse, or dragged into it, or even drugged with morphine and carried in? Could she have been lowered into the pit, to hide her or silence her? Or maybe pushed in? Or had she fallen while fleeing? Had she landed next to the hot coals, or been placed there? Or against the furnace itself?

Could the unexplained burn scars on Marie's nose and ear have been caused by direct exposure to the searing heat of this dark machine?

It was fully night now. The great black furnace stayed asleep. Ray Schindler was done with his hurried search. He left the eerie greenhouse and went back to the Seacoast Building, back to Frank Heidemann.

CHAPTER 19

What Kind of Fellow He Was

*

November 27, 1910
Asbury Park, New Jersey

It was the colossal power of heat and steam that brought Frank E. Heidemann to America.

The slender German was twenty-six in January 1910 when he traveled one hundred fifty miles north of his hometown of Dortmund, an ancient city on the Ruhr, to the major port city of Bremen, on the River Weser. At the harbor in Bremen, he boarded the modern, magnificent SS *Kronprinz Wilhelm*, a twin-screw, four-stack steamship capable of an astonishing thirty-three thousand horsepower and a top speed of twenty-three knots. The 637-foot-long *Wilhelm* carried two six-cylinder, quadruple-expansion engines and sixteen massive boilers that consumed 550 tons of coal a day. A year after launching in 1901, the *Wilhelm* set a new world record for a transatlantic crossing—from France to New York in five days, eleven hours, and fifty-seven minutes.

In 1910, Frank Heidemann paid sixty-seven dollars and fifty cents to travel second cabin aboard the *Wilhelm*. He joined fifteen hundred passengers and a crew of five hundred for the weeklong, westward voyage, traveling from Bremen to Southampton, England, and on to Cherbourg, in northern France, and finally across the Atlantic and into the busy New York Harbor, the *Wilhelm*'s great steel hull maneuvering slowly past the Statue of Liberty, its copper then a rich brown that was only beginning to green.

More generally, on that day, Frank Heidemann joined an immense human wave of immigrants heading to America from all parts of the planet around the turn of the century.

In the five decades between 1880 to 1930, more than 27 million people left their countries for the shores of this more welcoming place, as political conditions changed in their nations, and technological wonders like the *Wilhelm*—using less fuel to propel more tonnage—made crossing the Atlantic more tolerable.

In 1910, when Heidemann made his voyage, there were already around 2.3 million German-born immigrants living in the United States, and more than five hundred German-language newspapers thriving across the country. Germans were the fourth-largest immigrant bloc, behind the Irish, the Austro-Hungarians, and the Russians. When Heidemann stepped off the *Wilhelm* onto U.S. soil on January 18, 1910, he became part of the grand experiment and promise of democracy—one more anonymous dreamer blending into the rich, unfinished fabric of America.

It was his chance to start over. In Germany, Heidemann had been a loner. His father, a tailor, sent him to boarding school when he was twelve, and when he got older he worked in a Dusseldorf cemetery as an assistant florist. He had no wife or friends. He had three sisters but was close with only one. On his first day ashore in New York City, he rented a room at the Union Square Hotel in lower Manhattan, and in his first weeks he bounced from hotel to hotel, each lowlier than the previous one, as his funds—a total of four hundred dollars—began to run short.

Early on, Heidemann took out a "Situation Wanted" ad hoping to get a job in the floral industry. It took him three months to find work as an elevator man in a German hospital at 77th Street and Park Avenue in Manhattan. He was soon promoted to night telephone operator, earning twenty dollars a month. He stayed there until October 1, when he noticed a help-wanted ad for an assistant florist. The ad gave a contact number for Max Kruschka in Asbury Park. Heidemann left his job at the hospital and traveled sixty miles south to his new home on the Jersey shore.

This, at least, was the clean, uneventful timeline of his life that Frank Heidemann gave Ray Schindler during his interrogation in Sheriff Hetrick's office. As Schindler would soon discover, not all of it was true.

During the interrogation, Schindler was informed that a reporter digging into Heidemann's background discovered he might have worked at the German hospital in Manhattan as early as 1906—four years before he claimed to have first landed in America.

Meanwhile, Schindler's own detective, T. P. Bowers, had been canvassing lower Manhattan for any details of Heidemann's life there in early 1910. Bowers found William Beckman, the owner of a rooming house where Heidemann had stayed. Beckman and his wife told Bowers that Heidemann was a problem tenant. He rarely left his room except to walk up and down 14th Street, "watching the women who frequent that vicinity," Bowers reported. One such woman, dressed shabbily and looking no older than seventeen, called on Heidemann and spent time in his room. Heidemann told the Beckmans she was his fiancée. He also claimed to be a detective, and showed off a badge, a club, and handcuffs.

When the young woman's brother showed up at the rooming house demanding to see Heidemann, however, the German refused to leave his room for four days.

Bowers then went uptown, to the German hospital on 77th Street. A superintendent there, Mr. Kortum, confirmed that Heidemann—using the name Frank Hardenburg—first worked there as a messenger starting in August 1906. He left after a year but returned in 1910, and was hired again, this time as Frank Heidemann.

Schindler confronted Heidemann about the two different names, but he was ready with an answer—he claimed to have fled Germany to avoid military service, and used the alias to avoid detection in the United States.

In New York City, Bowers also learned that Heidemann worked in a Jewish hospital at the corner of Clausen Street and St. Mark's Avenue in Brooklyn. The superintendent there, Mr. Strasser, confirmed that

Heidemann—again, as Hardenburg—worked as a hall man, night clerk, and telephone operator starting in September 1907. In the summer of 1908, he was fired. Bowers pushed Strasser for details about why Heidemann was dismissed, but Strasser insisted he couldn't say. In a second interview a few days later, Strasser offered the vague statement that Heidemann was let go for "unsatisfactory services." Bowers pushed harder. "Well," Strasser finally said, "when I don't like the habits or morals of one of our employees and don't wish to let him know in so many words my reason for doing so, I wait until he makes a mistake of some sort and then tell him or her that their services are no longer required, and get rid of them as soon as possible."

"As in the case of Hardenburg?" Bowers asked.

Strasser laughed and replied, "I cannot say."

*

Working on another tip, Bowers found the owner of the Bay View Hotel in Long Island, where Heidemann—calling himself Frank Heitman—worked as a driver and handyman for a few months in 1908.

"He was always talking about women," a hotel worker told Bowers. "He used to tell about a French doctor somewhere in New Jersey who caught him committing adultery with his wife."

On Bowers's second visit to the Bay View Hotel, another employee, Lizzie Gerdt, pulled him to the side. The young woman wanted to tell him something she had never shared with anyone except for the wife of the hotel owner. But first Bowers had to promise to keep her name out of the newspapers. Bowers assured her that he would.

"I always mistrusted Frank," Gerdt said, before sharing her story. One morning, she explained, when she was cleaning an upstairs room by herself, Heidemann quietly opened the door and snuck in. "I turned around and saw him in his nightshirt," Gerdt said. "The way he looked at me frightened me terribly. I gave him one yell and I ran into the adjoining room and down the stairs."

Later, Heidemann found her in the lobby and asked her not to tell on him. She agreed, as long as he promised to stay away from her.

"I shouldn't have told you this," Gerdt said to Bowers, "except that it might help to show what kind of fellow he was."

More incriminating stories followed. Mr. Kortum from the Jewish hospital said that in the weeks before quitting and going to Asbury Park, Heidemann "appeared mentally upset, very nervous and excitable." A nurse at the German hospital called Heidemann "a smart alec" and "fresh guy" who seemed "extremely nervous" most of the time. Schindler's detectives found two men who had traveled aboard the SS *Kronprinz Wilhelm* with Heidemann in 1910, and roomed with him in their early days in the United States. They confirmed Heidemann was preoccupied with taking women out on dates and spending money on them. Most of the women, they told Bowers, were prostitutes working on 14th Street.

At the time of his interrogation of Frank Heidemann, Schindler did not have all of this information, and did not realize quite how brazenly Heidemann was lying to him about a number of things—how long he'd been in America, his employment history, his obsession with women.

But from his hours of questioning him, and his visit to Heidemann's bedroom, Schindler *did* feel certain the suspect was hiding something. The way Heidemann refused to go back over the details of his whereabouts the morning Marie Smith disappeared. The way his lower lip quivered and his body shifted in his chair when Schindler announced, "Bring in the girl." The provocative postcards in Heidemann's room.

Schindler was also realizing, in the course of the interview, that Heidemann was not about to incriminate himself. He betrayed some measure of guilt through his expressions and his evasiveness, but he never came close to caving in and delivering a sobbing confession.

"It was Heidemann's practice throughout to admit only to such things questioned of which he was assured data had come into possession of the questioner," Schindler concluded. "It was apparent he would not admit to anything of a damaging nature. All through his examination he took good care to protect himself."

Schindler felt sure Heidemann was lying, but he couldn't prove it, at least not in any way that would hold up in court. Heidemann shrugged off the suggestive postcards as jokes. He said anyone who claimed he'd been in the United States in 1906 was flat wrong. And Grace Foster's story was, after all, the testimony of a child. In fact, not a single bit of hard evidence connected Heidemann to the murder of Marie Smith.

Schindler knew his team would have to work harder. Heidemann, he now understood, was skilled at deception. In his time in America he had used three names and secured several jobs without arousing much suspicion. He was odd enough to be mistrusted, even fired, but he hadn't crossed over to criminality. He was cagey and secretive, but he wasn't reckless. Whatever evil existed in his heart, it had only yet to reveal itself as immorality—so far as anyone could prove.

The interrogation of Heidemann lasted ten full hours, until 8:00 p.m. When it was over, Sheriff Hetrick marched Heidemann across the street to police headquarters, had him fingerprinted, and booked him as a material witness in the investigation of Marie Smith's murder. When Heidemann couldn't pay his two-thousand-dollar bail, an officer put him in a cell in the police station. It was the same cell that Thomas Williams— still locked away in the Freehold jail despite not being charged—had been put in the night an angry mob came calling for him.

When the iron bars closed behind him, Heidemann pleaded his innocence, and then loudly wept.

After the interview, Schindler returned to the Marlborough Hotel for a late meeting with the coroner, Robert Purdy, and Peter Smith's boss, Randolph Miller. Schindler filled them in on the interrogation, and they discussed strategy going forward. With Heidemann's arrest, at least Schindler and his team could rest easier, knowing where he was.

Then, during the meeting, Schindler was handed a message. It was not good news. Max Kruschka had hired a lawyer to represent his German employee, and, shortly before 10:00 p.m., the lawyer posted bail.

Frank Heidemann was free.

CHAPTER 20

Afraid of What They Might Find

*

November 28, 1910
Asbury Park, New Jersey

That night, Schindler restarted round-the-clock surveillance of Heidemann. The next day, Heidemann's arrest and interrogation were big news. The *New York Times* covered the story under the headline "German Nurseryman Held." Heidemann, the article said, endured "a scathing fire of questions," but did not crack. "Though no formal charge of murder is made against him," the paper declared, Heidemann's interrogators "virtually accuse him of the crime."

The biggest surprise for Schindler, though, was the coverage of events in the *Asbury Park Press*. When Schindler picked up the paper and read the front-page story, it was clear that Heidemann, after being bailed out, quickly met up with the *Press* reporter Alvin Cliver and shared his side of the story. It was a complete refutation of all the evidence that made Heidemann a leading suspect, right down to his lies to Schindler during the previous day's interview. Alvin Cliver, handed exclusive access to such a prominent figure in the investigation, gave Heidemann all the space he needed to build a case for his innocence—and against the detectives brought in to solve the case.

"I know I am innocent," Heidemann told Cliver, "and it makes me so mad to think they are trying to implicate me in the crime."

What about the biggest lie Heidemann told Schindler—that he'd never been in America prior to 1910? That *was* a lie, Heidemann admitted, but he told it for a reason.

"He withheld this part of the story because of his dislike of one of the questioners"—Ray Schindler—"and his belief that [Schindler] was endeavoring to fix the crime on him," Cliver wrote.

"I didn't like him," Heidemann was quoted as saying. "He made me so mad with his questions, over and over again."

What about the incident with Grace Foster? Did Heidemann tell her to come around to see him alone?

"I did not tell her that," Heidemann told Cliver. "The Foster boy and girl came up to me when I was working in the yard and I gave the girl a piece of candy. 'Have you got any more, Frank?' she asked me. I told her that I didn't have any more, but when I got some more, I would give her some. I said nothing to her about sneaking back. The Foster boy, Albert I think it is, said I give him five cents one day and told him to give it to Grace. I did not do this." Instead, Heidemann claimed, he paid Albert Foster five cents to load a wheelbarrow with wood.

Heidemann's conversation with Cliver changed the way he was perceived in Asbury Park. After the article ran, people who encountered Heidemann in public went up to him to shake his hand and tell him they believed he was innocent. Men and women all over the town crossed streets and avenues to get to Heidemann and announce they were on his side. It was a strange and instant celebrity for someone who until then had been all but invisible in Asbury Park.

One person who seemed to agree that Heidemann was being railroaded was John S. Applegate, the county prosecutor who'd been left out of the decision to bring Schindler into the investigation. Applegate was on record as believing Tom Williams was Marie Smith's murderer. The day after the Heidemann interrogation, Applegate told one of Schindler's operatives that their interview with Heidemann hadn't produced any new evidence. Grace Foster's testimony, Applegate said, was worthless because it wouldn't stand up in court. Similarly, any information about Frank Heidemann's past life in New York City was not relevant to the murder case, since none of it had resulted in any time served for a crime. By Applegate's estimate, Schindler and his men had been on the job a full week and gotten exactly nowhere.

As for Frank Heidemann, he had only recently emerged as a suspect in the murder. But just as quickly, the case against him, at least in the court of public opinion, had fallen apart.

*

It had never been part of Ray Schindler's plan to ignore Tom Williams as a suspect. Even before he interviewed Heidemann, Schindler devised a scheme to interrogate Williams, who was in a jail cell in Freehold and telling the same story to all his many interrogators—that he was innocent and knew nothing of the crime. Schindler's method would not be a formal interview. Instead, he was going to "rope" Tom Williams.

One day after the Heidemann questioning, Schindler finalized his plans with a Burns detective whose identity was closely guarded, even in company reports. Known only as R.W.E., the black man would pose as a criminal named "Russell," and—through Schindler's arrangements with the warden of the Freehold County Jail—be placed in a cell either with or next to Tom Williams. There he would gain Williams's trust and find out how much Williams knew about the murder.

Once the plan was activated, it worked quickly, and well. In his first evening in jail, "Russell" befriended Tom Williams and got him talking. Russell asked him what he was in for, and Williams told him about Marie Smith. Williams said that on the night before Marie disappeared, he stayed out late drinking, which caused him to get up late and miss an appointment with a man who had hired him for a job. After that, Williams said, he went to the saloon at Griffin's Wanamassa Hotel to drink some more. He never saw Marie Smith that day, and knew nothing about her disappearance. The next day, he helped Marie's father, Peter, search for the girl in the woods.

There were thousands of people all through the woods where the girl was found, Williams told Russell. *That stretch of woods was trampled over every inch. The girl must have been put there the next night.*

Russell mentioned that he had a white lawyer, and Williams asked if the lawyer could represent him, too. Williams was particularly interested in having a white lawyer, and said he wouldn't trust a black one. Here was a chance to have another "rope" question Williams.

"Advise that a white man be sent to" impersonate the lawyer, Russell suggested in his report. "Advise that [Ray Schindler] come himself, as Williams is crazy to see my lawyer at once."

*

Ray Schindler liked the idea. He was anxious to question Tom Williams himself, and here was the perfect opportunity to do it without betraying that he was a detective. Not long after Russell's first encounter with Williams, Schindler showed up at the Freehold County Jail late one afternoon. He spoke with Deputy O'Brian about the plan, and O'Brian led him to the anteroom where prisoners met with visitors. Tom Williams was waiting for him there.

Schindler asked Williams if he had requested to see a lawyer. Williams said that he had. *I need a good lawyer*, Williams explained, *as it is my intention to bring a lawsuit up against the state for false imprisonment.*

Schindler sat across from the prisoner, and they talked over the proposed lawsuit. Schindler wanted to take him through the details of the case, but the room was too public for that. Instead, they discussed how Williams planned to pay for his defense: he claimed to have friends in New York who would raise funds for him, and he promised to give their addresses to Schindler in his next visit to the jail.

That's when I'll tell you all the details, Williams said.

He also assured Schindler that he had a good alibi, and that plenty of witnesses—including Mollie Williams and some employees at Griffin's bar—would stand up for him. He claimed to have a clean record except for a single arrest for drunkenness—something Schindler knew was a lie. Williams left out his conviction and prison term for armed robbery.

Still, Schindler concluded, Williams was "apparently frank in his answers." It wasn't the interrogation he'd hoped to conduct, but in his short time with Williams, Schindler hadn't seen any sign that he was struggling to conceal his role in a brutal murder. Instead, Williams's focus was entirely on the lawsuit he wished to bring against the state.

*

Meanwhile, Schindler's detectives continued their rounds through the woods and streets and corners of Asbury Park, interviewing witnesses, following up on tips, going over familiar territory again and again. On Wednesday, November 30, Charles Scholl made his way to the Bradley School, where several people who'd seen Marie Smith leave after morning recess the day she disappeared had already been interviewed.

At the school, Scholl noticed Police Officer Walter Ireton, one of the two men, along with Thomas Broderick, first assigned to the case by Police Chief William Smith. Scholl asked Ireton if they could talk, and the officer said no. He didn't want to do or say anything that would upset the chief of police. Scholl persisted. Could Ireton just go over the events of the morning of November 13—the day Marie's body was found?

Reluctantly, Ireton agreed. Then he told Scholl something the detective did not yet know. Ireton said that, early on the morning of November 13, he saw Max Kruschka and Frank Heidemann walk out of the Wanamassa woods.

The men told Ireton they were cutting bits of laurel from trees and shrubs to use for a funeral piece. Scholl asked about their demeanor.

I can't say that Max Kruschka acted suspiciously, although he was noticeably garrulous, Ireton said. *Heidemann didn't act suspiciously, either.*

That was all Ireton would say. He'd already told his story in a report to Police Chief Smith, and there wasn't anything more to tell.

Scholl walked from the school to Kruschka's home to find out more. There he encountered a brash and belligerent Max Kruschka. Scholl asked him about the morning of November 13, and Kruschka confirmed he and Heidemann had been in the woods collecting laurel. Scholl asked him to show him the spot where they had made the cuts. Kruschka led the way into the woods and eventually pointed out a shrub. He showed Scholl where he had made cuts using shears, and where Heidemann had made cuts using a knife. Scholl wasn't convinced.

"There appeared to be a good deal of bluster about Kruschka's demonstrating, which was altogether unwarranted," Scholl later wrote.

Scholl and Kruschka walked out of the woods and back to Kruschka's home. Now Frank Heidemann was there, and Scholl asked him the same questions about the morning of November 13. He asked him if he, too, could show him where they'd cut the laurel. Heidemann took Scholl into the woods, but used a different route to go in and come out. The two versions of events were inconsistent. *What had Kruschka and Heidemann really been doing in the woods just hours before Marie Smith's body was discovered?*

Kruschka had his own theory about Marie's body, which he repeatedly shared with Scholl—he insisted the body had been in the woods all along, since the day Marie disappeared and was murdered. It hadn't been found, he claimed, because—contrary to all public accounts—that section of the woods had not actually been searched.

They assigned schoolboys to search the woods, and they didn't do so, Kruschka said. *They didn't do it because they were afraid. They were afraid of the woods and afraid of what they might find.*

Scholl, finished with his interviews, thanked the men and began to walk off the property. Max Kruschka's wife stopped him on the front lawn. The elderly woman seemed distraught and close to tears.

"I am so worried and nervous over this affair," she told Scholl. "I do not sleep nights and my sorrow is so deep. I can only compare it to the feeling I would have if I lost through death my own dearest child."

Then Mrs. Kruschka turned and walked back into the house.

CHAPTER 21

The Agonies of the Damned

*

December 2, 1910
Asbury Park, New Jersey

Pressure was mounting on Robert Purdy, the town coroner, to hold an official inquest into the murder of Marie Smith. He'd postponed it more than once, hoping Schindler and his men could produce fresh evidence, but now three full weeks had passed since the killing, and Purdy was out of time. He finally announced the inquest would be held on December 2, and he issued thirty-three subpoenas. Max Kruschka and Frank Heidemann were both summoned, but Tom Williams, the only named suspect, was not.

To many, that seemed like a violation of Williams's right to hear the evidence against him and testify on his own behalf. But having him testify would mean moving him from the Freehold County Jail to the Asbury Park Council Chamber, a fairly small room on the second floor of the Independence Hook & Ladder Company building on Mattison Avenue. Williams would need several prison guards and police officers to make the trip with him, and at least as many to protect him once he got to Asbury Park—where he would be surrounded in the council chamber by dozens of people convinced of his guilt. After the near riot outside the police station that almost got Williams lynched, no one wanted to take any more chances. So Purdy left Williams off the subpoena list.

Six jurors were selected, all white: the foreman, John Labaw, a well-respected grocer and steward of the Cranbury Fire Department; George Henderson, operator of an Asbury Park awnings business; Grandon Layton, a teamster; William Whittle, a tile and slate roofer and auxiliary police officer; Harold Jacques, a popular local athlete who went into the tire repair business; and William Truex. There was a general curiosity about which direction the questioning would lean. "Will an effort be made to place the crime on Thomas Williams," Alvin Cliver wondered in the *Asbury Park Press*, "or will the prosecution direct especial effort against Frank Heidemann, the German florist?"

One indication that there might be an anti-Williams bias was the man in charge of deciding which witnesses to call, and then questioning them—Monmouth County Prosecutor John Applegate, who was known to believe firmly in Williams's guilt. Cliver wondered if Applegate would show his full hand and conclude the inquest with a sole suspect, or hold back some key evidence as his investigation continued.

Before 10:00 a.m. on the morning of the inquest, police officers ushered the thirty-three subpoenaed witnesses into empty rooms in the firehouse. They would be brought into the council chamber one by one, so none could hear the testimony of any other witness. By then, more than one hundred people were crowded outside the firehouse, hoping to get a seat inside the chamber. Though the inquest was open to everyone, there wouldn't be much room for spectators—just a few rows of open seats, and some standing room in the back. When the doors opened at 10:00 a.m., more people were turned away than got in.

Ray Schindler and Charles Scholl already had their seats. Schindler was anxious to hear the testimony of the two doctors who performed the autopsy, Joseph Ackerman and Earl Wagner. He had studied their reports and found them lacking. The doctors disagreed on certain key points, and neither could say with any certainty what had caused the burns on Marie's nose and ear, or if the scars were even burn marks. Schindler needed to know more—much more.

At 10:30 a.m., Applegate called the inquest to order. The first witness was Marie's father, Peter Smith.

Gaunt and weary, Smith took a seat in the front of the chamber. Applegate asked him about the day his daughter went missing.

"I saw Marie last Wednesday morning, November 9, before I left for work," Smith said. "That was about 6:30. She was getting dressed. I left at 6:45. I never saw Marie alive again."

Applegate asked him to describe the morning Marie's body was found. Peter Smith took a deep breath. He didn't show any emotion, but he didn't show any life, either. He looked defeated and spent. "A pathetic figure," one paper wrote. Slowly, he forced himself to talk.

"I had no idea that the child would be found dead," he said. "I was hoping she would be found in good health. I thought maybe somebody had kidnapped her to play a trick on me."

And when he came upon his daughter's mangled body?

"The body lay with the head to the east," Smith said, "with the coat and dress pulled up and the legs exposed. I look until I saw a cut in the back of her head. Then I could stand it no longer, and I went away."

Do you know who committed this crime? Applegate asked.

Peter Smith said, "I wish I did."

*

Peter's wife, Nora, was next. She was dressed head-to-toe in black, with a heavy black mourning veil over her face. She, too, seemed impossibly tired. She explained that she had four children—but that only two of them, Thomas and Joseph, were still alive.

Applegate asked about her drinking, and if she ever drank with Delia Jackson—the woman who had hired Tom Williams to work on her property the day Marie didn't come home.

"Yes, a bit of beer occasionally," Nora answered. "Sometimes she would come in my place and drink."

"Did Tom Williams ever buy beer for you and bring it into your house?" Applegate asked.

"He did. He bought me two bottles of beer on three occasions. I never drank with him and he never saw me drink anything."

"Did you ever have any quarrel with Williams?"

"I never did," Nora said.

Could Delia Jackson, perhaps, have had anything to do with her daughter's murder? Applegate asked.

Nora Smith, like her husband, answered with hopeless resignation. "That I don't know," she said.

The two doctors, Ackerman and Wagner, soon followed. They talked about compound fractures, brain tissue, incision sizes. They both believed the strange marks on Marie's nose and ear were burn marks, most likely the result of Marie "coming in contact with direct heat," Ackerman testified. But neither seemed all that convincing.

Schindler listened to their findings and knew he would need more information than what they had provided. Why couldn't the doctors be more specific about the weapon used to strike Marie? Was it a knife? A hatchet? An ax? Were there any substances in Marie's blood? Morphine, perhaps? Had the burn marks been examined microscopically? Why hadn't more testing been done before the child was buried?

There was more testimony. Delia Jackson confirmed that she had lunch with Frank Heidemann on the day Marie Smith vanished, as Heidemann claimed. She also said she hadn't seen Heidemann until they sat down to eat "soon after the twelve o'clock whistle had blown." She could not provide him an alibi for the previous ninety minutes, which was when Marie went missing. Even so, was it possible that Heidemann could have committed such a gruesome crime and then casually sat down for lunch with Delia Jackson, as if nothing had happened?

Heidemann's boss, Max Kruschka, also took the stand. His answers were short and he didn't say anything he hadn't already told reporters.

"Is this man Heidemann addicted to any bad habits?" John Applegate asked him. "Does he ever take any narcotics?"

"Not that I know of," Kruschka answered.

Had he discussed Marie's murder with Heidemann?

Yes, he had, and Heidemann told him he didn't have anything to do with it. Kruschka testified that he fully believed this denial.

Frank Heidemann himself was next to the stand.

*

Much like Ray Schindler had, Applegate took Heidemann through his life history. This time Heidemann gave a more truthful version, which included arriving in America in 1906. His story at the inquest matched the story Alvin Cliver had published. There was nothing new or surprising about his testimony. Then Applegate—who knew that drugs had been found in Heidemann's room—asked him if he had ever used morphine. This was the first that anyone in Asbury Park was hearing about Heidemann's drug use. Heidemann, however, was unfazed. He was ready for the question.

I occasionally take morphine tablets to produce sleep, he said. *At times I am very nervous, and I take a tablet about once every two or three weeks.*

Heidemann reached into his vest pocket and took out a small vial of morphine tablets. He showed it to the prosecutor, who took it and logged it as evidence before returning it to Heidemann. It was as if he had known the matter would be raised, and was prepared to answer the question in a way that made his use of morphine seem inconsequential.

In fact, Heidemann *had* been prepared for the question. It later emerged that the two Greater New York detectives, Johnson and Cunningham, had warned Heidemann the question would likely be asked—and had advised him to bring a vial of his medication with him to the inquest, as a way to defuse the whole situation. Heidemann followed their advice, and Applegate soon dropped the line of questioning.

Next, he asked Heidemann if he had gone to see Marie Smith's body in the woods. Heidemann admitted that he had. "Chief of Police Smith was in the road near where the body was found," he said. "I asked him if I could go down and see the body. He said I could. I told him if he wanted me I would be down there."

Why, Applegate wondered, had he bothered to tell Chief Smith where he could be found, in case, as he put it, the police "wanted me"? Why would the police want to see him?

Again, Heidemann was ready with an answer.

I knew I was under suspicion because of the many visits the detectives had paid me since the child disappeared, he said calmly. *I didn't want the chief to think I would try to get away.*

Throughout his testimony, Heidemann remained composed. "His very frankness in telling of his use of [morphine] and his production of the only tube he had opened had a good effect," Alvin Cliver wrote in the *Press*. "His story was told in his usual frank manner, and produced the impression that he was guiltless of any implication in the crime."

Several more witnesses testified: County Detective Elwood Minugh, who had arrested Tom Williams; William Griffin, owner of Griffin's Wanamassa Hotel, where Williams drank in the hours before Marie disappeared; John "the Cripple" Carlton, the bartender who sold Williams whiskey; William Wynn, who was at the rooming house where Williams had spent most of three days in bed. One of the last people to testify was Martha Coleman, a black twenty-six-year-old resident of Asbury Park. Coleman had already signed an affidavit, on November 21, swearing that, four days before Marie Smith vanished, she had heard Tom Williams say "that there was a little white girl he was going to get familiar with if he got the chance."

On the stand, she repeated her assertion, and testified that Williams had said the girl was at "Mrs. Jackson's"—the home of Delia Jackson, where Marie Smith and her parents were living, and where Williams was working a job. The implication was clear—Tom Williams was talking about Marie Smith.

Coleman's statement had already been refuted by two men she said also heard the remark. Yet the prosecutor, John Applegate, chose not to subpoena either man. He also decided to make Martha Coleman the second-to-last witness to testify, adding more weight to her claim.

Applegate also left Grace Foster off his witness list, denying jurors the chance to hear her describe Frank Heidemann's offer to her. He chose not to present any testimony about Tom Williams's criminal record, either, but to some, Applegate's choice and placement of witnesses seemed highly strategic. Besides the news about Frank Heidemann's use of morphine, Martha Coleman's testimony was the biggest revelation of the day. Her claim capped off the testimony on a decidedly anti-Williams note. Indeed, the *Asbury Park Press*'s headline blared: "Woman Heard Him Say He Would Possess Tiny Victim."

After the final, inconsequential witness—the elderly Mrs. Thomas Sculthorpe, who was confused by Applegate's aggressive questioning—Robert Purdy read the coroner's charge to the six male jurors.

"Gentlemen," he said, "you are sworn upon your oaths to declare of the death of Marie Smith, whether she came to her death by murder, manslaughter, misfortune, accident or otherwise, and where and when and by what means and in what manner, and if by murder, who were the principals and who were the accessories, and if by manslaughter who were the perpetrators, and with what instrument the stroke or wound was in either case given."

At 5:45 p.m., Detective Minugh escorted the six jurors to a room behind the chambers and locked the door behind them.

Just twenty minutes later, the jury foreman, John Labaw, was ready with a statement: "We, the Jury, find that the said Marie Smith came to her death at the hands of a person or persons unknown to the Jury."

That was it. No decision. No progress. No new suspect was named, nor was Williams found to be guilty. Three weeks into the investigation, nothing of note had been determined, not even what weapon had been used to strike the child. Not a single piece of hard evidence connected anybody to the crime. Even so, John Applegate decided to keep Tom Williams imprisoned as a suspect.

Frank Heidemann, on the other hand, had the conditions of his bail rescinded at the close of the inquest, by law. He was no longer considered an official suspect. Without any reservations, Heidemann was free to do as he pleased. He had every right to leave Asbury Park and disappear, if he wished to.

The inquest left many in Asbury Park feeling hopeless, as if the best chance to catch Marie Smith's killer had already come and gone.

"Whoever committed this awful crime must be suffering the agonies of the damned if he has any senses," read an uncharacteristically resigned editorial in the *Press*. "He will never have a minute's peace until he has made his full and complete confession. Herein seems to lie the final hope of solving this awful mystery."

A full and complete confession—the last best chance.

With that in mind, three men—detective Thomas Broderick, Asbury Park's enforcer, along with B. F. Johnson and George W. Cunningham, the Greater New York Agency detectives—waited for two days after the inquest before getting in a car and driving to the county jail in Freehold. There they asked a prison official to see the prisoner Tom Williams, and a guard took them to Williams's cell.

The three detectives asked to go inside the cell to talk to Williams, and the guard said that would be fine. He unlocked the bars and slid them open, and the men walked inside, and the guard closed the cell door behind them with a loud clang.

CHAPTER 22

Nobody Seen Me Do It

*

December 4, 1910
Freehold, New Jersey

Police officers and beat reporters had a name for it—"the third degree." It was, in the kindest possible interpretation, an interrogation technique. A way for investigators to get information out of reluctant suspects—a tactic, along the lines of good cop/bad cop, or building rapport with a prisoner. If deliberate questioning didn't work, the third degree was a way to ratchet up the pressure, often severely.

To administer the third degree meant to either physically beat a prisoner, or psychologically browbeat him. Which of these two was used depended on the character of the interrogator, and on the perceived moral or mental weakness of the suspect. Both were meant to obliterate a prisoner's defiance and shatter his will, leading, finally, to a confession.

In the early 1900s, third-degree tactics were commonly used in police departments across the country. They were also illegal. The U.S. Supreme Court handed down an 1896 ruling in the case of *Wilson v. United States,* which involved a man accused of murder and interrogated in front of a threatening mob until he gave a confession. "The true test of the admissibility in evidence of the confession of a person on trial for the commission of a crime," the Supreme Court ruled, "is that it was made freely, voluntarily, and without compulsion or inducement."

Several other similar rulings continued to invalidate confessions that were coerced through the use of the third degree.

And yet, the practice was far from abandoned.

On December 4, 1910, the three detectives entered Tom Williams's cell around 9:00 a.m. and showed him their badges. Williams knew Thomas Broderick from around Asbury Park, but he didn't recognize the two other men. They explained why they were there, and said they wanted to run Williams through the events of November 9, the day Marie Smith went missing, one more time. Williams agreed to talk.

The questioning went on for hours. Broderick stayed back and let the detectives take the lead. B. F. Johnson stood over Williams and described precisely how he believed Williams had killed Marie Smith. How Williams had lurked on the edges of the woods on the north side of Third Avenue, waiting for Marie, and then snatched her and attacked her and murdered her, and carried her body deeper into the woods, to the spot where she was found, before making his escape along Brickyard Road. How Williams had gone into hiding until his arrest four days later. There was no doubt in Johnson's voice—this is how it had happened.

We have many witnesses to verify this claim, Johnson told Williams. *We have a complete case against you. The story you told has been proven false. There is no chance for you to escape all of this.*

Yet Williams, as he had at every step, denied he had anything to do with the crime.

The questioning went on. All three men aggressively challenged Williams's story, over and over, crowding him in the small jail cell. The interview stretched into its sixth hour. There is no official record of what happened in that jail cell during those hours, beyond a report filed by Johnson and Cunningham. In that report, there is no mention of any of the interrogators so much as touching Tom Williams at any time. Alvin Cliver, who spoke with the detectives before and after the interrogation, simply wrote that they "put the negro through a rigid examination in an effort to get a confession."

Tom Williams, however, claimed the men tortured him in his cell. He told a friend, "They did pretty much everything to me except kill me."

At the end of the questioning, the detectives dropped any pretense. Johnson described yet again how he believed Williams committed the crime, then abruptly stopped and screamed into Williams's ear.

"You know you killed that little girl!"

"It's a lie," Williams said.

"But this woman swears she saw you!"

"She didn't see me. Nobody seen me."

Johnson paused.

"Are you sure nobody saw you?"

"I know nobody saw me," Williams said. *"Nobody seen me do it."*

It took Williams a moment to realize what he'd done.

"What am I saying?" he asked of himself.

And then, surprisingly, he laughed.

"Oh, go ahead and finish it, if you say so," Williams said. "I guess it won't make much difference if one more nigger gets it. It only means one less nigger."

*

The headline in the *Asbury Park Press*, in large type spanning nearly half the length of the paper, was damning:

"NOBODY SEEN ME" DO IT
SAYS NEGRO IN BLIND RAGE

Cliver's description of the interrogation was steeped in the biased and stereotypical language of the time, florid and breathless, and clearly prejudiced against Tom Williams. The suspect, Cliver wrote, "crouched his heavy six-foot frame and, wild-eyed and panting, faced three detectives who had coaxed him up with questions until his round and wooly head apparently was near the noose." During questioning, Williams's eyes "narrowed into slits thru which the bloodshot white shone craftily. Then in a moment they blazed forth in rage." The detectives "succeeded in driving the sneering bravado from his ebony face."

And yet, through it all, Williams had not confessed. Even Johnson and Cunningham were impressed by Williams's stubbornness. "After six or seven hours he was as strong as ever while we were tired out," they wrote in their report. "He is no one new at this game, for he wouldn't talk when we pressed him too close."

Still, there were Williams's words: "*Nobody seen me do it.*" Cliver's article, with its portrait of Williams as a raging monster, implied that this assertion might be enough to finally fix Marie's murder on Black Diamond. Cliver reported that, after their questioning of Williams in his cell, the two Greater New York Agency detectives were called back to New York City, their job in Asbury Park complete. Cliver also reported that "the Burns Agency men"—Schindler and his team—"have quit, and the case has apparently been dropped."

Publicly, at least, the story was set. Tom Williams was the killer, and at last he'd been tricked up, shaken off his song of innocence, brought closer to his reckoning, left in his lonely cell to face his final fate.

CHAPTER 23

The Watchtower

*

October 5, 1892
Lyric Hall, New York City

I da Wells tried hard not to cry. A thousand miles from home, largely friendless in a strange new city, she stood in front of hundreds of people and felt the tears coming on, and she tried to fight them off. But they came anyway—tears of loss and loneliness.

Five months earlier, a mob of white men demolished the offices of her newspaper, *Free Speech,* in Memphis. Wells fled to Brooklyn, New York, a sprawling city unlike any small southern town she had known. She lived by herself in a rented apartment on Gold Street, in a mostly residential neighborhood called Vinegar Hill, more commonly known as Irishtown, wedged between the Brooklyn Bridge and the Brooklyn Navy Yard. There she lived under the threat "of hanging or burning at the stake," the *Boston Herald* declared, should she ever dare return to her home in Memphis. Wells was thirty years old.

The same month Wells left Memphis for Brooklyn, May 1892, her friend T. Thomas Fortune offered her a weekly column in his newspaper, the *New York Age.* Wells took the job, she would say, with a new sense of purpose and resolve. "Having lost my paper, had a price put on my life and been made an exile from my home for hinting at the truth," Wells wrote, "I felt that I owed it to myself and to my race to tell the whole truth now that I was where I could do so freely."

Her first article for the *Age* ran across seven columns, covering nearly the entire front page of the June 25, 1892, issue. It was titled "The Truth About Lynching." It was, in a way, a continuation of the antilynching article that led to the destruction of the *Free Speech* offices in Memphis, except that it was, as Wells had promised, a fuller, freer, and more graphic denunciation of the racism, terror, and violence inflicted on the colored race in the South.

It was unlike anything ever written by a black journalist before.

Wells set out to do two things: debunk the accepted premise used to justify lynching—the rape of white women by black men—and vividly describe the true horrors of lynching in a way that would change perception of the practice. "It is with no pleasure I have dipped my hands in the corruption here exposed," she wrote. "Somebody must show that the Afro-America race is more sinned upon than sinning, and it seems to have fallen upon me to do so."

Wells did not hold back. She listed more than seven hundred instances of lynching, and provided the dates, places, and names of victims—"the awful death-roll that Judge Lynch is calling every week." She described the barbaric sameness of many of the crimes—white mobs dragging black men out of jail cells; brutal hangings in town squares; already-murdered victims riddled with bullets or dismembered. "The flaying alive of a man in Kentucky, the burning of one in Arkansas, the hanging of a fifteen-year-old girl in Louisiana . . . until the dark and bloody record of the South shows seven-hundred twenty-eight Afro-Americans lynched during the past eight years," she wrote.

Of those victims, Wells noted, only a third had even been accused of rape; the rest were lynched under a variety of other justifications, including, in one instance, "acting sassy." Of those charged with rape, Wells insisted most were surely innocent. "Nobody in this section of the country believes the old threadbare lie that Negro men rape white women," she argued. She insisted here as she had before that the charge of rape, therefore, was largely a pretense—the real aim of lynching was to keep the black race economically subjugated through the use of terror and violence. The lynching of her close Memphis friend, Thomas Moss, had, after all, been precipitated by an economic clash—Moss's black-owned grocery posed a threat to a rival white-owned store. In the end, Moss's lynching led to the destruction of his store, and to its stock and customers being absorbed by the very rival who saw to it that Moss was lynched.

Wells believed the same was true of most acts of mob violence against blacks across the country. The white southerner, she wrote in her auto-biography, "had never gotten over his resentment that the Negro was no longer his plaything, his servant, his source of income." Without the practice of slavery to keep black citizens under their control, white southerners instead branded the Negro as a race of wild rapists—people who needed to be brutalized in order to be tolerated. By so thoroughly and graphically cataloging the reality of lynching throughout the South, Wells, for the first time, provided a solid factual argument against the foundational lie that justified the practice.

And because Wells anticipated a backlash that would suggest she'd exaggerated or fabricated her descriptions of lynching, she did some-thing shrewd—she used only white sources for her catalog of crimes. All her information came from white journalists and white-owned news-papers, and if she made a personal observation, she backed it up with secondary reporting. These are known facts, Wells was saying—all she had done was compile them into an unspeakable whole.

Wells's approach to the topic helped elevate the *New York Age* arti-cle from daring journalism to something larger and more profound. Wells's antilynching statement would go on to become, according to the author and professor Anita August, "the founding rhetorical text in the anti-lynching movement." Wells assembled a uniquely vivid, factual, and coherent portrait of the practice in America—the first fully contextualized analysis of lynching, and of the willful indifference of white law authorities to it, as seen from the side of the victims.

That, on its own, ensured her article's impact. But that was not all Wells did. Despite avoiding sentimentality, she also managed to invest her writing with a deep and undeniable humanity, a beseeching demand for reason and decency. "The Truth About Lynching" was a moral clarifier, a call to action, so persuasive it could not be dismissed. Wells did not hope to reflect public opinion—she meant to *shape* it.

T. Thomas Fortune printed ten thousand copies of the June 25 issue of the *New York Age* and sent them out across the country. More than one thousand copies were sold in Memphis alone. These were not staggering numbers (black newspapers like the *Age* had limited circulation) but they were signs Wells now had her largest audience yet.

The article, which carried the byline "Exiled," did produce a predictable backlash against Wells. One Boston newspaper editorial called her "a licentious defamer of Southern women" and "a harlot," while the governor of Virginia and former Confederate colonel Charles T. O'Ferrall said "the slandering utterances of Ida Wells are calculated to do harm rather than good, and intensify rather than mollify the spirit of violence." O'Ferrall argued that the crime of black men raping white women "caused all the lynching in the South, with rare exceptions," and that Wells and other blacks should "frown down upon it and cry out against it, and not exert their energies to a denunciation of the lynching."

But, crucially, Wells's article also made it into the hands of one of the most prominent black women in Brooklyn—an accomplished schoolteacher and activist named Maritcha Remond Lyons.

Lyons began teaching in 1869, the same year she became the first black girl to graduate from Providence High School in Rhode Island. Over the years Lyons gained, as she put it, "some little recognition as an elocutionist"—a public speaker whose powerful voice could reach the highest rafters. Lyons met Ida Wells through the Brooklyn Literary Union, one of the leading literary clubs in the city. The Union held its meetings at the Everett Assembly Rooms on Willoughby Street, in halls rented out for twenty dollars an evening. In one of the Union's featured debates, Lyons squared off with the club's invited guest, Ida Wells. Lyons later wrote that her own performance "won the plaudits of the members."

As for Wells, her performance in the debate gained her a lifelong friend in Lyons. Fourteen years older than Wells, Lyons was impressed by Wells's "grit and determination," and agreed to "coach her in the art of extempore speaking." Lyons taught Wells her two main rules of public oratory: "1 - Be so familiar with your subject that you are literally saturated with it; think, meditate and reflect to develop all the points in logical sequence. 2 - Learn how to manage the voice; if thought is prolific, expression of ideas will become automatic."

Not long after the debate, Lyons received her copy of the *New York Age* that featured "The Truth About Lynching." The article had its desired effect—it moved Lyons to action. Together with Victoria Earle Matthews, a journalist and early reformer in Brooklyn's black settlements, Lyons arranged local meetings to read and discuss Wells's writings, and in the following weeks the meetings grew in size. Matthews and Lyons decided they wanted to help Wells financially—and perhaps even raise enough money to allow her to publish the *Free Speech* again. They organized a committee of two hundred fifty women, announced an event in honor of Wells, and invited her to give a speech to their expanding circle.

Wells agreed to attend, and a date and place were picked— October 5, 1892, at New York City's Lyric Hall, an elegant dance palace that normally hosted wedding receptions and society balls.

*

On the evening of October 5, 1892, Wells crossed the Brooklyn Bridge— free for walkers, three cents for drivers—and headed north toward the Manhattan neighborhood known as Longacre Square.

Around her, the city was rising. In lower Manhattan, the new emigrant office at Ellis Island was now processing the many millions of immigrants streaming into the city each year. A mile inland from the harbor, Joseph Pulitzer had just finished constructing the world's tallest office building— his golden-domed, twenty-six-story World Building on Park Row. Farther north, the stately, marble, seventy-seven-foot Washington Square Arch, flanking the south end of Fifth Avenue, had just been completed. "Let us raise a standard to which the wise and the honest can repair," read the inscription atop the arch. "The event is in the hand of God."

Wells made her way north to 42nd Street, the wide thoroughfare that spanned the island from the East River to the Hudson River. The street was anchored on Fifth Avenue by the massive, aboveground Croton Reservoir, a stone fortress with walls that were fifty feet tall and twenty-five feet thick, built to hold more than twenty million gallons of pure water piped down from the Croton River forty-five miles upstate.

One block west of the Reservoir, between 42nd and 43rd Streets on Sixth Avenue, sat Lyric Hall.

Ida Wells walked past newsboys and pretzel vendors and entered the hall, and once inside she was surprised by what she found. Matthews and Lyons had gone to some lengths to prepare the hall for her speech. Behind a large main platform, a string of lights spelled out IOLA, Wells's pen name. The evening's programs were designed to look like miniature copies of the *Free Speech*. The hall was filled with "the leading colored women" of Boston, Philadelphia, and New York, Wells noted—"a brilliant array." The event, Matthews and Lyons declared, "was the greatest demonstration ever attempted by race women for one of their number."

Matthews began the program with an introduction. Then a few short speeches and the reading of resolutions, followed by music and singing. Finally, Ida Wells took the stage. Matthews, Lyons, and several other prominent activists took their chairs behind her on the platform, and in front of her a crowd of several hundred sat and waited. Wells looked out over their faces, took a deep breath, and began to tell her story.

And then, as she would recall, "a panic seized me."

*

Wells was not yet a confident speaker. She'd stood before people and spoken before, first in school, then in recitals and plays. She was comfortable going door-to-door and giving short speeches to sell news-paper subscriptions. She'd even addressed respectable gatherings: in 1891, she talked about her life in front of the Afro-American League in Knoxville, Tennessee, and in September 1892 she gave a speech titled "The Afro-American in Literature" to a literary circle in the Concord Baptist Church of Christ in Brooklyn. She also had the benefit of Marit-cha Lyons's public speaking lessons.

Even so, Wells admitted, "When the committee told me I had to speak, I was frightened." Her speech at Lyric Hall would be different from anything she'd ever done. It was expressly political, and it was at the request of—and in the presence of—her most prominent fellow activists.

"This was the first time I had ever been called on to deliver an honest-to-goodness address," Wells wrote—the first time she'd actually written down the words of a speech, rather than simply speaking from memory. Wells was being asked to transform herself yet again, from a journalist into a bona fide public speaker—someone who could not only command a crowd, but also stir it to action.

Wells also understood that, as part of her speech, she would have to discuss the violent lynching of her Memphis friend Thomas Moss, a trauma that was only a few months old. She had no idea how talking about Moss would affect her. And, to her surprise, it overwhelmed her.

Onstage at Lyric Hall, not too far into her speech, Wells lost her focus. While describing the events surrounding Moss's murder, "my mind went back to the scenes of the struggle, to the thoughts of my friends who were scattered throughout the country," Wells later wrote. She felt shaken by "a feeling of loneliness and homesickness for the days and the friends that were gone." And then, she said, "I felt the tears coming."

Wells struggled to control her emotions, or at least prevent the prom-inent people behind her from seeing her cry. "I was afraid that I was going to make a scene and spoil all those dear good women had done for me," she wrote. "I kept saying to myself that whatever happened I must not break down, and so I kept on reading." But Wells could not stop her tears—and she realized she didn't have the handkerchief she usually carried with her. She'd left it on a seat behind her.

Wells did not stop speaking. Instead, she put her hand behind her back and signaled for help. Victoria Matthews came forward, and Wells asked for her handkerchief. Matthews got it and brought it up to her. "I wiped my nose and streaming face," Wells wrote, "but I kept on reading the story which they had come to hear."

It was without doubt a powerful story. "On the morning of March 9, the bodies of three of our best young men were found in an old field, horribly shot to pieces," Wells said in her clear, even voice, even as tears still ran down her face. The details of the killings, and the dispute that led to them, were dramatic enough, but Wells, who was friends with Moss's widow and godmother to his daughter, also spoke of events and moments that could not be found in newspaper accounts. She spoke of the loss of the three young men—of her friends—in starkly human terms.

"The baby daughter of Tom Moss," Wells said, "too young to express how she missed her father, toddles to the wardrobe, seizes the legs of the trousers of his letter-carrier uniform, hugs and kisses them with evident delight, and stretches up her little hands to be taken up into the arms which will nevermore clasp his daughter's form.

"And his wife holds Thomas Moss Jr. in her arms, upon whose unconscious baby face the tears fall thick and fast when she is thinking of the sad fate of the father he will never see, and of the two helpless children who cling to her for support she cannot give."

Many people in Lyric Hall quietly wept. "Do you ask a remedy?" Wells said at the end of her speech. "A public sentiment strong against lawlessness must be aroused. Every individual can contribute to this awakening. When a sentiment against lynch law strong, deep and mighty as that roused against slavery prevails, I have no fear of the result.

"The voice of the people," Well concluded, "is the voice of God."

*

When she was finished speaking, Wells felt mortified. "I had not been able to prevent such an exhibition of weakness," she later wrote. In fact, her speech was a success. The crowd gave her a long, loud ovation, and afterward several people assured her that her emotions had only lent her words more drama and power. One preacher told Wells her speech "did more to convince cynical and selfish New York of the seriousness of the lynching situation than anything else could have done." One newspaper account of the speech read "All eyes were turned on Ida B. Wells, for it was she herself a victim of the portrayed outrages, and she was moved to grief. Miss Wells was the star of the convention; though modest in appearance she shone with intellectual brilliancy."

Wells's speech at Lyric Hall changed her life again. She gained an almost instant renown as a fiery activist and forceful public speaker, giving her the platform she needed to spread her antilynching message. The event raised four hundred dollars, which was handed to Wells, along with another one hundred dollars, to use toward publishing her *New York Age* editorial as a stand-alone pamphlet that could be more easily distributed around the country. Her new friends Maritcha Lyons and Victoria Matthews also presented Wells with a gold brooch in the shape of a pen. The brooch had the word *mizphah* etched on it.

Mizphah is the Hebrew word for "lookout" or "watchtower."

It was a sort of benediction. The expanding circle of black New York–area activists had appointed Ida Wells their lookout, their eyes and ears—the tip of their spear in the fight for the rights of black citizens.

Wells continued to inspire the movement through her writings and through many more powerful speeches—hundreds of them over the next several years. Some women's clubs even chose to name themselves after Ida Wells. Her influence on the movement led directly to the formation of the National Association of Colored Women Club, which helped to clear a path for the eventual founding, in 1909, of the National Association for the Advancement of Colored People—the NAACP.

The next three years were a nonstop storm of action and advocacy for Ida Wells. With the money raised by her Lyric Hall speech, Wells and T. Thomas Fortune published *Southern Horrors: Lynch Law in All Its Phases,* a pamphlet that featured pages of lynching statistics and more of Wells's powerful, graphic narrative about the true nature of mob violence.

The pamphlet sold for fifteen cents, and found readers across the country. Wells followed it up in 1895 with another even bolder pamphlet, *The Red Record,* which ran to one hundred pages and delivered more vivid reporting about the rising tide of lynchings in the United States. The pamphlets were financially successful and earned Wells more fame as the leading female activist of her time. "The salvation of the colored people of the south," read one editorial, "may yet come through a woman." Wells was becoming, in the words of another columnist, "the most famous colored woman in the world."

*

In 1894, more than one hundred people, a surprising number of them white, crowded into the main pews and balcony seats of the Bethel A.M.E. Church, an ornate, Gothic Revival building with towering arched windows overlooking Sullivan Street, in New York City's Tenderloin district. They were there to hear Ida Wells speak.

Her friend T. Thomas Fortune introduced her to the congregants, before Wells—wearing a plain black dress with her mizphah gold brooch, and a white braided leghorn hat pinned with white ostrich feathers—strode forward and stood confidently before the gilded, wood-paneled altar and the church's large silver crucifix. By then Wells had delivered more than one hundred public speeches on the subject of lynching, including several speeches in the United Kingdom, where she had been invited for a series of talks.

"The colored people of this country should organize themselves from one end of the country to the other," Wells told her listeners in the church, her plea for action now sharpened into a militaristic charge. "They should at least contribute the sinews of war with which to fight the battle. It is our duty to see that every story published from the South, in which a Negro is accused of some fiendish act and lynched for it, is run down by our own detectives. There are two sides to every lynching."

Every story. Every accused black man. Every last one. This was the task Wells set for herself, and for her race. They would all be detectives now, searching for truth and justice, no matter the cost or danger.

"I am occasionally threatened to this day with death if I do not cease my work against lynching," Wells told one reporter in 1895.

"Does it scare you any?" the reporter asked.

Wells closed her eyes, took a moment, and smiled.

"I haven't quit yet," she said.

CHAPTER 24

Two Coffins

*

December 15, 1910
Brooklyn, New York

R ay Schindler was not pleased with the autopsy performed on Marie Smith. It was incomplete and inconclusive. After the disappointing coroner's inquest, Schindler made an unusual and extraordinary request of the coroner, Robert Purdy, and Sheriff Hetrick. The men listened to his reasoning, and agreed to his plan.

A few days later, midmorning on December 15, 1910, the Burns detective Charles A. Severance crossed over the Brooklyn Bridge and walked into an elegant five-story, white-marble building set inside the triangle formed by Flatbush Avenue, Willoughby Street, and Fleet Place. The building housed the offices of the Brooklyn Board of Health. Severance was there to get the signature of a local New York City undertaker, James McCanna, on a permit, to go along with permits already signed by Robert Purdy and Peter Smith.

Once he had the third signature, the way would be clear for Ray Schindler to exhume the body of Marie Smith.

Peter Smith, who was needed to identify his daughter's remains, came along with Severance. Sheriff Hetrick and Randolph Miller, as well as a stenographer, Edward Handley, also traveled up from Asbury Park. The coroner of New York City, Otto H. Schultz, would perform the second autopsy, aided by a noted Manhattan surgeon, Walter H. Bishop. Raymond Schindler would join them later for the procedure.

After McCanna arrived and signed the permit, Severance paid an eight-dollar permit fee and phoned a supervisor at the Holy Cross Cemetery in the Flatbush section of Brooklyn. He was told the grave site would be ready for them by 2:00 p.m. All the talk of exhumation was too much for Peter Smith, who told Severance he felt sick. The detective took him to a nearby saloon for lunch and a hard drink. In the Catholic faith, it was no small thing to pull the dead up from the ground. Burials were meant to be acts of finality, allowing the deceased to rest in peace until their flesh was resurrected in the glory of a risen Jesus. To disinter a body was to interfere with one of the most essential principles of the faith. It should only be done for the most solemn of reasons.

After their drinks, Smith and Severance made their way to Tilden Avenue and the arched stone entrance gates of the Holy Cross Cemetery, and through them several hundred yards to Marie's plot in the St. Alban's section of the site. Marie had been buried just outside the shadow of the Chapel of the Resurrection, beneath which, in catacombs, lay the diocese's pioneer priests, and some of Brooklyn's oldest Catholic families.

By the time they got to Marie's plot, the dirt had already been dug and heaped in a pile besides the grave. The coffin remained in the ground. Severance and Smith stood around the hole, along with Hetrick, Miller, Otto Schultz, and Walter Bishop. Six cemetery workers used ropes to raise up the outer burial vault—the rough box—and placed it in the grass. The box was marked with a metal plate identifying Fred E. Farry as the embalmer, and a pasted paper label from the manufacturer, Morris Manufacturing Company. Sheriff Hetrick turned to Marie's father.

"Mr. Smith, do you recognize this grave?" he asked.

"Yes, sir. It is the grave in which my child, Marie, is buried."

Hetrick pointed at the box.

"Does that box contain the coffin in which your daughter Marie was buried?"

"Yes, sir," Smith answered.

"Your daughter—Marie Smith?"

"Yes, sir."

Hetrick waved at the workers, and they loaded the box into a wagon provided by the local undertaker, James McCanna. Peter Smith sat in front of the wagon and rode along the one mile to the office of P. McCanna & Sons, at 804 Flatbush Avenue. An autopsy room in the back quickly filled up: the surgeons Schultz and Bishop, Hetrick, Miller, Severance, and Charles Scholl, another Burns detective. The men crowded around the embalming table, on which workers had placed Marie's coffin.

Otto Schultz took control. The city coroner was small and serious, his owl-rimmed glasses only slightly softening a scowl. He spoke in a droning monotone, as if "he was weary of murders," one reporter suggested. The town of Asbury Park would pay Schultz the considerable sum of seven hundred dollars for performing this second autopsy—by far the biggest expense yet incurred by Ray Schindler and his team.

Schultz gave the instruction for the coffin to be opened. When the lid came up, Marie Smith was there, white and bruised in her funeral dress and shoes. Schultz turned to her father.

"Look at the body," Schultz told him. "Tell us who lies there if you can."

"That is my daughter, Marie," Smith said.

"Do you positively identify the body was that of your daughter Marie?"

"Yes, sir, I am positive."

"Now," Schultz said, "don't you think you had better leave the room, Mr. Smith?"

"No, sir. I want to stay."

Schultz would not have it. He knew what was to come.

"But *we* think you had better leave the room," he said.

Smith lowered his head. Charles Severance led him out of the room, and to another saloon for another hard drink. Smith was badly shaken, and Severance let him talk about it. Smith explained that he had seen something when the workers raised up Marie's box at the cemetery. There, at the very bottom of the hole, he had seen the second box.

The box that held the coffin of his firstborn child, John, who died at eighteen months of age after swallowing horse liniment.

Smith had his drink, and got ready as best he could for when his second child to die would be lowered into the earth once more.

*

In the airless, unsterilized embalming room, Otto Schultz pulled an apron over his suit clothes. Around him, the tools of autopsy—a broad-bladed postmortem knife; a seven-inch brain knife; long-bladed scissors for cutting through stomach, bowels, air passages, and heart cavities; rib shears, bone forceps, various scales and weights, needles, twine, sponges, sawdust, graduated vessels, and glass bottles.

Once Peter Smith was out of the room, Schultz asked Randolph Miller to serve as a second witness and identify the body. Miller confirmed it was Marie. Schultz began by surveying the surface of the corpse for evidence not included in the first coroner's report. Charles Scholl, standing next to him, did the same. "Nothing of a startling nature was revealed," Scholl would write, "except that when the skull was laid bare there were two distinct fractures revealed."

The first autopsy had listed only one compound fracture at the back of the head, slightly above the neck.

Schultz called out his findings for the stenographer.

Fracture on the right side extends down to one-quarter inch from the base of the skull, just above pyramidal portion of right temporal bone. Fracture in left side extends down to the base of the skull at the junction of the outer wall with the floor of middle fossa.

Scholl asked Schultz about the fractures. Could one of them have resulted from a fall into a pit? Schultz answered that yes, a fall into a pit with a concrete bottom, with the head striking something on its way down, could also cause such fractures. Scholl noted the length of one of the fractures—two inches. "It will be remembered that two inches in diameter is about the measurement of the iron pipe standing in the furnace pit at Kruschka's greenhouse," Scholl reported. The pipe had been mentioned in the first coroner's report as a theoretical cause of the fracture. Now Schultz confirmed it was possible. Both fractures, he concluded, would have required a very severe blow.

By then, Raymond Schindler had arrived at the undertaker's office. The autopsy itself, he was told, had not revealed anything new or meaningful beyond the second fracture, which only confirmed the severity of the death blow. Further analysis of Marie's organs might shed more light on what happened, but that would take some time. For Schindler, this was disappointing news. He had hoped to be able to settle on a murder weapon, at the least. All that had been accomplished, then, was a strengthening of Schindler's leading theory—that Frank Heidemann had lured Marie into the greenhouse and killed her there.

Otto Schultz ended the autopsy. Schindler joined up with Severance, who was back from the saloon with Peter Smith. Schindler stayed with Smith until they could be sure Marie's body had been properly re-dressed and reburied. It was the last grim task of a grim day. That Smith had not been present to see what remained of his daughter after Schultz's procedure was the only small mercy of the afternoon.

And when Marie went back into the earth later that day, she, too, had played her final part in the case, and had given all she possibly could to help the men in their hunt for her killer.

CHAPTER 25

The Hellhound

*

December 1910
Asbury Park, New Jersey

Ray Schindler and his men were out of options.

They'd been in Asbury Park for more than a month and uncovered no hard evidence linking anyone to the murder. They'd combed the Wanamassa several times, and spoken to just about everyone with any connection to the case. The coroner's inquest hadn't been helpful, and now the second autopsy hadn't yielded any leads. Grit and legwork had only taken Schindler's men so far, and perhaps as far as they ever would.

Their diligent interviewing and reinterviewing of witnesses did yield some results. Charles Scholl, for instance, was deliberate in going after Marjorie Coleman, the woman who claimed to hear Tom Williams say he would "get next to" Marie Smith. The county prosecutor, John Applegate, presented her claim as vital evidence against Williams at the coroner's inquest. Scholl asked around and learned that Williams allegedly made the remark at an impromptu afternoon party in Asbury Park. He tracked down everyone who was there and spoke to them all. He got three of them to sign affidavits declaring Tom Williams never made any remark about any child, much less about Marie Smith.

Scholl also paid a return visit to the ramshackle boardinghouse where Tom Williams was arrested. There he met a woman named Carrie Higgins, who had insight into two key pieces of evidence—the small towel and the faded blue blanket found near the room where Williams slept. Mysteriously, both items appeared to have blood on them, and were collected as proof of Williams's guilt.

But now Higgins had an explanation for the red stains. She told Scholl the blood on the blanket belonged to her son, who had been sick and suffered a nosebleed. As for the towel, Higgins said she hung it on a clothesline just beneath a red underskirt, which dripped on the towel and stained it with red dye.

Scholl accepted Higgins's explanation about the towel, but he checked with a local physician about her son's nosebleed. The doctor confirmed the story. Scholl, then, was able to discount three crucial bits of evidence aimed at Tom Williams—the bloody towel and blanket, and Marjorie Coleman's claim.

Yet all that did was weaken the case against Williams. It did nothing to build a case against anyone else.

Schindler knew the investigation was losing momentum. For a long time, the spectacular crime had absorbed the town's citizens completely. There had been at least one major story about Marie Smith in local newspapers for twenty-seven straight days. But by mid-December 1910, more than a month after the murder, interest was waning. People were getting on with their lives, and the headlines disappeared. The *Asbury Park Press* and Alvin Cliver stopped their front-page coverage of the case on December 9. There simply wasn't anything new to report.

Here is where Raymond Schindler's inexperience as a homicide investigator proved helpful.

Marie's killing was his first murder case, and in many ways he was still learning on the job. He understood the investigative protocols and parameters put in place by Williams Burns, but he didn't have a deep well of prior work to draw on. He had yet to be buttoned into any one way of working a case, and he was freer to take chances and follow his instincts than a more seasoned detective might have been. There was room in his still-forming methodology for invention and imagination. For creativity.

That is how Ray Schindler pushed through the dead spot in the investigation and devised a new plan.

Admittedly, it was a plan "which on its face seemed foolishly theatrical," Schindler later confessed. "It was like the wildest sort of fiction, but we hoped it would work."

Two people inspired Schindler's plan—the experimental German psychologist Hugo Münsterberg, and Sir Arthur Conan Doyle.

Schindler's interest in the psychological underpinnings of crime, as studied and articulated by Münsterberg, led him to believe that, under pressure, human beings could not help but betray their true emotions. A suspect who was guilty would, under the right circumstances, manifest his guilt through some kind of physical tic. "The lips and hands and arms and legs, which are under our control, are never the only witnesses to the drama which goes on inside," Münsterberg wrote in his seminal essay collection, *On the Witness Stand*, published two years before Schindler joined the Marie Smith case. "If they keep silent, others will speak." Investigators, Münsterberg believed, should look for "the involuntary signs of secret excitement"—human nature slowly revealing itself.

Münsterberg pushed to have his theories adopted by law enforcement professionals, who he felt would hugely benefit from applying experimental psychology to crime detection. His great frustration was that almost no one in the field took him seriously.

He had a fan in Raymond Schindler, though, and now Schindler was about to put Münsterberg's controversial theories into practice.

Schindler, a devoted reader of literature, turned for direct inspiration to one of the most popular current works of crime fiction—*The Hound of the Baskervilles*, written by the famous English author Sir Arthur Conan Doyle, and serialized in a magazine for the first time in 1901. The book featured Doyle's greatest creation, the uncommonly intuitive detective Sherlock Holmes. In the story, Holmes takes on a murder case in Devon and confronts the legend of a fearsome, oversize hellhound prowling the moors of England's west country. Holmes succeeds in proving the devilish beast is just a bloodhound-mastiff mix painted with luminescent phosphorous to make it look supernatural.

While the legend persisted, however, the phantom hound was deeply terrorizing, and convinced a family that it had been fatally cursed.

Here was the tale of people under pressure projecting their own fear and guilt onto a harmless animal. Could Schindler somehow apply the same kind of pressure to Frank Heidemann, to flush out his "secret excitements"? It was, Schindler concluded, worth a try.

Years later, when he wrote about the case, he explained his thinking at the time. "It is not so much a detective's business to catch a criminal," Schindler believed, "as it is to make a criminal catch himself."

*

Schindler knew Frank Heidemann's second-floor bedroom in Max Kruschka's house had a small window overlooking the backyard kennel where Kruschka's big watchdog slept.

One night, shortly before 12:00 a.m., Schindler positioned one of his men, Thomas Bowers, the assistant manager of the New York Bureau, in a dense cluster of bushes and branches behind a fence that ran along Kruschka's backyard. From that spot, Bowers was roughly twenty yards from both Frank Heidemann's window and the backyard kennel.

Bowers had several stones in his pockets. His instructions were simple—at midnight, he was to throw a stone at the kennel, aggravate the hound, then slip out of view. Bowers was told to do the same thing every hour until daybreak. From his discreet perch, he would watch for Heidemann's reaction to the disturbance, and report back to Schindler.

The first night in the thicket, Bowers waited until midnight, threw his rock at the kennel, and dropped back into the bushes. The big watchdog ran out howling, his long chain rattling behind him.

The dog kept up his furious barking, and Bowers watched as the lights came on inside the house. In a moment both Kruschka and Frank

Heidemann came out into the yard and walked around the property. They found nothing, and Kruschka scolded the dog before going back inside.

One hour later, at 1:00 a.m., Bowers threw another stone. Out came the howling hound again, and again the lights came on. This time Kruschka stuck his head out the front door and yelled and cursed at the dog. Eventually the barking stopped.

At 2:00 a.m., another stone, more yelping. Neither Kruschka nor Heidemann came out. Bowers, however, saw the light come on in Heidemann's room. The dog barked until he got tired and went back to his kennel. An hour later, another stone brought him out again.

This went on until dawn. Bowers reported that Kruschka soon blocked out the barking, but at every hour, the racket caused Heidemann to switch on his lights. Ray Schindler sent Bowers back to the same spot for a second night, and a third night. According to Schindler, the hourly harassment went on for either nine or ten straight nights. Heidemann's bedroom light, Schindler later noted, "stayed on longer and longer. His shadow could be seen on his window shade. It was evident that he was pacing the floor."

Yet after more than a week of continuously agitating his suspect, Schindler had nothing to show for it. Beyond pacing in his room, Heidemann did not betray any secret, hidden emotion besides annoyance. In his later writings, Schindler said he never expected his *Hound of the Baskervilles* ploy would cause Heidemann to confess to murder. Instead, he claimed, he simply wanted to get under Heidemann's skin.

"The howling of a dog at night is supposed to be a bad omen—to be significant of death," Schindler wrote. "We wanted very badly to unnerve the gardener. We wanted to get him out of that house—out of Asbury Park, if possible. Where a man can't rest, he won't live."

The plan, it seemed, did not work. In the days that followed, Frank Heidemann appeared unfazed. One Burns detective noted in a report on Christmas Day that Heidemann "seemed to feel good, and many times during the day he played with the dog in the yard."

Two days later, on December 27, Charles Scholl was called in for a meeting with Clarence Hetrick and Randolph Miller in the sheriff's office. The news he was given was bad. "It was requested by the Sheriff, and seconded by Mr. Miller, that surveillance upon Heidemann be called off," Scholl reported.

Ray Schindler wasn't pleased. He told Scholl to go back to Hetrick and stress how crucial the surveillance on Heidemann was to the case. Hetrick didn't budge. On New Year's morning, Schindler himself spoke with Hetrick, but that didn't work, either. So far, the Burns Agency had billed the county $3,634.17, plus the seven hundred dollars Schindler paid Otto Schultz for the autopsy. This was well past the original three-thousand-dollar budget—and the money spent hadn't produced a breakthrough.

So, in his meeting with Hetrick and Miller, Schindler was told to begin to wrap up his work. "It was decided to have Charles Scholl bring together all the tail ends of the investigation, so that by the end of the week we would be in a position to present the matter to Prosecutor Applegate so he could see exactly what the status of the case is to date," Schindler wrote. If, at that point, Hetrick could be persuaded to keep Schindler and his men on the case, they would move forward.

If not, Schindler concluded, "it would probably be useless to continue the investigation as there would be little chance of success without the cooperation of the Prosecutor."

So that was it. Schindler was to gather all his evidence and build whatever case he might have—which, he well knew, was no case at all.

By Sheriff Hetrick's order, New Year's Day would be the final day of surveillance on Schindler's primary suspect, Frank Heidemann. What Schindler had called an intense "system of espionage" came to an official end on January 2, 1911, nearly six weeks after it began.

Ray Schindler's mangy hellhound had not, as he hoped, laid bare a murderer's guilt.

*

Or had it?

On January 4, 1911, two days after the end of surveillance, Max Kruschka helped Frank Heidemann put a big steamer trunk in a covered wagon and take it to the North Asbury Park train depot. The trunk was marked with the number 929687 and routed for delivery aboard a ferry to New York City's West 23rd Street dock. The next day, in the predawn darkness, Heidemann, dressed in a suit, quietly left Kruschka's home and steered a wagon west to the train depot. At the depot he asked a steward with a thick red mustache to help him unload his other bags. Heidemann had a ticket for the 6:15 a.m. train, scheduled to arrive in its destination at 8:17. Just before boarding, Heidemann looked behind him, and to his left and right. He saw nothing troubling. Then he got on the train, which left the station right on time, and carried Frank Heidemann out of New Jersey.

Schindler later learned that Heidemann had asked Max Kruschka for two weeks' vacation time, so he could go to New York City to marry a hospital nurse turned chorus girl named Mabel Brightel.

But there was no wedding, and there was no Mabel Brightel.

Frank Heidemann was fleeing Asbury Park for good.

CHAPTER 26

The Hands of Parties Unknown

*

June 27, 1895
Chicago, Illinois

They came by the hundreds to see Ida Wells, from the North and South, from California and New York, to a place that would soon be called the Black Metropolis—the colored Douglas neighborhood on Chicago's South Side, a few blocks from the shore of Lake Michigan.

More than nine hundred of them—businessmen and politicians, lawyers and activists—made it inside the magnificent A.M.E. Bethel Church and filled its pews to capacity. Many dozens more lined the streets around the ornate church. Built of massive stone blocks and St. Louis pressed brick, the Romanesque structure stood on the corner of Dearborn and 30th Streets and was, according to one newspaper, "a monument to the enterprise of the colored race." The Douglas neighborhood, though run-down and neglected, boasted several new black businesses and culture centers. It was only fitting that so many would come to see her there, in the heart of Chicago's Black Belt, at the start of what was called the Colored Renaissance.

Yet they did not come to hear Ida Wells give a speech.

They came to see her get married.

She would wed Ferdinand Lee Barnett, an accomplished black lawyer ten years older than she. Barnett's first wife died five years earlier of heart disease, when their children were four and two. Wells had worked with Barnett on a libel case she filed against a Memphis newspaper in 1893. That same year, they collaborated on a pamphlet protesting the lack of black representation at the Chicago World's Fair.

The Nashville-born Barnett, like Wells, was a journalist, activist, and civic leader. At twenty-six, he cofounded Chicago's first black newspaper, the *Conservator*, and published a steady collection of antilynching stories and columns. He was popular and dashing, fond of silk hats and Prince Edward coats, and when he fell for Ida Wells he made sure she had a letter from him waiting at every stop of her speaking tour. They were, it seemed, wonderfully suited for each other.

Yet Wells postponed their wedding three times, in order to deliver antilynching speeches. She did not want a big, fancy ceremony, until a Chicago women's club inspired by and named for her asked for permission to manage the affair. Wells agreed, and her wedding became a major social occasion, with finely printed invitations, a long guest list of notable figures, and a front-page mention in the *New York Times*.

"The interest of the public in the affair seemed to be so great," Wells would write, "that not only was the church filled to overflowing but the streets surrounding the church were so packed with humanity that it was almost impossible for the carriage bearing the bridal party to reach the church door."

The ceremony, set for 8:00 p.m., was late to start. Ten women from the Ida B. Wells Club, dressed in white, served as ushers. The young Rev. D. A. Graham, with his fierce muttonchops beard and logical, practical oratorical style, waited at the altar. The organist Gertrude Johnson played Wagner's "Bridal Chorus," the wedding march from the opera *Lohengrin*. The flower girl, Betty Womack, sprinkled petals down the aisle, followed by Wells's sisters Annie and Lilly, wearing lemon crepe dresses with white ribbons, slippers, and gloves. Ida Wells was next.

Then thirty-three, she wore a white satin wedding gown trimmed with chiffon and orange blossoms. She walked down the church's left aisle, ahead of two groomsmen, R. P. Bird and S. J. Evans, who came down the right side. Ferdinand Barnett took his bride-to-be's hand at the altar. The organist played a sweet rendition of "Call Me Thine Own," and Rev. Graham proclaimed the couple man and wife. Mendelssohn's "Wedding March" rang through the church as little Betty Womack led the procession back down the aisle, scattering more petals as she went.

Rather than give up her own last name, Ida Wells became Mrs. Ida Wells-Barnett.

By all accounts, the wedding was a simple and beautiful celebration of love and community, and for Wells—who'd spent the previous three years traveling relentlessly throughout the United States and Great Britain on her antilynching crusade—a deserved respite and blessing.

And yet many saw it as a betrayal.

As soon as Wells's wedding was announced in June 1895, "there arose a united protest from my people," she wrote. "They seemed to feel that I had deserted the cause, and some of them censured me rather severely in their newspapers for having done so." Many argued it would be impossible for Wells to devote the necessary energy and passion to the movement she created once she was married and raising a family.

Even the reformer and women's rights activist Susan B. Anthony, who had become friendly with Wells, seemed unhappy with her decision to wed. A year after the birth of her first child, Wells was a guest in Anthony's home while both were working on launching the Afro-American League, a collective that would protest racial injustice. After a few days together, Wells noticed how Anthony "would bite out my married name when addressing me," she wrote. "Finally, I said to her, 'Miss Anthony, don't you believe in women getting married?'"

"Oh yes," she remembered Anthony replying, "but not women like you who had a special call for special work. I too might have married but it would have meant dropping the work to which I had set my hand."

Anthony did not try to be diplomatic. She blamed Wells for a loss of momentum in the movement for black rights. "I know of no one in all this country better fitted to do the work you had in hand than yourself," Anthony said. "Since you have gotten married, agitation seems practically to have ceased. Besides, you have a divided duty. You are here trying to help in the formation of this league and your eleven-month-old baby needs your attention at home."

Wells wasn't happy with the criticism, which she believed was misguided. The real reason she was scaling back her public activism was that "I had been unable to get the support which was necessary to carry on my work," Wells wrote. "I had become discouraged in the effort to carry on alone." Her detractors, she was disappointed to learn, "were more outspoken because of the loss to the cause than they had been in holding up my hands when I was trying to carry a banner."

Wells was also disheartened by a growing number of challenges to her leadership role, most of which she felt were political. Earlier in 1895, a group of Methodist ministers asked her to leave a meeting before she could defend herself against charges that her views on lynching were too radical. Wells was weary from all the scrambling for political position in the antilynching movement, and worn out, physically and emotionally, from years of grueling train travel and dozens of wrenching speeches. She believed she had earned the right to step back.

Wells had never longed to have children. She lacked a strong maternal pull, she said. Her guess was that, because she'd been forced to be a mother to her younger siblings at a very early age, that burden might have "smothered the mother instinct." But as she got older, the idea of having a family of her own began to appeal to her. She decided not to answer her critics, and instead move forward with her new direction in life. Nine months after her wedding, in March 1896, Wells gave birth to a son, Charles, the first of her four children with Ferdinand Barnett.

But even then, Wells did not stop working. In fact, in the year after her wedding, she hardly seemed less busy than she had been the year before. She merely shifted her energy back to what she called "my first, and might be said, my only love"—journalism. Wells took ownership of her husband's newspaper, the *Chicago Conservator,* and was in its offices, serving as publisher and editor, the Monday after her Thursday wedding.

Four months after giving birth to Charles, Wells traveled to Washington, D.C., for a meeting of the Association of Colored Women's

Clubs, at which she was a delegate. Wells took along her baby, and her husband hired a nurse to go with her. Later that year, Wells gave speeches in several cities across Illinois, once again traveling with infant Charles. At every stop, her local hosts provided a nurse to watch over the baby while Wells delivered her speech. It was a juggling act, and Wells performed it for as long as she could. Yet she felt pulled in two directions.

Wells remained convinced of the urgency of her antilynching message, and she never left the movement completely. However, she also believed her children needed their mother to be with them as much as possible. She'd suffered the loss of her own parents at a cruelly young age, and that only made her feel more devotion to her new family. Despite her claims that she lacked a nurturing instinct, as a parent Wells "was kind and loving, but firm and strict," her youngest daughter, Alfreda M. Barnett Duster, wrote many years later. "She impressed upon her children their responsibilities, one of the most important being good conduct in her absence." When she was present, Duster remembered, Wells didn't need to say a word to express disappointment: "Her 'look' was enough to bring under control any mischievous youngster."

In 1897, Wells stopped working at the *Conservator,* and soon after gave up the presidency of the Ida B. Wells Club. By the time she had her fourth child in 1904, she resolved not to accept any work assignments that took her away from her children for long stretches until her youngest, Alfreda, was eight years old. "The duties of wife and mother were a profession in themselves," she wrote, "and it was hopeless to expect to carry on public work."

It was not exactly a full-blown retirement. Wells traveled locally to give speeches, often with a young child in tow. She stayed involved in the politics of her movement and lent her voice through letters and appearances when it was necessary. As hard as she thought it would be for her to "carry on public work," she did so as events required.

But for more than ten years after her marriage to Ferdinand Barnett in 1895, Wells was, by design, a much-diminished presence on the national scene. She had retreated from the front lines. She found rich and surprising rewards in being a wife and mother, and she did not regret her decision to refocus her life. "What a wonderful place in the scheme of things the Creator has given women," she wrote. "I cannot begin to express how I reveled in having made this discovery for myself."

All around her, however, the lynchings did not stop.

*

In the small town of Danville, 145 miles south of Chicago, a swelling mob of white men and women—as many as five thousand—surged down East Main Street, headed for the county jail.

It was the night of July 25, 1903, and they were coming for James Wilson, a black man accused of attacking a white farmer's wife. Along the way, completely by chance, the crowd swept into another black man, John Metcalf, and there was pushing and shoving. Metcalf "became involved in an altercation with some of the men in the mob," one newspaper reported. "They started after him, and he pulled a gun."

Metcalf fired a shot, killing Henry Gatterman, a young butcher.

Police officers caught up with the fleeing Metcalf and sped him to the police station. The mob, diverted from their original mission, was not far behind. Rather than put Metcalf in a cell, the officers locked him inside the vault used to store police records. Several men from the mob forced their way into the station, and were told Metcalf had already been taken out a back door and whisked away in a buggy. No one believed it.

Instead, some of the men left and returned with sledgehammers and railroad ties. They broke the lock on the vault door and dragged out John Metcalf. They took him six blocks back to East Main Street, hanged him from a telephone pole, and shot his body full of bullets.

The mob never got to James Wilson, their original target. But it took the men of Danville less than seventy-five minutes to encounter, provoke, pass judgment on, and end the existence of John Metcalf.

"When Danville is aroused," one of them told a reporter, "it does things in a rush."

*

The murder of John Metcalf haunted the mind of Edward D. Green, a candidate for the Illinois State House in 1904. When, that November, Green won election to the 44th General Assembly, out of Cook County's First District, he became the only black legislator in Illinois. He took an office in the Capitol Building and "scarcely sat down in his seat," one newspaper said, "before he began laying out his plan."

Green's plan was to ensure that John Metcalf's death meant something—and to write a law that would make lynching a state crime.

There existed laws that dealt with murder and mayhem, but no language that specifically addressed mob violence, the majority of which befell black Americans. Green wanted to change that. In February 1905, he introduced the Suppression of Mob Violence Bill, which one paper called "drastic in its revisions and calculated to be far-reaching in its effects." Green's bill—which referenced Metcalf's lynching—would give new legal definition to the term "mob," shrinking it to five or more persons with intent to offer violence. It would introduce jail time and financial penalties for anyone found to have participated in a lynching.

Its most provocative feature, however, was section 6:

> If any person shall be taken from the hands of a sheriff, or his deputy, having such person in custody, and shall be lynched, it shall be *prima facia* evidence of failure on the part of such sheriff to do his duty, and upon the fact being made to appear to the Governor, he shall publish proclamation declaring the office of such sheriff vacant, and he shall thereby and thereafter immediately be vacated.

Green's idea was to hold white sheriffs accountable for the lynching of men wrested from their custody. This was important because of the near-total lack of accountability for the actual participants in mob lynching. It was well understood that, while most murderous mobs were made up of common townspeople—farmers, grocers, saloonkeepers, friends, fathers, sons, even local officials—no one would be identified to authorities afterward. Witnesses by the dozens would swear they didn't recognize a single guilty party, even when they had witnessed the crimes from just a few feet away. Most coroner's inquests into lynching ended with the same cold conclusion, the same calculated wording—the killings came "at the hands of parties unknown."

This blind-eye practice became an unwritten code of conduct—and gave legal cover to lynch mobs. Lynching was simply considered beyond the scope of state or federal action. Mob violence, therefore, was a local issue, best left to local authorities.

Edward Green's bill sought to upend that unwritten rule and replace it with an ironclad law.

It would not be an easy sell, but Green was the man to sell it. He was friendly and popular, a natural politician, "very polite and always with a smile on his good-natured face," one paper declared. Green also enlisted the support of the Chicago Bar Association, and of the best-known antilynching crusader of the day, Ida Wells.

In 1904, Wells was still on self-imposed leave from her leadership role in the movement. She had not been especially prominent in the antilynching debate in the past few years. In 1903, she did not even write about the lynching of John Metcalf, even though it happened not too far south of where she lived. By 1904, she and her husband Ferdinand had four children—Charles, Herman, Ida Jr., and Alfreda. Her focus was largely on her family. Even so, she lent her support to Edward Green's bill.

Three months after it was introduced, Illinois governor Charles S. Deneen signed twenty-nine bills into law.

One of them was Green's Suppression of Mob Violence Act.

It was enacted by the 44th General Assembly, entered the Illinois Criminal Code as Section 256, and went into effect July 1, 1905. It was considered an enormous victory for the black race, and Edward Green was celebrated as a hero. "If he never performs another noble act in his life," one essayist wrote, "he has covered himself over in glory and immortalized himself." Ida Wells—who gave a speech in honor of Green at Chicago's Olivet Baptist Church that September—said the passage of the act "had given lynching its death blow in this state."

Tragically, she was wrong.

CHAPTER 27

Frog James

*

August 14, 1908
Springfield, Illinois

Three years later, in August 1908, a terrible, three-day spasm of violence struck Springfield, Illinois, the hometown of Abraham Lincoln. It was a scene of the bitterest hatred and bloodshed, involving thousands, a race riot of ghastly scope and horror. It was, one newspaper reported, a flat-out "war between the negroes and the white man." While the city of Springfield prepared for the upcoming centennial of Lincoln's birth, its streets were suddenly overrun, its stores set ablaze, its citizens plunged into anarchy. "As the blood red prairie sun sank tonight into the fields of waving corn that hedge about the city," one reporter wrote, "where lie the bones of him who said: 'With charity for all and malice toward none,' the people trembled with terror and alarm."

The riot, triggered by a white woman's allegation that a black man pulled her out of bed and tried to rape her, included some five thousand white citizens, many armed with axes and hatchets, rampaging through the Levee and the Badlands, the two black neighborhoods in Springfield, laying waste to black businesses and burning down homes. Just blocks from the two-story, twelve-room house where Lincoln had lived, angry rioters chanted, "Lincoln freed you, we will show you where you belong."

In three days of rioting, many dozens of black homes and businesses were destroyed, and at least sixteen people were killed, nine black and seven white. The 1908 Springfield Race Riot was a cruel reminder that, four decades after Lincoln freed the slaves, the once-improving plight of blacks was being forcefully and often violently reversed, the subjugation of slavery replaced by the determined quashing of black enterprise, community, and life. "Springfield's riot occurred in the context of the steady and marked deterioration of blacks' security in the United States that began in the late 19th century and continued after 1908," wrote the professor and author Roberta Senechal de la Roche in her study of the event. "Race riots and lynching represented the most extreme attempts by whites to subordinate blacks."

Here was the core of Ida Wells's antilynching crusade—the reality that mob violence against blacks was primarily a means of economic suppression. Despite Wells's years and years of work and sweat, and all the national attention she had drawn to the issue, lynching and suppression of black businesses and communities remained a governing practice across the country. The number of mob killings had dropped—89 of them in 1908, down from 161 in 1892—but there still existed a barbaric and relentless appetite for such crimes. For the three decades surrounding the turn of the century, an average of one black American was lynched every four days.

The Springfield Riot triggered a series of smaller acts of anti-colored violence around the country. Abraham Lincoln's damaged hometown had not yet been fully repaired when, one year later, 160 miles south of Springfield, another mob gathered in Cairo, Illinois, a poor former railroad town by the Ohio and Mississippi Rivers.

*

Katherine Boren, three years old, was playing in the alleyway behind her family's home in Cairo when she saw something frightening. She ran home to tell her mother, and her mother called the police.

There in the narrow alley lay the crumpled, naked body of Mary Pelley, a white, twenty-four-year-old shopgirl. Beside her lay her broken umbrella. She had been dragged into the alley, raped, and murdered. Town officials quickly announced a one-thousand-dollar reward for the capture of her killer, and sent for bloodhounds from a nearby city.

Before nightfall, six black men were in custody.

One of them was William James, who was known to everyone as "Frog" or "Froggie," and who worked as a driver for the Cairo Ice and Coal Company. There wasn't any physical evidence against him, except for his size and bulk, which police said justified naming him the main suspect and locking him away in a cell.

The next night, the town's rage over Pelley's murder began to boil. Separate mobs, each hundreds of people thick, swarmed the courthouse, police station, and Frog James's house.

The Alexander County sheriff, Frank E. Davis, feared the worst. Before dawn on November 10, Davis and his deputy, Thomas Fuller, snuck James out of the jail and onto an Illinois Central train heading north. They got as far as the Donegal station, twenty-seven miles north of Cairo, before hearing about mobs gathering at depots along the train route. Davis and Fuller rushed James off the train and into the woods of the town of Karnac. They walked for twenty-four hours without food or water, and finally lay down on the side of a hill to rest.

A man hunting in the woods recognized Sheriff Davis, and knew right away whom he had stumbled upon. Word spread fast, and before long one thousand people were on the hill.

Sheriff Davis protested as the mob encircled him, but he was ignored. A man slipped a rope around James's neck and dragged him down into town. The mob commandeered a Big Four Route train at the depot in Belknap and brought James back to Cairo.

There another five thousand men and women were waiting at the station. The massive horde marched James to the center of town, "sweeping the streets like a flock of sheep might tread a narrow lane," one witness said, until they arrived at the most public place in Cairo—a towering steel arch strung with electric lights across Eighth and Commercial Streets.

It was the women in the mob—friends and relatives of Pelley, the wives of prominent town officials, even elderly church workers—who led the assault. According to one report, a gray-haired woman got up in front of the mob and delivered a rousing call to violence: "Men, men—and women, too—will you be cowards? Will you see a black demon escape? Will you see your daughters murdered by a black fiend? I call on you to take this Negro murderer and give him the fate he deserves."

The arch lights were switched on, and a rope was hoisted high over its top. Hundreds of women got their hands on the rope and pulled James, pleading for mercy, into the air. Before the rope could strangle the life out of him, it snapped, and James fell to the ground.

The instant he landed, "hundreds of revolvers flashed and 500 bullets crashed into the quivering form of the negro," one newspaper reported. "The riddled dead man was then dragged through the streets of the city to the spot where the Pelley girl was assaulted and slain."

There someone sawed off Frog James's head, stuck it on the end of a pike, and held it up for all to see. Someone else set the bloodied corpse on fire, and the mob cheered and howled at the flames. Later, when all that remained was a charred mass, members of the mob took it apart with knives and bare hands, keeping parts of Frog James—an ear, a finger, a bone—as souvenirs of their triumphant day.

*

Illinois governor Charles Deneen placed Cairo under martial law. He ordered the National Guard and ten companies of militia to the town. By one estimate, as many as ten thousand people formed the mob that effectively took control of Cairo for a full day, rendering it lawless. That figure represented every white citizen of Cairo, plus another one thousand people from elsewhere. Governor Deneen called the incident "an outrageous proceeding and a disgrace to the State of Illinois."

But the governor had another obligation. Under the terms of Edward Green's 1905 Suppression of Mob Violence Act, the governor was bound to dismiss Frank E. Davis as sheriff of Alexander County for allowing a prisoner in his custody to be lynched.

At the opposite end of Illinois, nearly four hundred miles north of Cairo, the Chicago newspapers graphically covered the horror of Frog James's lynching. When Ida Wells learned of it, she searched for news about Sheriff Davis, to see if he'd already been dismissed. He hadn't been.

"The newspapers quoted the governor as saying that he did not think it mandatory on him to displace the sheriff," Wells later wrote.

Wells and her husband sent a telegram to the governor, demanding that he follow the law. The pressure worked, and Deneen dismissed Davis from the office of sheriff. Deneen also sent a telegram back to Wells advising her that, under the terms of the 1905 act, Davis was entitled to appeal the decision, and he had already done so. A reinstatement hearing was set for December 1.

Frank Davis had good reason to believe he could get his job back at the hearing. Many people had seen him pleading for the mob to let James go, both on the hill in Karnac and under the arch in Cairo. Davis even had to be dragged away by the mob to clear the way for James's lynching. The sheriff was popular in Cairo, both with whites and blacks, who were pleased to see he hired black deputies. And Davis had strong political connections in Illinois. He would surely bring a team of prominent supporters to attest to his character at the hearing.

In Chicago, Wells, Barnett, and a small group of activists gathered to discuss the upcoming hearing. For Wells, it simply didn't matter how well liked Davis was, or even that he might have spoken up for James. What mattered was that the 1905 mob suppression act had to be enforced. If, for any reason, it wasn't, Wells believed other sheriffs around the country would have license to ignore the law. Wells had also heard from two separate black eyewitnesses who claimed to have seen Davis give a hand signal that helped the mob find Frog James. In either case, the only fact that really mattered was that a prisoner in the custody of a sheriff had been lynched, which meant the sheriff had to go.

It was also clear that, to ensure this happened, someone needed to be there to speak against Davis's reinstatement at the hearing.

Wells and Barnett worked to recruit representatives to testify to the facts of James's death. But everyone they approached, including the eyewitnesses, turned them down. When they and "others were reminded that it was their duty to fight the effort to reinstate the sheriff," Wells wrote, "they still refused."

Two days before the hearing, they still hadn't found anyone to speak up for Frog James in court.

In their two-story home on the South Side of Chicago, Wells and her family sat at the dinner table for their evening meal. Barnett brought up the hearing and told his wife they were out of options.

"And so it would seem that you will have to go to Cairo," Barnett said, "and get the facts with which to confront the sheriff."

Wells said she would not go.

"I had already been accused by some of our men of jumping in ahead of them and doing work without giving them a chance," Wells would later recall of her decision not to go to Cairo. "It was not very convenient for me to be leaving home at that time, and for once I was quite willing to let them attend to the job."

"You know as well as I do how important it is that somebody gather the evidence," Barnett impatiently told his wife. "If you're not willing to go, there is nothing more to say."

With that, Barnett picked up a newspaper, fanned it open, and hid himself behind it. Wells was through with the discussion, too. She picked up her youngest child, Alfreda, and went upstairs. She got in bed and sang her baby to sleep, as she did every night, and then fell asleep herself.

A while later—Wells couldn't tell how long—she heard a voice.

"Mother, wake up."

It was Charles, her handsome eldest son, ten years old and nearly as tall as she was.

"Mother, Pa says it's time to go," Charles said.

"Go where?"

"To take the train to Cairo."

Had his father put Charles up to it? Or had Charles, who heard the entire discussion at the dinner table, decided on his own to talk to his mother? Wells did not know. But it didn't matter. Wells was not going to Cairo. There was nothing more to say.

"I told your father downstairs that I wasn't going," Wells said. "I don't see why I should have to go and do the work that others refuse."

"Mother," Charles said, "if you don't go, nobody else will."

A scripture came to Wells's mind—Psalms 8:2. "Out of the mouths of babes and sucklings hast thou ordained strength." Then Wells had another thought: "If my child wants me to go, I ought not to fall by the wayside."

"Tell Daddy it is too late to catch the train now," she said to Charles. "I'll go in the morning."

The next day, Wells's husband and four children went with her to the train station to see her off. She had vowed not to leave them for any stretch of time, yet here she was, boarding a train for a full day's ride south. Before midnight, she would be in Cairo.

CHAPTER 28

The Rope

*

January 5, 1911
Union Square, New York City

It was morning in New York City, and a hard blast of sleet and snow that buried third rails and crippled train service had moved north, giving way to a cold but mostly clear winter's day in Manhattan.

Here was the densest borough in the densest city in the world, with 106,000 people squeezed into every square mile. At that moment in time, a moment of great demographic flux and tidal sweeps of immigrants flooding its streets by the tens of thousands, Manhattan was the most populated island city in all of history.

One more immigrant, traveling discreetly, could arrive and proceed with no heed or notice at all.

The young German, Frank Heidemann, left Asbury Park in the morning dark and rode a New York & Long Branch railroad train to the Central Railroad Terminal in Jersey City, arriving shortly after 8:00 a.m. From there he took a small ferry across the Hudson River to Manhattan's Pier 63, which sat at the northern end of 23rd Street.

Heidemann rode a taxicab ten blocks south and nine avenues east to 306 East 14th Street, a four-story brownstone building a few steps from Second Avenue and across from the New York Eye and Ear Infirmary, a prominent hospital with a pavilion designed by Stanford White. The brownstone at 306 was a furnished rooming house, and Heidemann booked a room in the front of the building, on the ground floor. That afternoon, he left the brownstone and hailed a green taxicab, marked No. 29329. He told the driver to take him back to the 23rd Street Ferry Terminal. There he collected his big steamer trunk, loaded it into the taxi, and brought it back to the rooming house on 14th Street.

Now Heidemann was settled in, and ready for his first night in his new neighborhood. He was in the heart of Union Square, a onetime potter's field and squatter's park named for the union of Broadway and Bowery Road, on the northern edge of lower Manhattan. Union Square was a gathering place, a walking place, rich with history. The city's first electric streetlights, built by the Brush Electric Light and Power Company, lined its streets in 1880; two years later the city's first Labor Day parade featured twenty-five thousand people marching through the square, calling for a ban on child labor. The area was also a working place, filled with skilled German and Jewish immigrants, and restaurants and meeting halls to accommodate them. It would be easy for Frank Heidemann to blend into the human traffic on its wide, elegant streets.

For his first night there, Heidemann dressed in a clean shirt, tight-fitting blue trousers, and black shoes. He slipped on a dark gray three-quarter-length overcoat and pulled a pearl gray Alpine hat down low on his forehead, the front rim nearly covering his eyes. He walked three blocks to a restaurant on Third Avenue and stayed for twenty minutes. When he paid his bill, he took a thick roll of five- and ten-dollar bills from his trouser pocket. To anyone who noticed it, the roll appeared to contain at least two hundred dollars, probably more.

In fact, most of the bills were fake—advertisements made to look like real money.

Heidemann kept up his tour of the square. He found a saloon on 15th Street, sat at the bar, and drank alone. When he left the bar he stood out front and simply watched people walk past. His eyes followed the younger women, one after another. In just a few minutes, one of the women caught his gaze and stopped. A bit later that night, Heidemann and the woman spent one hour in a room at the Hotel Irvington. Afterward, Heidemann went drinking at Holberg's Saloon on Third Avenue, before taking to the streets again and watching women walk by. Finally, at 11:00 p.m., he tired and went to his room. He took off his spiffy outfit and fell asleep, his aimless day of adventure over at last.

Heidemann had fled Asbury Park to escape unwanted attention, and here on the wide boulevard he found what he needed most—a place to disappear, to catch his breath. On his first day on the run, Frank Heidemann surely felt safe from whispered judgments and peering eyes, a sort of dream come true.

But it was only a dream.

*

In Asbury Park, Sheriff Clarence Hetrick shut down surveillance of Frank Heidemann—but he did not forget about the German just yet.

Early on January 5, Hetrick received a tip that Heidemann had taken a carriage to the train depot. Hetrick ordered an officer to go to the station and discreetly fetch more details. Then he called the New York City office of the Burns Detective Agency and left a message—a steamer trunk belonging to Frank Heidemann had been routed to the West 23rd Street Ferry in Manhattan.

Charles Scholl picked up the tip and called the ferry terminal. He had a station agent gather whatever information he could about the steamer trunk and where it was headed. Scholl then called Raymond Schindler at Schindler's apartment on West 109th Street, two blocks from the Hudson River in Manhattan's Upper West Side. Schindler had already left for the office, and Scholl caught him there.

Schindler was not surprised to hear that Heidemann had fled Asbury Park. After all, he had wanted to dislodge Heidemann from the cover of Max Kruschka's home. He wanted Heidemann out in the open, where he could watch him and track his movements and behavior. Now that had happened—Heidemann was on the run.

But what if the plan had worked too well? What if Heidemann were not only leaving Asbury Park, but leaving America?

Schindler quickly pulled four detectives on the case. They all started work in the very early morning hours on January 5. Charles Scholl took a train south to Asbury Park, where he spoke with a station agent, N. E. Warner, at the train depot. Scholl got a description of Heidemann's steamer trunk—an old-fashioned model with four strips of wood, stained yellow and fixed decoratively around its middle. Another Burns detective, T. P. Bowers, went to the West 23rd Street Ferry Terminal and had a station agent look up the record of arriving luggage. Bowers got the tag number assigned to Heidemann's steamer trunk—No. 929687.

A third detective, Charles Severance, dug around for information about transatlantic voyages from New York City to Germany. He learned the steamship *America* was leaving for Germany at 11:00 a.m. that very morning. Severance went to the offices of the Hamburg-American Line in Hoboken, New Jersey, to comb through the ship's passenger list. He didn't find Heidemann's name, but he couldn't be sure the German hadn't used an alias. Schindler instructed a fourth detective, S. S. Brody, to rush to the departure pier in Hoboken. Brody got there one hour before the *America* was scheduled to leave. He boarded the steamship and walked through as much of it as he could, searching for Heidemann, to no avail.

Just a short while later, Severance got a call from T. P. Bowers, who was still at the West 23rd Street Ferry Terminal. Bowers had found Heidemann's trunk. It was there, at the terminal, which meant it had not been routed to the Hamburg-American pier in Hoboken.

Which meant Heidemann likely wasn't leaving for Germany.

S. S. Brody left Hoboken and joined Bowers at the Ferry Terminal on 23rd Street in Manhattan. The men found hiding spots from where they could survey the luggage area without being seen. They waited for more than two hours with no sign of Heidemann. Then, at 3:00 p.m., they saw him. They had shadowed him for days and days in Asbury Park, and they knew him on sight. The detectives watched as Heidemann claimed his steamer trunk and had it loaded into a green taxicab. As soon as the cab door shut, Brody and Bowers hailed another cab and told the driver to follow Heidemann's taxi.

A few minutes later, both taxis arrived at 306 East 14th Street.

Brody and Bowers got out and watched with quick glances as Heidemann had a hotel worker take his trunk into the rooming house. They waited outside, a safe distance away, for fifty minutes until Heidemann appeared out front again. He was dressed up now, in his Alpine hat and dark overcoat. The detectives followed Heidemann as he began his city adventure. For the next eight hours, the detectives kept their target in sight. It wasn't always easy. Heidemann stopped often to leer at women walking past him—which made it more difficult for Brody and Bowers to stay unnoticed behind him. They had to frequently duck out of view. Luckily, Brody reported, the target "did not appear suspicious of being watched."

At 9:00 p.m., Brody told Bowers to go home. Brody stayed and followed Heidemann to his final stop—the rooming house on 14th Street. He watched the entrance for another twenty minutes before he felt sure his subject was in for the night. He stopped surveillance at 11:30 p.m.

By dawn, Detective Brody was back outside the rooming house.

*

Raymond Schindler's new plan was under way.

It was a largely secret strategy, mentioned only in passing in Schindler's January 2 agency report as "the plan outlined." He'd discussed it with Sheriff Hetrick and Randolph Miller in their final one-hour meeting on the day Hetrick shut down surveillance of Frank Heidemann in Asbury Park. Hetrick didn't agree to go along with it, at least not right away. He wanted to see if the first step of the plan—Heidemann fleeing Asbury Park—would come to pass, as Schindler predicted.

When Heidemann did leave on January 5, Hetrick saw Schindler had been right, and agreed to let the Burns detectives stay on the case.

Heidemann had absently wandered straight into Schindler's sights. Just thirty city blocks south of Heidemann's rooming house, Schindler kept track of his target's movements from his Burns Agency office in the stately Park Row Building in lower Manhattan. He received regular reports from his "shadows"—the detectives following Heidemann—and he began to search for patterns. His plan depended on anticipating Heidemann's behavior—on understanding his impulses.

Schindler's intention was to "rope" Frank Heidemann—the old trick he'd learned from Walter J. Burns while working corruption in San Francisco. The rope, as Schindler described him, would be a detective "assigned to form the acquaintance of Heidemann, the object being the establishment of friendly relations with him, which would develop into intimacies, with a view to obtaining his confidence, securing a knowledge of his character, his antecedents, his means and mode of living, his associates and affiliations—all for the purpose of securing direct evidence as to his knowledge, culpability, or innocence of the Marie Smith murder."

In other words, Schindler was after a full and detailed confession from Frank Heidemann—his only remaining hope to solve the case.

It was an unusually elaborate plan, expensive and labor-intensive, with little precedent in murder cases and any number of ways to fail, starting with Heidemann figuring out he was being tailed. One careless slip at any point could doom the whole operation. And even if it worked perfectly, and the rope managed to befriend Heidemann and gain his full confidence, there was no assurance Heidemann would ever confess.

Schindler, however, believed that every criminal, as Hugo Münsterberg suggested, desperately needed to "give up his identity with the criminal and eliminate the crime like a foreign body from his life." Schindler believed Heidemann *needed* to confess his sins, and *would* confess them, under the right amount of pressure.

The most crucial decision was picking the right rope. Schindler selected a detective named Carl R. Neumeister. His qualifications included "many years experience in this particular branch of detective work," Schindler wrote, as well as a reputation as "one of the best qualified experts in the business." Like Heidemann, Neumeister was born in Germany and spoke the language fluently, and he had "a thorough acquaintance of the German Empire," Schindler wrote.

Neumeister also projected a sense of calm authority. He had a sturdy build and a square face, and he wore his thick black hair swept up and high over his forehead. He had a substantial mustache and eyebrows, and his appearance was precise but warm. He could have passed as a banker or businessman, or even a friendly politician.

Schindler set up a fake identity for Neumeister. He would use his real name, but pose as a longtime resident in America and a recent arrival to New York City. His story would be that a relative back in Germany had died, and named him in the will as a beneficiary. He was in Manhattan to work with an international banker and clear the way for him to receive his inheritance. In the meantime, he was receiving seventy-five dollars a week from the estate. Schindler arranged for an actual New York City banking firm, Knauth, Nachod and Kuhne, to provide Neumeister with phony bank records and assist him in the ruse.

One thing Schindler did not do was brief Neumeister on the details of the Marie Smith murder case. He didn't want the rope to know what Heidemann had been accused of, or why he was being followed. He believed that knowing what had been done to Marie might affect Neumeister's emotions and actions. It would be better to feed him information as he needed to know it.

Neumeister went to work on January 6, 1911, Heidemann's second day in Manhattan. He showed up at the Burns Agency on Park Row, and traveled with Detective P. T. Bowers to 14th Street, where Heidemann had his room. Two other detectives, including S. S. Brody, were already there staking out the entrance. Neumeister went into the rooming house and found the landlady. He asked to rent a room for himself, but none were available. Neumeister's first contact with Heidemann would have to happen elsewhere. He stayed on 14th Street just long enough for

Bowers and Brody to discreetly point out Heidemann to him. Now he knew the man he was roping. The strange ballet had begun.

*

Bowers and another detective spent most of that day following Heidemann on and around 14th Street. Heidemann's second day in the city was much like his first—saloons, restaurants, movie houses. He spent some time in a popular German restaurant named Reinken's on Third Avenue—a likely place for a German new to the city to wander into. Someone like Frank Heidemann—or the illusory Carl Neumeister. Ray Schindler approved Reinken's as a place to begin the roping.

The next day, January 7, the detectives were back on watch on 14th Street. Neumeister was with them, waiting for his moment. The men spotted Heidemann leaving the rooming house at 8:30 a.m., and they followed him to Reinken's Restaurant. They waited several minutes for Heidemann to get settled. Then Carl Neumeister walked inside alone.

He spotted Heidemann sitting at a long table, and without hesitation sat across from him. Neumeister opened a German newspaper, the *Staats Zeitung*, and started reading, paying no attention to Heidemann. Schindler had one important rule for his rope—he could not be the one to make first contact. He was to sit and wait until Heidemann made the first move, even if it took several trips to Reinken's.

Luckily, it didn't take long. Heidemann, speaking in German, commented on an item in the newspaper, and Neumeister answered him.

"I engaged him in conversation," Neumeister later reported. The two men, speaking only German, introduced themselves and had their first breakfast together.

A connection had been made, and it was a good one. After breakfast, Frank and Carl, as they called each other, went for a walk down Third Avenue, toward the Bowery section of Manhattan—not all that far from Schindler's headquarters. There they went into a saloon on the corner of Bleecker and Lafayette Streets. They drank together, then went for another stroll through Chinatown and Little Italy. At every stop, Frank— seemingly eager to talk—shared details about his life.

He told Carl he'd been drafted into Dusseldorf's Hussar Regiment of the German Army in 1904, and had been caught abandoning his post without leave. He was fined two hundred marks and deemed unfit to serve any longer. Eventually he made his way to America, and was now on two weeks' vacation from his job as a gardener in Asbury Park. He planned to go back to his job if he failed to find a new one in the city.

Frank also told Carl he was friends with a prostitute who worked along 14th Street, and had known her for more than a year. She was now living with him in his rooming house, he said.

How was it that the secretive Frank Heidemann, so careful and closed off in Asbury Park, had so quickly opened up to a new friend in Manhattan? Was it loneliness? Schindler was counting on that, but even he was surprised by how quickly his rope took hold. On their first day together, Frank felt comfortable enough to show Carl a private side of himself—a side that was dark and incriminating. He could not help but share with Carl his fondness for young women.

In Little Italy, the crowded neighborhood of some ten thousand Italian immigrants, Frank pointed out a particular store to Carl.

"This is where one can get Italian emigrant girls, young and tender," Frank told him. The girls were imported for that purpose, he said, and they only cost fifty cents.

"They always treat customers right," he added. "If you're afraid to go, I'll go with you one night."

After spending the morning together, the men agreed to meet later for drinks. That evening, Carl went to Reinken's three different times, but saw no sign of Frank. He walked by Heidemann's rooming house, hoping to run into him, but had no luck. He stayed in the area for nearly seven hours before quitting for the day.

Had Frank figured it out? Had he realized it was unwise for him to trust anyone with any part of his life story?

Carl Neumeister was back to 14th Street the next day, January 8—Frank Heidemann's fourth day in the city. Carl returned to Reinken's, and this time he ran into Frank on the way. There was no sign anything had changed. They had lunch together and went for a walk. Frank even brought Carl up to his rented room. He said he wanted "to see if his woman was still in bed reading the Sunday papers," Carl reported. She wasn't, but the men stayed in the ground-floor room and talked.

It was then that Carl saw the first evidence of what could be called a guilty conscience. He noticed Frank pulling the drawn curtains aside and peering out to the street. "It is evident he expects to be shadowed," Carl wrote. "I asked him why he was looking around so much and he replied, 'I think I am being followed.'"

This was good news for Schindler and his team. Frank was suspicious—but he did not suspect Carl Neumeister. He did not realize his pursuers were as close to him as they were.

By then Carl had found a way to deepen his target's trust in him. It had to do with how often Frank spoke about young women. Frank freely shared that he was drawn to little girls "with well-developed legs," Carl reported. He would point them out on the street and make remarks in German "such as, 'That one would be a nice fuck,' and 'Look at the fat legs of that one; I'd like to get her in bed, wouldn't you?'"

Carl played along. Eventually he began to establish his own dark side as a way to further gain Heidemann's trust. He made up a story about a crime from his past that had now come back to haunt him, a crime involving an abortion.

"A midwife who performed a criminal operation on a girl has been arrested," Carl told Heidemann. "I am in trouble in consequence of it."

At that moment, perhaps, Frank Heidemann saw in his new friend someone who might understand the harsh cruelty of misfortune.

"Gee," he said, "then you're in a fix, too."

CHAPTER 29

Immoral Thoughts and Expressions

*

January 10, 1911
Union Square, New York City

Frank Heidemann didn't elaborate on the kind of fix he was in, and Carl didn't ask. It wasn't time yet. He'd only known Frank for two days. Asking too many questions too early could scare him off. And the roping, he understood, had started well. Some measure of trust and friendship had already been established. Frank freely shared stories about his life, and in particular about his prowess with women. He bragged to Carl about the brothels he visited on the Heiligengeiststrasse in the German city of Essen. He told him about a Manhattan prostitute who was, in his words, "dead gone on me." He called her "my woman." He claimed she liked him so much, she paid him not to sleep with other women.

Frank also let on that he disliked Manhattan. "This New York is not quite enough to suit me," he said. "I would rather go South or far West. I like Texas." The desire to escape to a distant place became a theme in their conversations. It didn't take much to get Frank pining for a new beginning someplace else, far away from his past.

"I would walk out to Kentucky tomorrow if I knew what's what," Heidemann once said. "Say, Carl, let's go there. I'm ready if you care to come along. I wish someone would lend me enough money to get out

West. You would if you knew me longer. I would repay you and thank you from the bottom of my heart."

Ray Schindler had guessed Frank Heidemann did not have much money with him, and he was right. The German was running out of funds. It was an opening, and Schindler exploited it. He had Carl offer to pay for many of Frank's expenses—ten cents for a cigar, a dollar for supper, fifty cents for drinks at a saloon.

Frank, who believed Carl was receiving seventy-five dollars a week from the estate of a relative, accepted the money every time, and soon came to expect his friend to sponsor their days of eating and drinking. It was a way for Carl to gain more of his target's trust, but also to make him financially dependent. And that dependence would make him vulnerable.

Meanwhile, Carl continued presenting himself to Frank as a ruthless and cunning criminal—someone who could understand his predicament. Carl had mentioned the illegal abortion that was troublesome for him, and now he told Frank about a friend in Chicago who was helping him get out from under it. He would stay in New York City to wait for his inheritance, Carl explained, as long as his friend from Chicago assured him the police weren't closing in on him.

"In case my friend warns me the police are looking for me, I may not even wait for you to skip out in a hurry," Carl said. "I would leave you some cash at Holberg's so you could meet me in some other town."

The news panicked Frank.

"No, Carl, don't leave without me," he pleaded. "Wait at Holberg's for me or come to the room. I have not got anyone to rely on. Do that for me, will you? You don't know what it means to me."

Then Frank looked at Carl and confessed to how desperate his situation really was.

"If the river was not so damn cold, I would jump in and leave this rotten world," he said. "What is life anyway? I am tired of it."

*

"What is life anyway?" Heidemann's question might as well have been a rephrasing of Hamlet's famous query: "To be or not to be?" Ray Schindler knew *Hamlet* well. He'd read all of William Shakespeare's plays. He saw Shakespeare as a master at revealing the psychological desires, fears, and motives of his characters through dramatic speech and action. The characters in *Hamlet*, for instance, are haunted by crimes and guilt—by the terrible understanding that balance in nature can be restored only through retribution for sins. Even ceasing to live— ceasing "to be"—offers no escape from the anguish of guilt and remorse. Our mortal sins, if unconfessed and unpunished, will follow us into the afterlife.

In formulating his plan to wring a confession out of Heidemann, Schindler turned for inspiration to William Shakespeare—specifically, to *Hamlet*'s Act III. In the play, Hamlet's father, the King of Denmark, has been murdered. A ghost tells Hamlet that his uncle Claudius is the killer. But how can Hamlet be sure? He commissions a play that depicts the poisoning of a king, and arranges for Claudius to see it. He plans to measure Claudius's guilt by his reaction to the murder scene. When Claudius flees the theater, Hamlet has the evidence he needs.

"Murder has no tongue," Hamlet explains, "but miraculously it still finds a way to speak."

Ray Schindler needed to make murder speak. So he lifted Hamlet's scheme and moved it to Manhattan. "A detective must write his own play as he goes along," Schindler later told his biographer, "and act it with whatever actors may make their exits and entrances."

*

Schindler recruited the manager of a movie theater near 14th Street and paid him eighty dollars to show a particular film on a specific night. The film Schindler picked was known as a "two-reeler"—a cheaply made, sensationally gory foreign horror movie. Two-reelers were popular with American audiences, despite growing criticism of their immorality.

Schindler selected an Italian crime movie. It featured a scene in which a Mexican man strangles a young girl with strands of her own hair.

On January 10, Carl Neumeister persuaded Frank to see the movie with him. They went to an afternoon showing. Schindler sent in several shadows to fill the seats around Frank and watch for his reaction. The lights went down and the movie flickered on-screen, and halfway through, the crucial scene arrived. Frank watched in the dark as the villain bound the girl's hands and feet with rope and pushed her down a steep hill to her death. The film showed the girl's battered body lying on the ground.

During the scene, Carl heard Frank begin to breathe heavily. He asked him a question, and Frank "answered me in only monosyllables for about an hour afterwards," Carl reported. "At the end of the program he regained some good humor, but afterward and until I left him, he sighed very frequently and would say '*Gott Jah,*'" over and over again.

The German phrase translated into "God, yes."

That evening, Frank paced in his small ground-floor room. "He was very dejected and nervous," Carl noted. "He said, 'I wonder if the police inquire about me back in Germany.'"

Carl asked him why he was so worried about the police. Frank wouldn't say. Instead he offered his usual lament.

"I would rather go West as far as I can and start life anew. We could easily change our names, and everything would be all right."

There was no further confession. No discussion of Frank's past. If the goal of Schindler's movie ruse had been to unnerve Frank to such a degree that he blurted out his guilt, the ruse had failed. But, as usual, Schindler didn't see it that way. He would later say the scheme was designed to tighten the pressure on Frank Heidemann—to chip away a little more at his fragile psyche.

*

The roping continued. Frank, aware that his fellow German had a steady stream of income, complained to Carl that his money had all but run out. Soon he wouldn't be able to afford even his weekly rent at the rooming house. Schindler had Carl offer to pay for a room where they could both stay. Frank quickly agreed. On January 11, the two men walked to a boardinghouse at 129 West 15th Street, between Sixth and Seventh Avenues. Carl spoke to the landlady, Mrs. Freeman, and paid her five dollars for a second-floor room in the back of the four-story brownstone. Frank gave his name as "Frank Hallman."

Once they'd settled into their new room, the men resumed their routine. They ate breakfast in nearby restaurants and drank Manhattans in different cafes. They went to a toy store on Broadway near Tenth Street and brought a chess set, and took up the game. It was a good way for them to pass their idle days, and they played for hours. When he could, Carl snuck away and called Schindler from street corner pay phones, to update him on Frank's mood and condition.

The days passed. Carl was now surely his target's closest friend, his only true intimate. They spent hours together every day, talking and swapping stories about their lives and desires. Carl could not know how much of what Frank told him was true, and how much was boastful invention. But one thing was undeniable—Frank Heidemann had a very dark side. He was obsessed with young girls. Frank could hardly pass a young girl in the street without winking or whistling or making crude comments. The behavior was so pervasive that Carl kept a log of all the remarks Heidemann made after passing women in the street.

"This one I would like to have naked in bed."

"Look at the plump legs and breasts of that one."

"Hasn't this one a nice behind and pretty legs? A sweet girlie."

Heidemann called women over twenty "*alte hures*"—old whores. He was only interested in girls.

"He is a moral degenerate of the lowest type," Carl wrote of Heidemann in a report. "He is a dangerous criminal in immoral thoughts and expressions, and his mind dwells almost constantly on the shape and innocence of girls up to the age of about 15 years."

As the days passed, Carl noticed something else about Frank—the pressure of his situation was getting to him.

"Subject is losing weight since last week and appears to be worrying a good deal," he reported. "He sighs very frequently and has bad dreams, as I can tell from the moaning in his sleep."

Frank's angular face was now gaunt. His cheeks were sunken. He was a light sleeper and he paced constantly in his room, or he left to walk the streets for hours. Two women staying in the room next to theirs tried to strike up a conversation with Frank, "but the subject refuses to have anything to do with them," Carl noted. Instead, "he peeps at them through the keyhole" and "puts in much time looking through a drill hole in the door between our closet and our neighbor Minnie's room."

The weaker Frank became, the more Carl tried to shore up his fake persona—that of a hardened criminal. He told Frank he'd served five years in prison for highway robbery in Canon City, Colorado. "I have no scruples whatever when I need money," he said. He suggested he was responsible for an explosion at a train depot that killed fourteen men, and for the dynamiting of a mine shaft that caused two deaths.

"I have three notches in my .38-40 Colt," he bragged to Frank, "and that was before coming up to Cripple Creek and burning a farmhouse for revenge while heading East."

The act was convincing. "He thinks I am a villain of the deepest dye," Carl reported. "He says he would go to the limit with me in any crooked deal, and is anxious to have me leave New York with him."

And yet—Carl could not get Frank to talk about his own past.

In the moments when Frank revealed his true self, whether he was winking and whistling at young girls or pacing miserably in his room, Carl looked for his opening. He was waiting for just the right time to ask what he called "the final crucial question." Sometimes Carl would say nothing, sensing Frank was too closed off. Other times, he would try to steer Frank back to discussing his past, to whatever hidden crime was now causing him such torment.

But Frank would not be baited. If asked, he would share some small detail about his time in Asbury Park, but only reluctantly, and he never spoke of any women he knew there. Carl even dropped hints that he understood Frank's feelings about women. "I made him think I am love-sick, and have catered to such women by giving them candy"—a deliberate reference to Frank's offer of candy to young Grace Foster in Asbury Park. But that, too, failed to draw him out.

Carl stayed ready to pounce even in the middle of the night, in Frank's most unguarded moments, the times when his darkest demons ran rampant through his dreams. One night, Frank grunted in his sleep so loudly that Carl woke him up. Frank described an awful dream—he was holding a revolver and running away from a group of policemen and soldiers frantically chasing after him. Carl asked him what he was running from. Frank said he couldn't remember.

Frank was a clever man, Carl concluded, smarter than most, and he was sharp enough mentally to recover quickly should he let something damaging slip. He wasn't going to give his pursuers any easy openings. He would fight off, as long as he could, Carl's final, crucial question: What unthinkable evil did you commit in Asbury Park?

*

Ray Schindler understood that another ruse would be necessary to put even more pressure on Heidemann. He resorted to another trick he had used in Asbury Park—a phony article planted in a local newspaper.

He had his operative Charles Severance compose the fake article and arrange to run it in the February 1 morning edition of the New York *Staats Zeitung*, which Heidemann faithfully read. By then Carl and Frank had changed rooming houses again. His previous landlady, Frank complained, had been "too nosy." Carl paid for a room in a brownstone at 151 West 14th Street, and the men agreed to stay in the back parlor until repairs were made to an upstairs room. At 8:00 a.m. on February 1, a Wednesday, Carl announced he was going to the drugstore to buy soap.

Frank asked him to bring back a copy of *Staats Zeitung*.

A few minutes later, Carl returned with the paper.

"Here, Frank, read that, you old reprobate," Carl said, casually tossing him the paper.

Carl discreetly studied Frank's reflection in a mirror as his roommate scanned the paper. "He gritted his teeth continually while he read the article about himself," he observed. The article read:

For two months the Authorities in Asbury Park have done their utmost to find out who the murderer was of the ten-year-old Marie Smith, whose corpse was found in a lonesome spot. Then they let the matter rest to all appearances. In the last few days they have received new evidence however, which tends to implicate the gardener Frank Heidemann, who had already once been under arrest. Heidemann has absolutely disappeared as far as the authorities know. It is thought that he is in Europe.

Frank was clearly flustered by the article. Carl said nothing, but stood there and waited for an explanation. For the first time, Frank spoke at length about what happened in Asbury Park.

"I've never seen that girl in all my life," he said. "The negro is the one who broke her skull, but he's protected by politicians who don't care who they hang as long as the negro goes free."

Frank's story was that Tom Williams was a member of a Masonic lodge, and no lodge member had ever been convicted of murder in Asbury Park, and the authorities wanted to keep it that way.

Carl took the offensive. "It was not right for you to deceive me and make me think that you are an angel," he scolded. "I don't care whether you did it or not! In a fix a man will do anything to save his neck."

"No, you're right," Frank said dejectedly, before quickly changing the subject to Carl's inheritance. "You have to try and get an advance on it and take me West. Today if possible."

The men went for breakfast, but afterward Carl brought up the article again. He asked about Marie Smith.

"She was found with her head crushed in and besides that was strangled, but not misused," Frank told him. "The negro's axe was found nearby and he is the guilty party." Frank claimed that Marie's mother and Tom Williams were lovers, and together they conspired to do away with Marie. "Or she might have been killed by a passing automobile," he said.

Carl acted as if he didn't believe anything Frank was telling him.

"Next time, you leave the little girls alone," he said.

"Yes," Frank agreed, nodding his head.

"If you want to pinch little girls' legs again, don't take ten-year-olds." Frank said he wouldn't.

It was an opening. The murder of Marie Smith was now on the table. That night, Frank again begged to be taken west, to Colorado, or if not that far, to Omaha, and Carl seized on Frank's desperation.

"I still believe you did the crime," he said, "but if you were on the square with me and would tell me the truth—why, anybody can get in a fix like that when passion controls conscience. If you were to tell me right now you had to do it to save your neck, why, old man, I would go through Hell for you. I would help you get to Omaha in a minute.

"On the other hand," he continued, "if you are innocent of it, I don't see the necessity of getting away."

Which would it be—confess and escape the East Coast once and for all? Or continue to claim his innocence and be stuck in Manhattan?

Frank was silent. Carl waited. But an answer never came. There was no confession. Instead, there was only more begging.

"Help me get away as far as possible," Frank pleaded. "I would be your debtor all my life and would do anything you want me to."

Carl had finally asked his crucial question.

Frank Heidemann had simply refused to answer it.

*

Then, something unexpected happened.

On February 27, Carl and Frank rented a horse-drawn carriage from the Lowerre Stables in Yonkers, a northern suburb of New York City. They took a ride up and down snow-covered, tree-lined Midland Avenue. At 4:15 p.m., they saw an Italian man jump out of the woods and come toward them. The man asked for a match. Carl tossed him a matchbook and kept going.

"Don't you want your matches back?" the man snarled.

"To hell with them," Carl replied.

"To hell with you," the Italian said, spitting out curses.

The carriage stopped. There was an argument. Words and punches.

Three gunshots rang through the quiet woods.

When Carl Neumeister and Frank Heidemann pulled the carriage away and steered it hurriedly back to the stable, they left behind them a dead man lying facedown in the snow.

CHAPTER 30

Angels Could Do No More

*

November 28, 1909
Cairo, Illinois

The Illinois Central Railroad train—one locomotive, six coach cars—carried Ida Wells straight down the spine of the state, on her way to Cairo after the lynching of Frog James. The trip was neither speedy nor especially safe. Most steam engines could push trains to speeds above sixty miles per hour, but conductors rarely went faster than 40 miles per hour because of the poor condition of the tracks. Even so, in 1909 alone, there were several fatal wrecks and accidents along the Illinois Central line—a train crashed into a coal car, killing six; five dead when a train turned over; three dead and thirty-six injured after a train was upended by broken rails.

Wells rattled through dozens of towns—Kankakee, Champaign, Tuscola, Carbondale—before reaching the very last stop in Illinois—Cairo, nicknamed "Little Egypt." The trip took more than twelve hours. Wells had made arrangements to visit with Cairo's colored A.M.E. minister, and was met at the station and taken to his home.

There, in the minister's parlor, she made a shocking discovery.

When Wells asked the minister for his help in gathering facts about the lynching of Frog James, he said he believed James was guilty of murdering Pelley and deserved to be lynched. Most of the black people in Cairo, he added, felt the same way.

What was their belief based on? Wells asked.

"Well," the minister said, "he was a worthless sort of fellow, just about the kind of a man who would do a trick like that."

In fact, many black people in Cairo had already written letters of support or signed petitions in favor of Sheriff Davis, and sent them to the governor, asking that Davis be reinstated.

Wells was astonished. She jumped to her feet and stood above the minister in his chair.

"Do you realize what you've done in condoning the horrible lynching of a fellowman who is a member of your race?" she demanded. "Don't you know that if you condone the lynching of one man, the time might come when you will have to condone that of other men higher up than Frog James, providing they are black?"

The minister wasn't moved. Wells got her coat and bag. She'd been invited to spend the night, "but after he told me that, I had no desire to do so," Wells wrote. The minister provided the address of a friend, Will Taylor, a Cairo druggist, and Wells left for his home in the dark of night. The minister's wife went with her because it was so late.

Will Taylor was more helpful. He connected Wells to several black people in town, and spent the next day with her as she interviewed them. They spoke to twenty-five people that day. Taylor also took Wells to the alleyway where Mary Pelley was murdered, and to the steel arch on Eighth and Commercial Streets, where Frog James was lynched. That night, Taylor set up a meeting between Wells and the black citizens of Cairo. More people turned out than Wells had expected.

At the meeting, she gave a speech about her background and activism, and spoke to some of the men in attendance. She learned many of them were friends with Sheriff Davis and believed he was good to black people. Davis was a Republican, the party that was more favorable to blacks, and they preferred him over any Democratic replacement. Others felt it would be too dangerous for them to speak out or take action against a white sheriff. Wells understood their fear.

"I am willing to take the lead in the matter," she assured them, "but you must give me the facts. If we don't take a stand against this lynching, we are endangering the lives of other colored people in Illinois."

She asked a series of pointed questions.

Did Sheriff Davis use his great power to protect the victim?

Had he sworn in any extra deputies to help protect him?

Had he called the governor and asked for reinforcements?

No one who was present, including a few men who had served as sheriff's deputies under Frank Davis, could honestly say that Davis had done all he could to protect Frog James.

That was all that mattered to Wells. She put forward a resolution condemning Davis's actions and collected signatures for it. The next morning, she showed up uninvited at a meeting of Baptist ministers and asked for more signatures and support. One elderly minister confessed he'd already sent a letter of support for Davis. "I was told that when the mob placed the rope around Frog James's neck, the sheriff tried to prevent them and was knocked down for his pains," the minister explained.

Wells pleaded her case. She spoke of the horror and brutality of the lynching, and of why it mattered that the 1905 act be enforced.

"All your actions in support of Davis will mean that we have other lynchings in Illinois," she warned, "whenever it suits a mob anywhere."

By the end of her speech, Wells remembered, the Baptist minister was in tears. He agreed to sign Wells's resolution.

"When you meet with the governor tomorrow," he told her, "tell him I take my letter back and hereby sign my name to this resolution."

Her job in Cairo done, Wells got back on an Illinois Central train, churning toward Springfield, the state capital, 237 miles to the north. It was another long, hard ride, and Wells was anxious. Her husband had drafted a legal brief and sent it to the Springfield post office, where she would pick it up and have a very short time to read it, correct it, and prepare to use it in the hearing.

The good news, Barnett told her, was that—although there was no legal precedent for this kind of reinstatement hearing—it was likely the Illinois attorney general would be there to represent the people in the case against Frank Davis. Wells would not be alone.

And then at 10:00 a.m. on December 1, 1909, Wells walked into an elegant chamber in Springfield's grand State Capitol Building, an Italian Renaissance Revival masterpiece with a spectacular 361-foot-tall dome and hallways lavished with historic paintings and sculptures—a shining monument to white wealth and power.

As soon as she entered the chamber, Wells saw the truth of the situation—there was Sheriff Frank Davis, surrounded by a half dozen men in suits, including a former U.S. commissioner, a member of the state's Board of Equalization, and an elderly black man, T. A. Head, who was ready to speak on Davis's behalf.

Behind them was a gallery of spectators, all white. The attorney general had not come after all. Neither had any black supporters. There was no one to speak for James, except for a single black local attorney, Morris Williams, who'd heard about the hearing and showed up to offer Wells whatever little help he could.

*

At the head of the chamber sat the Illinois governor, Charles S. Deneen, forty-six years old and handsome, with wavy black hair and penetrating eyes. Deneen was popular in the state with both whites and blacks. He earned much credit for suppressing the Springfield Riot in 1908, and he'd just won a second term as governor, the first man to serve two four-year terms as head of the state. Deneen called the meeting to order and gave the floor to Davis's personal attorney, Walter Warder.

Warder, fifty-eight, projected all the confidence and authority of a successful career politician, and a man accustomed to getting his way. He was the best-known lawyer in southern Illinois. He'd spent nearly three decades in public office and served as president pro tempore of the State Senate. Twice he'd been named acting governor.

Warder also lived in Cairo and was good friends with Frank Davis. He stood up and read aloud Davis's petition for reinstatement. The sheriff's chief argument was that the lynching was not a result of any miscarriage of justice in Cairo, but rather due to the fact that the leaders of the mob, and many of its members, came across the border from Kentucky. They were not citizens of Cairo or Alexander County. What's more, they could not be stopped, no matter what level of heroics.

Warder followed up with another petition, this one from the business leaders of Cairo. He also offered letters, telegrams, and affidavits from dozens of prominent men—lawyers, bankers, shop owners, judges, military officials, clergymen, even the man appointed to temporarily fill the office of county sheriff. All of them insisted Frank Davis had done everything he could to prevent the lynching of Frog James.

Warder left his most persuasive document for last. He produced a petition signed by some five hundred black citizens of Cairo, including its leading ministers, who all supported the reinstatement of Davis as sheriff.

Wells already knew about the petition, which had been circulated among three black barbershops in Cairo. When she was in Cairo, Wells visited the barbershops and met a handful of men who had signed the petition. "To the few who happened to be standing around," Wells recalled, "I gave the most blistering talk that I could lay my tongue to."

But now, in Springfield, the petition spoke for itself. When he had finished reading it aloud, Warder, satisfied with his case, took his seat. The governor looked in the direction of Wells and Williams, who were sitting by themselves across the table from Davis and his supporters.

"I understand Mrs. Barnett is here to represent the colored people of Illinois," Governor Deneen said.

Not until that very moment, Wells would later say, "did I realize that the burden depended upon me."

*

She was not a lawyer. She had no legal experience. She hadn't even been sure she would be asked to speak at the hearing. And yet, here she was, on her own, expected to shoulder the entirety of the case against Frank Davis. Her eldest boy, Charles, had been right.

If not her, then whom?

Wells took the floor. In her strong and clear speaking voice she read the legal brief she'd picked up at the post office on her way to the Capitol Building. The brief emphasized the 1905 Suppression of Mob Violence Act, and Wells read the important words from Section 6. She stressed the unambiguous penalty for failure to protect a prisoner: "the Governor shall publish proclamation declaring the office of such sheriff vacant, and he shall thereby and thereafter immediately be vacated."

Wells then described her time in Cairo. She began to lay out the facts of the lynching, but before she could finish, the governor interrupted her. It was twelve o'clock. In country towns, all business stopped at noon so people could go home for dinner. The governor declared a recess. The hearing would resume at 2:00 p.m.

Wells had not prepared a formal speech, and had then been interrupted midway through her remarks. She had not been able to show her true power as an orator. Nor was the case she was presenting comparable in breadth and scale to the support for Frank Davis, so forcefully articulated by his attorney, Walter Warder.

The recess, therefore, came at a good time. Instead of accepting Morris Williams's offer to have dinner at his home, Wells retreated to Williams's Springfield office to work on the rest of her speech. She felt better prepared when Williams came to get her a little before 2:00 p.m.

Back in the State Capitol Building, Governor Deneen returned the floor to Wells.

The chamber grew quiet. Wells got up and continued reading from the resolution she had prepared in Cairo.

This time Walter Warder stopped her.

"Who wrote that resolution?" he asked.

"Don't answer him," Morris Williams whispered to Wells. "He's only trying to confuse you."

"Isn't it a fact," Warder said, "that you wrote the resolution?"

"Yes," Wells replied. "I wrote the resolution, and I presented it. But the audience adopted and passed it. It was done in the same way as the petition which you have presented here."

Wells turned to face the governor.

"But that's not all," she went on. "Governor, I have here the signature of the leading Baptist minister who has been so highly praised to you. I went to his meeting yesterday, and when I told him what a mistake it was to seem to condone the outrage on a human being by writing a letter asking for the reinstatement of the man who permitted it to be done, he rose and admitted his mistake. He wanted me to tell you that he endorsed the resolutions which I have here, and here is his name signed to them."

Wells passed the petition over to Governor Deneen. Walter Warder had no more questions for her. Wells went into her closing argument.

"Governor, the state of Illinois has had too many terrible lynchings within her borders within the last few years," she said, speaking directly to Deneen. "If this man is sent back, it will be an encouragement to those who resort to mob violence, and will do so at any time, well knowing they will not be called to account for so doing.

"All the colored friends in Cairo are friends of Mr. Davis, and they seem to feel that because his successor, a Democrat, has turned out all the Republican deputies, they owe their duty to the party to ask the return of a Republican sheriff. But not one of these, Mr. Davis's friends, would say that for one moment, he had his prisoner in the county jail, where the law demands that he should be placed, or that he swore in a single deputy to help protect his life until he could be tried by law.

"It looked like encouragement to the mob to have the chief law officer in the county take that man up in the woods and keep him until the mob got big enough to come after him. I repeat, Governor, that if this man is reinstated, it will simply mean an increase of lynchings in the state of Illinois, and an encouragement to mob violence."

With that, Wells sat down.

It was late in the afternoon, and all the testimony from both sides had been given. That should have been the end of the reinstatement hearing. But it wasn't.

Governor Deneen had something to say. He announced that he wanted the two opposing parties to get together and agree upon a statement of fact regarding the lynching in Cairo. And since he had to leave town the following day, he needed the parties to reconvene at the statehouse at 8:00 that night. Davis's lawyer, Walter Warder, was not pleased.

"He and his party expected to go through the form of presenting that petition, and then taking the afternoon train back to Cairo, arriving there in time for dinner," Wells observed. "Instead, we had to have night session, which would necessitate them remaining over" in Springfield.

Warder took Wells's petition and threw it across the table—"like a bone to a dog," Wells said—and told the governor there was nothing more to discuss. Deneen disagreed. They would reconvene at 8:00 p.m., he repeated. Wells, who had skipped lunch, was "quite willing to go home and get something to eat," she recalled.

But as she was on her way out of the chamber, the men who had been surrounding Frank Davis stopped her before she could go.

One of the men took Wells's hand in his, and shook it.

"Congratulations on that wonderful speech," he said.

Another man shook her hand and said the same thing. An Illinois state's attorney, Alexander Wilson, asked her if she was a lawyer. The land commissioner told her, "Whether you're a lawyer or not, you made the best speech of the day. And you were up against the biggest lawyer in southern Illinois."

Finally, to Wells's surprise, Frank Davis himself came over.

"I bear you no grudge for what you have done, Mrs. Barnett," he said. Then he shook her hand and walked out of the chamber.

*

They reconvened at the capitol at 8:00 p.m.

Wells noticed that the men in fine suits sitting with Frank Davis were less boisterous, less confident than they had appeared in earlier sessions. "There was all the difference in the world in their attitude," she wrote.

The hearing began. Walter Warder and Alexander Wilson had drawn up a statement of facts, and it was presented to Wells for her signature. Instead, she took a pen and began to cross out words.

"What are you doing?" Wilson asked.

"I am not a lawyer," Wells said, "but I do know a statement of fact when I see one."

The document drawn up by Wilson read, "The sheriff, fearing an outbreak by the mob, took 'Frog' to the railroad station." Wells drew a line through "fearing an outbreak by the mob."

"That is his opinion, rather than a fact," she said.

Wilson turned red and grumbled, but let it go.

Two hours later, the revised statement of facts was complete. The governor, waiting in his stately office in the capitol, asked the parties to come back the next morning to offer any final arguments.

Early the following day, Wells marched back up the steps of the State Capitol Building. The local Springfield attorney, Morris Williams, was by her side once again. At the building's entrance, Walter Warder and the rest of Frank Davis's legal team were waiting for Wells. When she approached, they took off their hats, out of respect for her.

"Mrs. Barnett, we have decided that if you are willing, we won't make another argument over this matter, but we will submit it all for the governor's action," Warder said.

It seemed no one wished to give Wells another chance to speak.

"Whatever my lawyer advises, that is what I will do," she said, handing the statement of facts to Morris Williams. Williams looked it over, and agreed it could be submitted directly to the governor.

And so it was. The hearing was over, and Charles Deneen would deliver his verdict in a few days. On the way out of the Capitol, Williams turned to Wells as they walked down the formidable steps.

"Oh, the governor's going to send him back," he said, meaning Deneen would surely reinstate Frank Davis. After all, Deneen owed a debt to the many friends and political supporters who had helped him get elected, nearly all of who were in favor of reinstating Davis. Very few people believed Deneen would turn his back on the political machine that swept him into office.

"I don't see how he can help it with such terrific pressure being brought to bear to have him to do so," Williams told Wells. "But, by George, if I had time to dig up the law I would have furnished him so much of it that he wouldn't dare do so."

Wells paused and considered her kind, new friend—the only one who, out of nothing more than a passion for the cause, had been there with her for the most important speech she would ever give in her life.

"We have done the best we could under the circumstances," Wells told him. "Angels could do no more."

They said good-bye, and Wells got on a train and headed home.

*

Governor Charles Deneen announced his final decision on the morning of December 6. It was one of the longest decisions he'd ever written as governor.

"The sole question presented is, does the evidence show that the said Frank E. Davis, as Sheriff of Alexander County, did all in his power to protect the life of the prisoners and perform the duties required of him by existing laws for the protection of prisoners?" Deneen asked. After all, Davis had the authority to deputize, and arm, as many citizens as he wished—ten, twenty, thirty, more. By law, no one eighteen or older could refuse his order to join the posse comitatus. What's more, Davis and his deputies would be "justified in taking life should these riotous persons refuse to disperse," Deneen wrote. The sheriff could also ask the governor to send as many National Guardsmen as needed—in fact, two militia companies happened to be stationed near Cairo, and could have been in the town within hours.

Frank Davis, Deneen noted, did none of these things.

Instead, he "took his prisoner almost without protection outside the County." Because of that, there was only one decision he, as governor, could reach: "Measured with these standards, it does not appear that Frank E. Davis, as Sheriff of Alexander County, did all in his power for the protection of the prisoners.

"Mob violence has no place in Illinois," Deneen concluded. "It is denounced in every line of the Constitution and in every Statute. Instead of breeding respect for the law, it breeds contempt. For the suppression of mob violence, our legislature has spoken in no uncertain terms.

"I must deny the petition of said Frank E. Davis for reinstatement as Sheriff of Alexander County."

Ida Wells had won her case.

The governor then appointed Fred D. Nellis, the county treasurer, to replace Frank Davis as county sheriff. Back in Chicago, the Bethel Literary and Historical Club convened a meeting and raised the grand sum of thirteen dollars and twenty-five cents, which they sent to Ida Wells to reimburse her for the cost of her trip to southern Illinois.

CHAPTER 31

Rope and Coal Oil

*

August 1910
Chicago, Illinois

A few months later, Ida Wells spent part of a midsummer morning at home, reading a newspaper. One story stood out.

It was about Steve Green, a black tenant farmer who had fled Arkansas a few steps ahead of the law. There had been a disagreement with a white landlord, Will Saddler, and Saddler shot a fleeing Green in the neck. Green grabbed a rifle and fired back, and Saddler was dead. Green left the state and moved from town to town in Illinois, hoping to escape the certain lynching that awaited him in Arkansas.

Then police caught Green in Chicago. A black friend betrayed him and turned him in. Officers put him in a jail cell and went to work on him. "Three times afterward they put me in a sweatbox for a day and a night, and gave me neither food nor drink for four days," Green told a reporter. In time, police wrangled a confession from him, and made arrangements to send him back to Arkansas.

In his cell, Green said, "I got to thinking what they had done to other colored men who had tried to defend themselves, and what they would do to me. It seemed to me I'd rather kill myself than wait to be burned, hanged, and shot by them."

And so, when his jailers weren't watching, Steve Green ate the tips of several matches, hoping the chemicals on them would kill him. When they didn't, he swallowed bits of ground glass. Police finally strapped him to a chair so he wouldn't try to kill himself again.

Ida Wells read the article and was moved by the details. That a man would swallow glass because of his dread of white justice struck her as especially heartbreaking. She also knew Steve Green was right—if he was returned to Arkansas, he almost surely would be lynched. She had seen it happen many times before, most recently in the Frog James case—a suspect pulled from police custody and hanged by an angry mob.

Now, here was another potential, even probable lynching, unfolding slowly in real time. Wells did not want to see it happen.

She put down the paper, picked up the telephone, and made a call.

*

One year earlier, Wells received an invitation to attend a three-day conference in New York City.

The conference, sponsored by a small group called the Committee on the Status of the Negro, was intended to outline a course of action in the cause of black rights. An even smaller group of people—five in all—had, only a few months earlier, led an effort that sparked the creation of the committee. They were, to varying degrees, active in the cause of black rights, and they were eager to make an even bigger difference. Still, they did not realize that they were changing history.

All five of these people were white.

They came together in the wake of the Springfield Riot of 1908. A young activist named William English Walling, born in Kentucky to wealthy parents, had spent time in Springfield and was horrified by reports of violence there. He and his wife traveled to the city in the middle of the three-day riot, and Walling wrote about what he saw.

"We at once discovered, to our amazement, that Springfield has no shame," Walling wrote in his article, "The Race War in the North," published in the *Independent* newspaper in September 1908. "She stood for the action of the mob. She hoped the rest of the negroes might flee."

In fact, many hundreds of blacks did leave Springfield after the riots, most driven out by continued threats and pressure from the city's white citizens. Walling closed his powerful piece with a plea for action.

"Who realizes the seriousness of the situation, and what large and powerful body of citizens is ready to come to their aid?"

What large and powerful body?

In New York City, a Brooklyn-born suffragist, Mary White Ovington, read Walling's article and felt so moved she sat down and wrote him a letter that very hour. Ovington was already deeply involved in black causes, and was living in a black tenement as part of her work as a social reformer. She and Walling arranged to meet in the first week of January 1909, in Walling's small New York City apartment.

Another reformer, Henry Moskowitz, joined them for the meeting. A fourth activist, Charles Edward Russell, a friend of Walling's, was set to be there but couldn't make it. "We spent the afternoon discussing the race question," Ovington later wrote, "and deciding on people to form a committee" to launch the movement Walling suggested in his article.

Afterward, they drafted a fifth person, Oswald Garrison Villard, the white editor of the *New York Evening Post*, to bring the number of their small group to five.

Villard, whose grandfather was the well-known abolitionist William Lloyd Garrison, was also already active in the cause of civil rights. He was excited by the idea of a national organization, and he wrote a rallying cry entitled "The Call," and made space in his newspaper to publish it. He cited the urgent need for a national conference "for the discussion of present evils, the voicing of protests, and the renewal of the struggle for civil and political liberty."

Such a committee came to be formed, the Committee on the Status of the Negro, and the group of five invited Ida Wells and six other prominent black citizens—as well as five times as many white citizens—to be part of it. Wells agreed to join the committee and attend its inaugural conference on May 31, 1909, in the Charity Organization Hall, on New York City's East 22nd Street.

*

The National Negro Conference, attended by some three hundred people, was contentious. Political fault lines in the movement split the committee. Some organizers believed any national black association had no chance of being effective without the leadership, or at least the support, of Booker T. Washington, the charismatic, Alabama-born educator and orator who was then the most popular black leader in the country. Others wanted to move away from Washington's emphasis on job training over education and activism.

One such Washington critic was William Edward Burghardt Du Bois, the first black man to earn a graduate degree from Harvard, and a history, economics, and sociology professor at Atlanta University.

Du Bois, who in 1905 cofounded his own civil rights organization, the Niagara Movement, believed in a much more radical approach to progress than did Washington. He demanded economic and social equality for blacks, and insisted on respect for the pride and humanity of his race. The schism between the two factions—those who preached patient, practical progress, and those who agitated for quicker change—threatened to throw the National Negro Conference into chaos.

Ida Wells, whose two decades of activism made her a natural ally to Du Bois, worked behind the scenes to assure people that Washington's supporters would not take over the conference, and possibly the new organization. She "tried to allay the [fear] by asserting that most of those present were believers in Dr. Du Bois's ideas," she wrote. Her assurances worked, and she was proven right: Washington did not attend the conference, while Du Bois assumed a prominent role.

The first day of the conference, May 31, was given over to speeches. There was a lecture on the myth of black inferiority to whites, and a talk from Du Bois on economics and politics. Ida Wells gave a version of her speech about lynching, and referred to the practice as "color-line murder." She sharpened her core argument that the purported justification for mob violence—black men attacking white women—"is the excuse, not the cause." And she broadened her scope as a nod to the goals of the conference. Lynching, she said, "[i]s a national crime, and requires a national remedy."

The second day's agenda was more troubling for Wells.

The order of business was to choose the members of an elite Committee of Forty on Permanent Organization, to be composed of the activists, advocates, and thinkers—some white, some black—most trusted to push a national movement forward.

Loud arguments about who should be on the committee continued up to midnight. Wells, however, was certain that after all of the arguing, she had been picked to be one of the Forty.

"I had seen the list of names," she wrote of the moments before the Forty were announced. "I had been elected."

Finally, after midnight, Du Bois—the only black person on a seven-member selection committee entrusted with picking the Forty—stood up in front of the thinned-out audience and read the names of the chosen.

"Then," Wells wrote, "bedlam broke loose, for although I had assured my friends that my name had been among those chosen, when Dr. Du Bois finished his list, my name had not been called."

It was true—at the very last moment Wells had been cut from the committee. In Charity Hall, there was outrage. Other omissions and selections angered different factions, but leaving Wells off the list was, to many, a complete shock. Wells, too, was stunned, "but I put the best face possible on the matter," she wrote, "and turned to leave."

She made it as far as the aisle before a flustered organizer, John Milholland, stopped her.

"Mrs. Barnett, I want to tell you that when that list of names left our hands and was given to Dr. Du Bois to read, your name led all the rest," he said. Omitting her name, he added, was "unthinkable."

Wells replied that it was clear someone did not want her on the committee, and "that as far as I was concerned I would carry on just as I had done." Then she pushed through the front door and left.

Now she made it to the sidewalk before the conference secretary, May Nerney, ran up and stopped her.

"Mrs. Barnett," Nerney said, "they want you to come back."

Wells refused, and instead sent in the friend who was accompanying her. She waited outside on the sidewalk, from where, she would recall, she watched Mary White Ovington, one of the original five, and a vocal participant in the debates over the Forty, "sweep by me with an air of triumph, and a very pleased look on her face."

Before long, Wells was persuaded to come back inside. Du Bois offered an unconvincing explanation that he had dropped her name in order to squeeze in someone he felt needed to be on the committee—a member of his own Niagara Movement. Years later, Mary White Ovington would write that Ida Wells was "fitted for courageous work, but perhaps not fitted to accept the restraint of organization."

Wells took the slight personally, and saw it as a reflection of behavior she understood all too well—a distaste, especially among white people but also among some blacks, for her forward, aggressive style.

At the Charity Hall, Du Bois offered to retrieve the final list, which had just been sent out, and put Wells's name on it again. Wells declined, and left the hall for good.

It was, she would later admit, a "foolish" move. "My anger at having been treated in such a fashion outweighed my judgment." Wells believed she had somehow let down her cause.

Nevertheless, Du Bois soon put her name back on the list, and she was included on the stationery of the Committee of Forty.

The New York City conference ended with a proclamation of principles and the incorporation of a national organization. The new entity was named the Committee for the Advancement of the Negro Race. The following year, the name was changed. Some objected to the new title, with its unwieldy eight words. But Villard, adamant that the word "advancement" be included, made sure the new name stuck.

From 1910 onward, it would be known as the National Association for the Advancement of Colored People—the NAACP.

*

Six months after the conference, Ida Wells won her big victory at the reinstatement hearing of Sheriff Frank James.

Word of her achievement made it back to the other members of the Committee of Forty. One of her advocates there, John Milholland, let Wells know the matter had been discussed at a recent meeting.

"The committee," he told her, "regarded that as the most outstanding thing done for the race" all year.

Despite the praise, Wells kept her distance from the new association. She missed five committee meetings in six months, and stayed out of organizational decision-making. She was already busy with the Negro Fellowship League, which she founded in the wake of the Springfield Riot, and which grew out of informal "indignation" meetings in her home. She was also frustrated with having to endure constant criticism and political maneuverings while fighting on the front lines, usually, as at the Frank Davis hearing, by herself. Reluctantly, she'd left her family to stand up for Frog James, but she had no interest in leaving them again to deal with infighting in New York City. Wells was forty-eight years old now, and she was tired.

Then, on August 15, 1910, she looked through a Chicago newspaper and read the story about Steve Green.

Wells did not know Green, but she knew his story. It could have been the story of any free black man struggling for a foothold in post–Civil War America. Green was born in Jackson, Tennessee, during the war. When he was a child, his widowed father gave him to a local policeman who also ran a grocery store. Green worked for the man and his wife under the system of peonage, which many considered to be slavery by another name. "I nursed their children for six years, and got my room and board as wages," Green told a newspaper reporter. He was kept out of school so he could work at the grocery store. "They promised me three dollars a week," Green recalled, "but I seldom got it."

At seventeen, he ran away to Cairo, Illinois, and worked on the railroad for one dollar and fifty cents a day. He saved his money and rented a farm in Putnam County in Arkansas, and got by as a tenant farmer. He took a wife, had two children, and moved to nearby Jericho, where the schools were better and his children could get a decent education. In Jericho, Green rented twenty-five acres from a farmer named Will Saddler for five dollars an acre. When Saddler raised his fee to nine dollars an acre, Green decided to leave.

Saddler wasn't happy and wouldn't stand for it. "He told me if I did not keep this place for a year, there would not be room in Crittendon County for him and me," Green said. "I told him I would not do so."

Green finished gathering his crop and got ready to leave the farm.

Two days before he left, Green's wife died of heart failure.

Three days after burying her, on a snowy February afternoon, Green was back at work on the farm of a new landlord, a man named J. H. Usher. "I was grinding an ax, getting ready to go down in the field, when Mr. Saddler rode up and called me," Green said.

Saddler, wearing a revolver, reminded him of his earlier threat.

"You would not try to hurt an old man like me because of that, would you, sir?" Green asked.

"I mean just what I said," answered Saddler.

With that he pulled out his gun.

Green broke and ran, and Saddler fired three shots. Green was hit in the neck, the flesh of his left arm, and the calf of his right leg. But no bones were broken, so he kept running, and he raced Saddler, and two of his armed men, back to his home on Usher's property.

"I ran in and got my Winchester and ran out the back door," Green said. One of Saddler's men shot at him and hit him in the shoulder.

Finally, Green raised his numb arm and fired his rifle.

"They say that the shot killed Mr. Saddler," Green told a reporter, "but I do not know, for I did not stop to see."

The *Daily Arkansas Gazette* declared, "Rich Planter Killed by Negro," and claimed none of the white men were armed.

The fugitive made his escape by wading across a nearly frozen lake and hiding in a tree for a day. A doctor later told him the cold water in the lake stopped his bleeding and saved his life.

Thinking on his feet, Green put pepper in his shoes and mud on his clothes to throw bloodhounds off his scent, and made it out of Arkansas. He hid away on an island in the Mississippi River for three weeks. Some friends raised thirty-two dollars to help him escape, and gave him food and blankets. He eventually made it to Cairo, Illinois, where he ran into some colored men he knew. One of them, Green would say, proved to be "a Judas." The man contacted the sheriff in Jericho and asked about the reward for Green's capture. One day after Green arrived in Cairo, on August 14, 1909, two policemen arrested him and put him in the county jail.

When Wells picked up the story, the Arkansas governor had already sent extradition papers to Illinois, and Jericho sheriff C. L. Lewis was already in Chicago, preparing to put Steve Green on a train and bring him back to Arkansas to face justice.

Wells got straight to work. She called two black Chicago attorneys, William G. Anderson and Edward H. Wright, and asked them to look into the matter. The lawyers petitioned the Cook County Circuit Court to get a writ of habeas corpus—a document claiming unlawful imprisonment—and sought resolution of that matter before any other matter. William Anderson, who one newspaper called "one of Chicago's most able habeas corpus lawyers," was granted the writ, and along with Rev. A. J. Carey, presented it to the Chicago police chief steward.

"We don't want to see Green go back to Jericho for trial," Carey told a reporter, "for fear that he will be mobbed and burned at the stake."

But they were too late.

On the morning of Monday, August 22, Jericho sheriff Lewis took Steve Green aboard the Illinois Central Passenger Train No. 1, bound for Arkansas. In less than twelve hours, the train would leave the south-ernmost station in Illinois—the Cairo station—and cross the state line. When that happened, Steve Green would be gone for good.

If Wells wanted to save him, she would have to find a way to get Green off the train before it left Illinois.

Wells devised a plan. She had the other attorney on the case, Edward Wright, petition the Cook County sheriff, Christopher Strassheim, for permission to offer a one-hundred-dollar reward to any law officer who returned Steve Green to Chicago. Strassheim signed off on the reward. Working out of Strassheim's office, Wright called or sent telegrams to the office of every county sheriff along the train route, informing them of the habeas corpus writ and the reward. While he waited for someone to respond, he reached out to his more prominent contacts in Chicago for help in raising the reward money.

The hours passed, and the train carrying Steve Green continued rumbling toward Cairo. Aboard the train, Sheriff Lewis and a deputy kept close watch over their prisoner.

Sheriff Lewis was no stranger to the handling of black prisoners, or to the practice of lynching. Just a few months earlier, a mob lynched two black men in his custody in the courtyard of the Jericho Courthouse. Though an excited crowd had circled the courthouse all day, Lewis went home at 10:00 p.m., saying he believed the threat of danger had passed.

Sometime after midnight, several men from the mob of three hundred took the keys from Lewis's deputy, Tom Williford, and pulled the prisoners—Bob Austin and Charles Richardson—from their cells. They took them to the yard and hanged them from a tree. "The mob was orderly and went about its work in businesslike fashion," one paper reported. Lewis insisted he only learned of the hangings in the morning. Since Arkansas had no law similar to the Suppression of Mob Violence Act that ousted Frank Davis in Illinois, Lewis kept his job.

Now Lewis was charged with bringing Steve Green back to Jericho. On the afternoon of August 22, the train carrying Lewis and Green was just a hundred miles or so from the Illinois state line. The weather turned, and a terrible summer storm moved in. "Rain and lightning," one witness said, "seemed to rent the very earth."

Time was running out. Back in Chicago, Ida Wells waited for word, and Edward Wright worked the telephone. Many sheriffs were skeptical.

On whose authority would they be able to take Steve Green off the train?

"By the authority of the state attorney's office in Cook County," Wright replied.

Still, no sheriff agreed to help.

Night fell. The Illinois Central train had reached the last station in southern Illinois, in Cairo—the town where Frog James had been arrested the previous year. The train stopped at the depot to load up on water, and Sheriff Lewis sent a man out to telegram his office in Jericho.

The telegram said they'd be leaving Illinois in minutes.

Steve Green, sitting beside Lewis, may have believed his fate was sealed. And if he didn't, Sheriff Lewis made sure that he did.

"Steve, you are the most important nigger in the United States today," he told Green as they sat in the stopped train in Cairo. "There will be a thousand men at the Jericho station when we get there, and they will have the rope and coal oil all ready to burn you alive."

Green later recalled the moment.

"Not until then did I give up hope," he said. "I told the Lord that I would never again believe there is a God."

And then, as the hard storm raged and the train prepared to leave the station, a man with a gun and a badge stepped on board.

*

It was a local sheriff. He walked up to Steve Green and put his hand on his shoulder.

"I arrest this prisoner by virtue of authority vested in me as sheriff of Alexander County," the man said.

He handed the writ of habeas corpus to Sheriff Lewis, who protested. He had more than enough men waiting in Jericho to protect Green from any mob, Lewis argued, and if needed to, he could also call in the militia. He also offered to put Green in a jail cell in Memphis, Tennessee, until the whole mess could be worked out.

The Alexander County sheriff said no. He had the authority to take custody of Steve Green and bring him back to Chicago, and that is what he intended to do.

That, it turned out, is what he did.

Just a few miles from the Mississippi River, which defined the Illinois-Arkansas border, Steve Green was taken off the train.

"When the sheriff stepped up and arrested me," Green later said, "that was a direct answer to my prayers."

The sheriff who stepped up, the only lawman in the entire state of Illinois who stepped up, was Fred D. Nellis—the very man who just months earlier had replaced Frank Davis as the sheriff in Cairo, after Ida Wells made sure that Davis paid the price for a lynching on his watch.

CHAPTER 32

The Premonition

*

February 27, 1911
Yonkers, New York

The headline in the *Yonkers Herald* was sensational:

ATROCIOUS MURDER DISCOVERED
ON MIDLAND AVENUE

The story reported that a passerby found the body of an Italian man in the snow along a trail. Police secured a good description of a stranger seen in the area. They were working the case hard.

Both Frank Heidemann and Carl Neumeister read about the murder in the *Yonkers Herald*. For Frank, the turn of events was a nightmare. The last thing he needed was more scrutiny from police. He could not afford to get caught up in a brand-new murder case, and he was desperate to leave the area immediately. He told Carl they had to flee the rooming house where they were staying, and he checked out so quickly he left behind a bag of laundry. But there was something he didn't know.

There was no murder. There was no dead man in the snow.

It was all part of the play.

*

Ray Schindler understood that the roping of Frank Heidemann, given the German's cleverness, had to be executed perfectly in order to succeed, which meant it would take time—a lot of time. Weeks, possibly months. Time Schindler did not have.

In Asbury Park, Tom Williams continued to languish in a jail cell. He still faced conviction for the killing of Marie Smith. The county prosecutor was eager to close the Smith case once and for all, and let it be known he'd be happy to try Williams for the crime. The longer Black Diamond stayed in prison, the greater the risk he might suffer an even worse fate, an ever-present possibility—being dragged from his cell by a frenzied, impatient mob and lynched, just as Mingo Jack and Thomas Moss had been. Even in a northern state like New Jersey, a black prisoner had no guarantee of safety in any jail anywhere.

So while Schindler trusted his rope, he realized Carl had failed to fully impress his target as a partner in crime—a truly malevolent man. "We've made Carl too respectable," Schindler said to his fellow detectives in a meeting. Somehow they had to speed things up. Schindler had an idea for how to convince Frank that his new friend was every bit as evil and cold-blooded as any other gangster he knew.

"Neumeister is going to commit murder," Schindler declared.

His plan was to stage a mock murder. A Burns operative traveled to meet the Yonkers chief of police, Captain Brady, who agreed to help, and suggested a location—a lonely country road that wound around the woods in northern Yonkers.

Brady also connected the detective to the editor of the *Herald,* Frank Xavier, who agreed to print eight copies of his newspaper with a phony story about the murder in it. Meanwhile, Carl paid $13.93 for a Colt revolver. Carl told Frank about his new gun, but not about the cartridge of blanks he'd also purchased.

Early on February 27, two of Schindler's operatives—Detective Brody and Joseph Sfoza, the agent chosen to play the murder victim—traveled to Yonkers and took their places, Sfoza in the woods, Brody atop the hill overlooking the road. Sfoza was dressed "in the ramshackle attire of a vagabond," Schindler reported.

Five long hours passed with no sign of Carl or Frank.

Finally, at 4:15 p.m., Sfoza spotted a horse-drawn carriage coming up the avenue. He recognized the two men sitting inside. He waited until the carriage reached him, then jumped out of the woods and stood in front of it.

"Got a match?" he asked Carl Neumeister.

Carl threw him a pack of matches. Sfoza lit a cigar. As planned, Carl quickly steered the carriage away.

"I called after them and approached them and asked [in a surly manner] if they didn't want their matches back," Sfoza reported.

"To hell with them," Carl said to the Italian.

"To hell with you," Sfoza replied, spitting out an Italian curse.

Carl swung the carriage around and asked Sfoza what he had called him in Italian.

"You know what I called you," Sfoza said, "and you can take it any way you want."

Carl jumped down from the carriage and punched Sfoza three or four times. Sfoza punched back. Carl landed another punch that dropped Sfoza on his back in the snow.

"I'll fix you," Sfoza said, jumping to his feet.

"You will, eh?" Carl answered, pulling out his Colt revolver.

As Frank Heidemann watched from the carriage, Carl squeezed the trigger and two shots rang out. The blasts startled the carriage horse, and Frank struggled to control him. Sfoza fell to his knees and pitched forward, facedown in the snow. Carl fired one more shot.

"Is he dead?" Frank asked.

"Yes," said Carl. "Let's beat it."

He climbed into the carriage and steered it away from the scene.

Sfoza, unhurt by either the fake punches or the blanks, stayed in the snow, motionless, for five long minutes, until he was sure the target was gone.

*

Frank did not suspect a thing. Carl didn't even have to push too hard to get them to leave the area, because Frank was desperate to go. They agreed to try Philadelphia, and Carl arranged to have the next day's edition of the local paper, the *Yonkers Herald*, forwarded to him there.

The two men packed their bags and traveled to New York City's Penn Station, where they boarded a train to Philadelphia's Reading Station. They paid for separate rooms in the Brogley Hotel, using phony names—Frank D. Baker and Ben Hamilton. They stayed at the Brogley for several days, and at night went out for whiskey and beer.

"I pretend to have taken to drink with him," Carl reported, hoping the key to getting Frank to talk was getting him good and drunk. "He is too cautious. I have to try to get him to lose his self control."

In fact, Frank was already falling apart. He'd been on the run for nearly two months, and his money was gone. He had trouble sleeping, and "he is becoming a nervous wreck through the nightly practice of self-abuse," Carl wrote. When Carl confronted him about it, Frank said he had no choice. "I know you would give me the money to go and see a girl, but what's the use?" he said. "I'm too weak now."

To keep the pressure on, Carl continued waking up Frank in the middle of the night to tell him he'd been screaming in his sleep, even when he hadn't been.

Then came the mock murder, which pushed Frank to a new level of despair and vulnerability. It was the right time for the plan's next step—bringing in a hardened gangster named Joe Springenberg.

Springenberg, of course, was not real. Schindler and his team invented him to be Carl Neumeister's Chicago-based criminal partner and mentor. Right after the mock murder, Carl allowed Frank to see him writing a letter to Springenberg, confessing to the reckless thing he'd just done. Now they would both wait for the reply. Carl assured Frank that when he and Springenberg finally fled the country, they would take him with them. Still, Frank worried the murder in Yonkers had changed things.

A few days after they settled in Philadelphia, the Springenberg letter—written by Schindler and his men—finally arrived. It had a single, unambiguous piece of advice for Carl Neumeister.

Leave the country, and leave Frank Heidemann behind.

Carl shared the letter with Frank, whose very worst fear—being abandoned with no money and no prospects—was right there in smudged ink. That evening, Frank had a breakdown, and sobbed for nearly two hours straight while Carl tried to reassure him.

"The psychological moment," Carl would report, "had arrived."

Frank begged Carl not to leave him. Carl told him Springenberg was right. He wasn't one of them. They couldn't afford to trust him. They had no choice but to part ways. Frank would be on his own.

"You need not call me an angel and hesitate to take me in as your third partner," Frank pleaded. "I am far from being an angel. I may have done something similar to what you did in Yonkers."

Carl leaned in closer.

What similar thing have you done?

Heidemann wouldn't say. Same as before, he offered no specifics. The moment passed. Frank's weeping fits went on into the night.

The next day, Carl tried again.

He took Frank to a botanical garden, and as they walked he tried to steer their conversation back to Asbury Park. Carl suggested he would even pay for Frank's bail should he ever be arrested, but in return, he said, Frank would need to confide in him fully. After all, Carl reasoned, he was more experienced in avoiding prosecution, and rather than tell some untrustworthy lawyer the truth, he should share it with him.

The ruse didn't work. Nothing had worked. Frank's true past remained a secret. He must have believed that as long as he kept his head down, he would be okay. The police couldn't hurt him if they couldn't find him. There was no need for him to confess his crimes to anyone.

*

In New York City, Schindler was frustrated by Frank's caginess. He'd experienced it firsthand in his ten-hour interrogation; he'd seen how adept Frank was at wiggling out from under tough questioning. The staged murder had increased the pressure on the target, as planned, but it hadn't been enough to make him open up. Something more was needed.

Something that would give Frank Heidemann a real scare. The scare of his life. Schindler had an idea. He knew what would frighten Heidemann to his very core. A certain person from his recent past.

Ray Schindler himself.

The plan: Carl would take Frank into New York City, where they would "accidentally" run into Ray Schindler.

"By putting a little fear in his heart," Schindler reasoned, "he may be an easier subject to work on."

Using the excuse of needing to see his New York bankers on March 6, Carl, together with Frank, took a 7:00 a.m. train to the Exchange Place Station in Jersey City. From there, the Desbrosses Street Ferry brought them to lower Manhattan. They booked a room in the Central Hotel, and Frank waited there while Carl pretended to visit his bankers.

In truth, Carl traveled to Park Row to see Ray Schindler at the Burns Agency headquarters. Together they finalized the plan.

At 12:20 p.m., Carl and Frank took the Ninth Avenue downtown L train to the South Ferry Station on Whitehall Street. A bit earlier, Schindler arrived at the station and took a spot on the elevated platform where the L train stopped. He waited as several trains came and went.

At 12:40 p.m., Carl and Frank got off the L train and ran straight into Ray Schindler. Frank clearly recognized him, and picked up his pace as he and Carl headed across the platform to take the Third Avenue train.

"Let's get in quick," Frank said.

But they missed the train. Frank was jittery and couldn't stand still. He was relieved when another train pulled into the station.

"Thank God we caught this other one," he told Carl as they waited for the train doors to close. "I just wish it would start."

Finally, the doors were shut. Frank nervously peered out the window. On the platform, Schindler now had a uniformed police officer by his side. He and the officer walked along the platform. Schindler, who had taken note of which train car Frank got on, made sure to walk past the car's window, the policeman right beside him.

When Frank saw them, Schindler reported, "he huddled up in a seat and turned his back toward me."

At last, the train lurched to a start and left the station.

"Well, that danger is past," Frank said. "Who do you think I saw, Carl? The manager of the Burns Detective Agency was at the South Ferry and saw me! He's the one who gave me the third degree for ten hours! I don't think he recognized me or he would have arrested me."

Still, Frank explained to Carl, he couldn't take that chance. If Schindler had failed to recognize him, he might remember him later. And when he did, he and his officers would scour the city searching for him. They needed to return to Philadelphia right away, Frank said.

Schindler and Carl knew they had to seize on Frank's heightened emotional state. They had to act fast. That very evening, Carl made plans for him and Frank to take a train to Atlantic City, sixty miles southeast of Philadelphia, where together they would wait for the arrival of Carl's criminal cohort, the fictitious Joe Springenberg. They packed up and left the Brogley Hotel and made a stop at the post office, where Carl picked up the *Yonkers Herald* that had been forwarded to him.

He let Heidemann read the headline: "Atrocious Murder Discovered on Midland Avenue."

The news that police had a description of possible suspects was bad enough, but Carl added a twist—he told Frank that, out of anger, he had shredded a second issue of the *Herald* sent to him, and in that issue it was reported that police had traced the Colt revolver used in the shooting back to the killer. Back to Carl.

The walls were closing in on Frank Heidemann.

*

Carl and Frank took the 9:40 p.m. train to Atlantic City. They booked a room at the Newark House hotel on South Carolina Avenue, near the ocean. Then it was a waiting game. Joe Springenberg was due any day. In the meantime, Carl kept up the pressure on Frank. He returned to the topic of Asbury Park as often as he could.

On March 9, three days after they arrived in Atlantic City, the strategy finally paid off. That morning, Frank volunteered a curious story.

They were talking about the Marie Smith case, as they sometimes did. This time, Frank told Carl that, on the morning Marie's body was found in the woods—specifically, fifteen minutes before she was discovered—he'd experienced a strange sensation.

In those minutes, Frank explained, his heart began to race. And then: "I had a premonition, Carl."

Frank said he suddenly felt something horrible was about to happen. He didn't know what, just that something awful was coming. A few minutes later, he learned Marie Smith's body had been found. He hadn't known she'd been murdered, he insisted. So hearing she was dead came as a shock. Carl listened attentively but didn't ask any questions.

Instead, that afternoon, Carl shut down.

He sat in their shared room at the hotel and sulked. Heidemann asked if he wanted a game of pinochle. Carl said no.

How about chess? Again, Carl said no.

"Don't bother me," Carl grunted.

Frank was confused. He told Carl he'd figured out why he was acting so strangely—he must have received another letter from Springenberg. He guessed they were plotting to flee to Honduras and leave him behind in Atlantic City. That was it, wasn't it?

"When Joe comes, both of you will disappear and leave me here all alone," he said, "without any money or friends."

Carl told him to go ahead and get a job.

"What makes you talk like that?" Frank asked.

"Why, this morning you told me about the premonition you had fifteen minutes before the girl was found," Carl said. "You claimed to me that you did not know that the girl was killed. You must take me for a damn chump to try and get me to believe that. And another thing—if you tell that lie to Joe, he'll simply turn around and walk off."

Frank began to protest.

"Don't interrupt me, you fool!" Carl snapped. "Just listen and I will tell you. We've been together for over two months now, and in that time you have dropped certain remarks, which convinced me that you killed the girl. Now, I don't give a damn whether you did or not, but I think you are not sincere by not having told me the truth right along from the start, as I have always told the truth to you. You have been lying right along to me in this matter, and I have no use for a lying friend."

Frank appeared wounded. This was the worst argument they'd ever had, and the angriest he'd ever seen Carl.

"Now," Carl went on, "you can send me and Joe to the electric chair, either by direct or indirect denunciation, at any time you please, and we've got nothing on you."

The implication was clear. The time had come for Frank to prove he was one of them. Not just a grifter, not just immoral, but a man fully capable of taking a life. Cold-blooded and murderous, like them.

Frank paced the room, back and forth, one side to the other, over and over, while Carl waited patiently for an answer.

"Carl," Frank finally said, "if it does you any good—yes, I did it."

Did what?

"I killed the girl."

CHAPTER 33

Once to Every Man and Nation

*

September 19, 1910
Chicago, Illinois

Sheriff Fred Nellis brought Steve Green back to Chicago on the same train line that took him away. Newspapers reported on the dramatic happenings at the Cairo station.

"The stoutest heart quivered and the weaker hearts stood still, for the last faint hope seemed to be glimmering away to failure," read a story in the *Broad Ax*. Nellis rescued Green "at the doorstep of certain death."

A hearing was scheduled for mid-September to resolve the writ of habeas corpus and, effectively, Steve Green's future. If a judge ruled Green had been properly turned over to Arkansas authorities, he would be given to them once more and taken back to Jericho—the fate Wells and her attorneys were desperate to prevent.

On Monday, September 19, 1910, a judge of the Circuit Court of Illinois, Cook County—the Honorable Richard Stanley Tuthill—took his place at the bench of the seventh-floor courthouse in the circuit court building in Chicago. Both the room—richly carved wood paneling, two brass, twin-shade lamps flanking the towering bench—and Judge Tuthill, with a dramatically trimmed Vandyke he'd worn for decades, were stately and imposing. Spectators, both white and black, filled every seat and every space in the room, anxious with expectation. The *Broad Ax* announced, "Never before in Chicago was there such a trial."

During the first day of arguments the previous Friday, Steve Green stood before the court and told his story. Now, on the final day, Green's black attorneys, William Anderson and Edward Wright, took over. Chicago's assistant corporation counsel, William Barge, represented the state. Shortly after 9:00 a.m., the proceeding began.

Arkansas's governor, George Washington Donaghey, had signed his name to an indictment and extradition papers, which were presented to the court. Judge Tuthill gave the floor to Edward Wright. Wright began speaking at 9:30 a.m. and did not finish until 4:00 p.m. He cited no less than forty legal cases, including a Supreme Court case, to bolster his central argument—the Chicago Police Department had no right to surrender Steve Green to an Arkansas sheriff. Wright claimed the paperwork sent from Arkansas, both at the time Green was taken from a Chicago jail, and submitted to the court that day, was faulty and inadequate. Wright found several technical reasons to render it invalid.

At the end of the trial, Judge Tuthill offered his verdict. The requisition from Arkansas to extradite Green, Tuthill ruled, was, indeed, poorly constructed. What's more, he said, the Arkansas governor could not be a very good lawyer, if he was a lawyer at all, to sign his name to such shoddy extradition papers.

Therefore, Tuthill concluded, he had no choice but to discharge Steve Green "from the custody of the court, from the officers of the police department of this city, and from all other officers, within the jurisdiction of the circuit court of Cook County."

Steve Green was free to go.

The Chicago *Broad Ax* heralded Wright and Anderson for winning "one of the greatest legal battles of their lives." Judge Tuthill's ruling set a precedent, not only for Illinois, but also for other northern states. Writers compared Green's rescue to the days of the Underground Railroad, when escaped slaves were spirited to safety through an elaborate network of secret safe homes. This time it was a phone call from Ida Wells that triggered a series of unlikely events and actions that, in ways daring and cunning, led to freedom for Steve Green.

But it was a tenuous freedom.

After the trial, Ida Wells arranged for Green to stay at a safe house in Chicago. It was assumed Arkansas governor Donaghey's lawyers would amend the extradition papers and try again to take Green. The risk that Green would be sent back to Arkansas was still high. Wells and Green had a decision to make. Would they take their chances with the Arkansas justice system? Or would they never let it get that far?

A meeting was held in the bedroom of one of Green's lawyers, who was ill. Wells and the men took up a collection, and the money raised was handed to Wells. The decision had been made. They did not trust any Arkansas judges or police.

So they were going to make Steve Green disappear.

Wells arranged for Green to leave Chicago and head for the Canadian border, a few hundred miles north. Very few people knew where he was going. When Arkansas governor Donaghey learned Green was missing, he offered a two-hundred-dollar reward for his recapture. But it was never claimed. Wells kept Green out of sight until, she wrote, Arkansas officials gave up their pursuit "as a hopeless job."

Eventually, the state of Arkansas did give up on bringing Steve Green back. They couldn't extradite a man they couldn't find.

Once interest in the case died down to nothing, Green returned to Chicago under an alias. He took a job and worked the night shift, and during the days he slept in the lodging house of the National Fellowship League. Even Ida Wells soon lost track of Steve Green. All she knew for sure was that he had not gone back to Arkansas against his will.

"Here is one Negro who lives to tell the tale," she wrote, "that he was not burned alive according to program."

*

Once again, word of Ida Wells's actions in Chicago reached the New York office of the newly named National Association for the Advancement of Colored People. Not surprisingly, the NAACP was also interested in Steve Green's case. It was the kind of injustice the organization had been conceived to confront.

In its first year, the NAACP was stumbling. It had survived an intense round of early criticism—of William Walling's alleged southern prejudices; of the presumptions of white liberals to start such an organization; of Booker T. Washington's absence from its leadership, which was seen as a damaging boycott of the group. "This little crowd falls down every time it attempts to do some essentially big thing," Washington wrote to a friend who briefed him on the association's early troubles. "These fellows will be troublesome for a few months, but will soon wear themselves out."

On top of that, the NAACP could not find a competent treasurer, and anyway had very little money to work with. Early on, Oswald Garrison Villard envisioned a grand endowment of one million dollars. The reality was shockingly different. In early 1910, the NAACP listed monthly expenditures of $243.65—including one hundred fifty dollars for six weeks' salary for a secretary, forty dollars for two months' rent, and just under ten dollars for postage and office supplies. In the same period, the group raised just over $311—two hundred of which came from Villard and his family. The NAACP had exactly $66.55 in cash on hand, plus ninety cents' worth of stamps.

By the next meeting of the executive committee, the cash reserve had built up to over $260, but that was still far short of the two thousand dollars needed to pay for the group's second annual convention in May 1910.

One month after the convention, the NAACP ran a deficit. Villard asked all the members of the Committee of Forty to help raise funds and contribute at least five dollars each. At one point, Villard's mother chipped in fifty dollars for expenses. There were times when Villard feared his ambitious new project would completely collapse.

It survived, but continued to struggle. Villard himself became the disbursing treasurer, and W. E. B. Du Bois started a monthly association magazine called *The Crisis*. Its mission was to "set forth those facts and arguments which show the dangers of race prejudice," and it took its title from "The Present Crisis," a poem by James Russell Lowell:

> Once to every man and nation comes the moment to decide,
> In the Strife of Truth with Falsehood, for the good or evil side;
> Some great cause, God's new Messiah, offering each the bloom or
> blight,
> Parts the goats upon the left hand, and the sheep upon the right,
> And the choice goes by forever 'twixt that darkness and that light.

Du Bois and *The Crisis* would also serve as the NAACP's fact-finders, locating and researching cases for the association to take on. There was no set protocol for how the NAACP decided to get involved in a case, except for areas of focus—cases that involved peonage, extradition, and police brutality. One such case came to the group's attention in the fall of 1910. It involved a sharecropper named Pink Franklin, who had been arrested for killing a white constable who entered his home, then tried and sentenced to execution. Two black lawyers argued Franklin's appeals, and the case reached all the way to the United States Supreme Court. Twice the Court upheld the conviction and sentence.

Franklin's case drew much media attention, and W. E. B. Du Bois mentioned it in the first issue of *The Crisis*, in November 1910. The NAACP got involved with the case and spent more than four hundred dollars lobbying to have Franklin set free. In the end, they did not fully succeed—Franklin's sentence was commuted from execution to ninety-nine years on a chain gang. This was the very first legal proceeding the NAACP ever got involved in, and some saw it as a failure for the group, given that Franklin's sentence still seemed especially cruel and unjust.

Around the same time, the fall of 1910, the NAACP heard about a similar case, and moved to get involved. So it was that the matter of Steve Green became the second-ever legal case to interest the NAACP.

*

Alongside his coverage of Pink Franklin in the first issue of *The Crisis*, Du Bois also included a column about Steve Green. By the time the NAACP got involved, Ida Wells had already managed to spirit Green out of the country and into Canada. Du Bois mentioned this accomplishment, but gave the credit for it to "the colored people of Chicago" and "Steve Green's friends." Ida Wells was not mentioned in the item, or anywhere else in the first issue of *The Crisis*.

In New York City, a newspaper article about Steve Green outraged a man named Joel Elias Spingarn, just as it had outraged Ida Wells in Chicago. Spingarn, then thirty-five, was a poet, writer, and literary critic who had recently been fired as a professor of comparative literature at Columbia University after protesting a colleague's treatment by officials.

A dapper dresser with short, wavy dark hair and an intense gaze, Spingarn was the son of a successful Austrian Jewish tobacco merchant, and he had the means to make his Columbia position the last paid job he would ever hold. Spingarn was also an expert gardener and a flower collector. At one point he had two hundred fifty species of clematis, making it the world's largest private collection of the flower.

Spingarn did not have a deep background in black civil rights, but Steve Green's story moved him nonetheless. By one account, he had a single thought after reading about him in a newspaper—*Steve Green will never be extradited to Arkansas*. Spingarn dug out his checkbook and sent one hundred dollars to the office of the NAACP, so that whatever legal measures were needed could be enacted without delay. He also asked Oswald Villard to help him get information about Green's whereabouts.

Oswald Villard sent a telegram to Ida Wells, asking her if Green needed money for his escape. By then Green had been taken out of the state and was on his way to Canada. Green "cannot read or write, so we do not know for certain whether he has reached his destination, and we are afraid to inquire," Wells told Villard in a return telegram. "Later on, a way will be found to communicate with him. If he needs money I will be glad to let you know."

Wells, who usually paid for case expenses out of her own pocket or through local collections, did not ask Villard to send her the one hundred dollars Spingarn had earmarked for the Steve Green case. She didn't ask for reimbursement of any kind.

Back in New York City, Oswald Villard was excited by Joel Spingarn's interest in the case. The NAACP was still struggling for donations, and Spingarn's gift was one of the largest made by a nonmember. But even more meaningful than the money, Villard told Spingarn, was finding "another man who is willing to stand up and be counted on the side of justice for the downtrodden race." Villard asked Spingarn to join the NAACP, and Spingarn agreed to join the group's executive committee.

Spingarn would soon be named chairman of the board, and his energy and passion would play a vital role in the development of the NAACP as a powerful legal advocate for black people. Together with his brother Arthur, a gifted attorney, Spingarn helped institutionalize the legal services arm of the NAACP, for which it would be known and celebrated for many decades to come.

In 1910, Spingarn also allowed his one-hundred-dollar donation to the NAACP to stand, even though it did not go toward the Steve Green case. Instead, it was applied to the association's coffers, and put toward what would become the third legal case ever handled by the NAACP.

That third legal case involved a black worker arrested on suspicion of killing a ten-year-old schoolgirl in Asbury Park, New Jersey.

CHAPTER 34

Still He Lay in Jail

*

December 9, 1910
New Brunswick, New Jersey

Winter on the New Jersey shore was a sad thing, the ocean unswimmable at forty-eight degrees, the boardwalk swept clean of people by the westerlies, a day's fifteen hours of sunlight down to a meager nine, overcast skies and empty promenades. In Asbury Park, it was only at Palace Amusements, the Victorian pavilion on Kingsley Street, that a familiar sound of summer could be heard—the swirling jangle of a Wurlitzer organ serenading the camels and goats and horses on Ernest Schnitzler's grand, gilded, year-round Carousel. But in winter, these sounds were a teasing echo of the true joy of summer music.

On such a dreary day in December 1910, two white men, Charles Brooks Ames and Walter Lester Glenny, both attorneys, entered the New Brunswick chambers of Willard P. Voorhees, a justice on New Jersey's seven-member Supreme Court.

Brooks and Glenny presented a writ of habeas corpus for Thomas Williams. Technically, Williams had not been charged with murder, and was being held as a material witness in the Marie Smith case. But that was just a technicality. Most understood that to the Monmouth County prosecutor, John S. Applegate Jr., Williams was his primary suspect.

The writ of habeas corpus called on Williams's jailers to justify his incarceration, or set him free. Justice Voorhees granted the writ and called for a hearing two days later to enact it. Then he reached out to the Monmouth County prosecutor, John S. Applegate Jr., to inform him of the writ and give him time to prepare for the hearing.

When he got the news about the writ of habeas corpus, Prosecutor Applegate was angry and defiant. A new grand jury was to be impaneled for the Williams case that January, and Applegate was adamant about holding Williams until the jury was in place, despite not having charged him with anything.

"Those who are working together to get Williams out of jail on a writ of habeas corpus are wasting their time," Applegate announced to reporters. "We have enough evidence to warrant keeping him in jail until an investigation has been made."

To keep the pressure on Applegate, the editors of the *Asbury Park Press*—steered by the anti-Williams reporter Alvin Cliver—ran a vaguely threatening editorial that warned against Applegate going soft on the lawyers. "The public prosecutor of Monmouth County has a strange conception of his duty if he does not have Thomas Williams, accused of the murder of little Marie Smith, held for the January term of the grand jury, and seek by every means in his power to have the man indicted and brought to trial," the *Press* declared. "If lynch law is to be held in check, our citizens must know that due process of law will mean trial in open court and not merely the opinion of some court officer."

Who were these white lawyers who marched into a judge's chamber and spoke up for a poor black prisoner? Such a display of legal strength on behalf of an itinerant black man accused of murder was simply unheard-of at the time—so where did these two come from? What was happening? Some newspapers struggled to identify the mysterious attorneys, reporting only that they represented "a colored association."

The *Asbury Park Press*, however, got it right.

C. Brooks Ames and W. Lester Glenny had been sent to New Brunswick by the National Association for the Advancement of Colored People, then too new to be known by just initials.

*

Brooks was a graduate of Princeton, class of 1905. He was the brother of a famous poet, Van Wyck Brooks, and enjoyed writing poetry himself. Glenny attended Columbia University, class of 1902. He was a champion amateur golfer. Both men came from prominent families in Plainfield, New Jersey, and both worked as lawyers in New York City. Glenny was counsel for the *New York Evening Post*, the newspaper owned by Oswald Garrison Villard.

Villard asked the men to take on the Williams case. The NAACP had no paid attorneys on staff, and Villard did not hesitate to borrow his *Post* counsel. The NAACP's National Legal Committee—to be overseen by Joel Spingarn, whose interest in the Steve Green case had just brought him on board—was not yet fully in place. The defense of Tom Williams would be paid for with money from the association's general coffers, which included Spingarn's recent one-hundred-dollar donation.

The NAACP announced its role in the case through a story in the third issue of *The Crisis*, published in January 1911.

"A little innocent schoolgirl is brutally murdered," wrote W. E. B. Du Bois. "A Negro vagabond is arrested. Immediately, the news is heralded from east to west, from north to south, from Europe to Asia, of the crime of this black murderer. Immediately a frenzied, hysterical mob gathers and attempts to lynch the poor wretch. He is spirited away and the public is almost sorry he has escaped summary judgment. What proof was there against this man? He was lazy, he had been in jail for alleged theft from gypsies, he was good-natured and he drank whiskey. That was all. Yet he stayed in jail under no charge and under universal censure. The coroner's jury found no evidence to indict him. Still he lay in jail."

On the morning of December 9, 1910, after Black Diamond had been imprisoned for twenty-seven days, Ames and Glenny arrived at Justice Voorhees's chambers in New Brunswick for the 11:00 a.m. habeas corpus hearing. Tom Williams was not taken from his cell to attend the hearing—Ames told Justice Voorhees they didn't need him there.

Representing Monmouth County—Prosecutor Applegate and County Sheriff Clarence Hetrick. Applegate told Voorhees they had enough evidence of Williams's guilt to justify keeping him in jail until he could undergo a thorough grand jury investigation.

Brooks, who took the lead, argued that no charges had been filed against Williams, nor was he plausibly a material witness. After all, he had not been called to testify at the coroner's inquest just weeks earlier. Williams hadn't even been deposed about his whereabouts on the day Marie Smith disappeared. There was no evidence whatsoever that showed Williams knew anything about the crime at all. Describing him as a witness, Brooks argued, was a ruse to keep him locked up.

Justice Voorhees asked Applegate for the evidence against Tom Williams. Applegate said he could not reveal it because it hadn't yet been presented to the grand jury. Voorhees had heard enough testimony, and delivered his verdict. He concluded Tom Williams had *not* been properly committed to jail as either a suspect or a witness.

Therefore, he ordered Williams released from the custody of the sheriff's office immediately.

With that, Tom Williams—who had never been an official suspect in the murder of Marie Smith—ceased to have any legal connection to the crime, save for the suspicions of many in Asbury Park who continued to believe Williams was indeed guilty of the savagery.

The judge's ruling meant Williams was free to go.

But, in truth, he wasn't. John Applegate had made sure of that.

*

Applegate had a surprise for the New York City lawyers. He produced an affidavit from Edward Cashion, the keeper of the Monmouth County Jail in Freehold. In the affidavit, Cashion testified that Williams confessed to voting twice in the gubernatorial election held on November 8, one day before the murder of Marie Smith.

According to Cashion, Williams admitted he was not eligible to vote because he'd served eighteen months in jail for a prior felony. Nevertheless, on November 8 he voted twice—once in the second district of the first ward in Asbury Park, and again in Oakhurst, a town four miles north—under the pseudonym Thomas E. Morris. Applegate also produced voting records that proved Williams had voted twice. This was clearly a crime, and Applegate had already prepared an arrest warrant, and he served it on Tom Williams in his jail cell two days earlier.

The NAACP lawyers were knocked off balance. Ames and Glenny did not challenge the new charge against Williams, but they did ask Justice Voorhees to set bail for their client. Voorhees had to get a sentencing book and look up the maximum penalty for voting after having lost the right of franchise. He found it was punishable by up to two years in prison and a fine of five hundred dollars. The penalty for voting twice was three years in prison and a fine of one thousand dollars. Voorhees totaled the monetary penalties and set Williams's bail at two thousand dollars.

The hearing was over. Justice Voorhees congratulated Ames and Glenny for their work on Williams's behalf but said he could do no more for their client. There was no way Williams could raise his bail money, which meant he would stay in jail. And as long as Williams remained in jail—and couldn't leave town, as Steve Green had done—Applegate had a chance to try him for the murder of Marie Smith. Despite the lack of a good case against him, it was not hard to imagine such a trial happening.

As one local newspaper put it, "It is admitted that the evidence against Williams is purely circumstantial—but many a man has been convicted on less."

CHAPTER 35

What Was Her Name?

*

March 11, 1911
Atlantic City, New Jersey

Carl Neumeister brushed off Frank Heidemann's confession, as if Frank's words—"I killed the girl"—weren't the very ones he'd been waiting two months to hear.

"Hell, anybody can say that," Carl answered dismissively. "Joe will simply think you say that to get us to take you with us."

"No, Carl, it is the truth," Frank insisted. "I did it. I could not help myself. I had to do it. There were no women around the house that I knew, and I had to have a woman. Under the circumstances, any girl, no matter how small, had to do."

Carl said nothing. He wanted his silence to convey skepticism. Frank kept talking, filling in his story with details, terrible details.

"I took her inside and played and monkeyed with her. She was perfectly willing to be loved, but I could not get it into her. She was too small." Then, Frank explained, things took a tragic turn. He said that as he was assaulting Marie, he began shaking from nerves, and his nervousness frightened the girl.

"So before we left the greenhouse, I decided to kill her."

Frank said he picked up Max Kruschka's hammer and took Marie into the woods, where "it suddenly came over me and I could not resist it, and I had to hit her on the head. I killed her."

The only thing that worried him, Frank said, was the fact that Emma Davison had seen him with Marie. But he felt her testimony would not be believed. "They have no evidence against me, and I will be free as long as I can keep my damn mouth shut," he said. "They have got that nigger now for the killing and they will probably hang him for it."

Even so, Frank boasted, if he had to kill again, he would do it, without hesitation: "I will do it two or three or a dozen times if I have to. It would not worry me a bit anymore. I will kill if I have to."

With that, Frank stretched out his hand and waited for Carl to take it. The men shook hands. Carl did not push for more details. He didn't want to seem overzealous. He would need Frank to repeat his confession in front of Joe Springenberg. There was no sense spooking him now.

That night, Carl snuck away from Frank long enough to send a telegram to Ray Schindler in New York City.

Confession obtained. Killed her with a hammer.

*

It was the news Schindler had been waiting so anxiously and so patiently to hear, and it had not come a moment too soon.

Around the time Carl was roping Frank into a confession, Schindler—according to his recollection of the case—was in Asbury Park meeting with Randolph Miller, Sheriff Clarence Hetrick, and the prosecutor, John Applegate Jr., the men financing his investigation.

They met to discuss the future of the case, and whether or not Schindler's unusual methods were working. The original estimate of Schindler's costs had been three thousand dollars, but now, his expenses had risen to more than six thousand. Applegate, in particular, had had enough. He still believed Tom Williams was guilty of the crime, and he wanted to get on with his prosecution. He wanted to cut Schindler loose.

Schindler asked for more time. He provided an update of events in the pursuit of the target, including the fake newspaper, the set-up movie, and the mock murder—techniques that couldn't be found in any kind of police manual. Applegate had heard enough, and exploded.

"Get out of my office!" Applegate yelled.

Schindler jumped to his feet and made a move toward the prosecutor, but Hetrick got between them. Applegate begged the sheriff to swear out a warrant for Schindler's arrest on the spot, on the charge of fraudulently bilking the county of money for his own enrichment.

"I'll arrest him myself right now," Applegate said.

Instead, Sheriff Hetrick played peacemaker, and the meeting ended without any blows or arrests. Even so, Schindler would later write, "we practically agreed that afternoon to drop the case."

Later that night, Schindler received Carl Neumeister's telegram.

*

Schindler didn't waste a moment. That day, March 11, he picked a stenographer and an operative to go with him on an evening train to Atlantic City. He sent a telegram to Carl, telling him to be prepared to meet that night. Schindler booked room 308 at Young's Hotel, just off a pier on the boardwalk. Carl joined them later for the meeting.

Their first decision was how to bring Joe Springenberg to life.

To play the part of Carl's criminal partner, Schindler selected the man he could trust most in the world—his brother Walter.

Walter Schindler, who did not resemble his brother enough to rouse any suspicion, had joined Ray's investigative team back in San Francisco, where he interviewed witnesses and testified in court in the Abe Ruef corruption scandal. When William Burns hired Ray to open a New York office of the Burns Agency, Ray brought along his brother. They hadn't worked together on many cases, but now Ray needed someone reliable. He called Walter and asked him to take a train down to Atlantic City the following day.

Meanwhile, in room 308 at Young's Hotel, Carl sat with the stenographer and relayed his best recollection of Frank's confession. The stenographer typed up notes for Walter Schindler to study. They needed Frank to give another full confession that the stenographer could take down, and they needed Walter/Joe to ask just the right questions, to get the precise details that would make Frank's confession useful in court.

At 6:00 p.m. on March 12, Walter Schindler took his place on the boardwalk, near South Carolina Avenue. Very shortly, Carl and Frank strolled up. Carl and Walter embraced like the oldest chums. Carl introduced Heidemann, naming him only as Frank. The three men sat on a bench and talked. An operative who was shadowing the meeting confirmed to Schindler that the plan was under way.

Walter took Carl and Frank to dinner at a cafe on the boardwalk and discussed several upcoming criminal jobs. Frank listened attentively and stayed quiet. From all indications, Frank fully believed Walter was the notorious Joe Springenberg. Walter felt confident enough to invite the men back to his room at Young's Hotel—room 306.

One room over, in 308, Ray Schindler and his team got into place. All the lights in the room were shut off, and only a small candle lit the stenographer's notebook, so he could write down what he heard. The men crept as close to the locked door separating the rooms as they could.

Before long, they heard the sound of a doorknob turning, and the shuffle of feet. Then the murmur of serious men talking.

In room 306, Carl and Walter continued their discussion of possible jobs and heists. Soon enough, the talk turned to the subject of Frank Heidemann. Should they bring him along, or not? Carl repeated his reservation—Frank had incriminating evidence on him, but he had nothing on Frank. As a result, he simply couldn't trust him. He needed to have some leverage of his own.

Frank knew what he had to do. He had to talk about Marie Smith. He could not stall or evade any longer—his life depended on it. When the questions came, this time he decided to answer them—in full.

What did you do to her? Did she put up a fight? How did you kill her? Did you hit her only once? Heidemann answered them all.

What was her name? Say her name.

"Marie Smith."

And how did you lure Marie Smith into the woods?

"I asked her if she wanted to take some flowers home for her father, and in that way I got her to go into the woods with me."

CHAPTER 36

On the Square

*

March 14, 1911
Atlantic City, New Jersey

That was enough questioning for the night. Carl and Frank returned to their own hotel room down the boardwalk. Once they were gone, Ray Schindler got word to Sheriff Hetrick back in Asbury Park. From the adjoining room they had heard every word of Frank's confession. Now, incredibly, they would need to get him to give a *third* confession, this one with Hetrick—and the prosecutor, John Applegate—listening in as well.

Frank Heidemann spent the day strolling the boardwalk with Carl. He seemed happier, more energetic, as if confessing his crime had lifted the awful weight he'd been shouldering for so long. He and Carl got haircuts and visited a palmist, and later went to a movie at the Savoy Theater. Quite possibly, Frank slept a little more soundly that night.

The next day, March 14, Walter Schindler rented two adjoining rooms at Young's Hotel—rooms 200 and 202. He resumed his role as Joe Springenberg, and joined Carl and Frank for the afternoon. They visited several brothels, and Carl lent Frank five dollars. Carl and Walter waited while Frank took a room with a woman named Rita. Afterward, Carl reported, "he told us revolting stories about his doings with her."

Later that afternoon, Schindler checked into room 200 at Young's Hotel. He brought along a new stenographer, Ed Handley. Neither

285

Hetrick nor Applegate could be there for the third confession, but Randolph Miller—Peter Smith's boss and the driving force behind the exhaustive pursuit of Marie's killer—did make the trip. The Asbury Park treasurer, Reuben Norris, was also there, serving as a disinterested party—someone unconnected to law enforcement who could be an impartial witness to events.

Schindler bought a small pendant cord and lightbulb to plug into a socket in the room, providing just enough light for Handley to transcribe the confession. Schindler also had three split-cane chairs sent to the room, but in the end he spread a blanket and pillows on the floor near the door connecting the rooms. The men lay down and put their heads as near to the space beneath the door as they dared. Operative Peterson knelt next to them and pressed his head near the doorjamb. Handley propped pillows around his lightbulb, dimming it even more.

A signal had been arranged. When Walter felt he had the full confession he needed, he would flush the toilet in room 202 three times, to let Ray Schindler know they were leaving. On his end, Ray worked out a plan with Handley; he would squeeze Handley's arm a set number of times to denote who was speaking in room 202—one squeeze for Walter, two for Carl, three for Frank.

At 8:20 p.m., the men heard the door opening and closing in the adjoining room. They listened in as Carl, Frank, and Walter, as Joe Springenberg, engaged in small talk.

"Well, it's warm tonight in here, isn't it?" Walter began. "Let me fix the window. Take off your coats. Frank, how is that little blond down there?"

"All right."

"Did you give her a run for the money?"

Frank mumbled something Handley couldn't hear.

The men talked about Honduras—Springenberg's preferred getaway destination. Honduras had no extradition treaty with the United States, which meant they could stay there as long as they liked. They talked about what boat they could take, and other measures that would help them get into the country unnoticed. Suddenly Walter brought up Asbury Park. He asked Frank to tell his story again.

Frank changed the subject.

A few minutes later, Walter brought it up again.

Again, Frank slipped out from under.

They knew he was cagey. They knew he was mentally agile enough to talk his way out of corners. And Carl had seen how hard it was to get Frank to talk about something he didn't want to talk about. Had his first confession frightened him? Was he starting to suspect something? Walter and his brother had worked out another plan—if Frank began to resist talking about Asbury Park, Walter and Carl should step out of the room under the pretense of buying cigars, and leave Frank alone with his thoughts. So they did just that.

From room 200, Schindler could hear Frank, alone in the next room now, pacing back and forth and nervously opening dresser drawers.

Then he heard Frank walking. Walking toward the door connecting to room 200. Walking toward him. The footsteps stopped. Frank Heidemann was standing mere inches away from his nemesis Ray Schindler, lying on the floor on the other side of the door. Schindler listened as Heidemann took the doorknob in his hand, and turned it.

The door was locked.

Heidemann turned it once more, then pulled on it, trying to force the door open. Schindler and his men held their breath. Finally, to Schindler's great relief, Heidemann gave up and resumed his pacing.

Soon Walter and Carl returned. The questioning continued. Walter and Carl were arguing now, and Walter was angry. He was angry with Carl about a discrepancy in Frank's first confession and what he had just told Walter. Had Frank taken Marie Smith into Kruschka's greenhouse, or had he taken her directly into the woods?

"You ought to know goddamn well I won't stand for anything like this," Walter yelled at Carl. "You never knew me all the time we have been together to take any chances. You knew damn well I was straight, and yet you stood for this, and you thought I was going to stand for it, too, didn't you?"

"I meant to tell you about it," Carl pleaded.

Frank was alarmed. What was wrong?

"You said you took that girl into the greenhouse," Carl said.

"No, I never said that. You misunderstood me."

"This is one proposition where there is no chance of misunderstanding," Walter interrupted. "He knows damn well that I never take any chances."

"I never said I took her in the greenhouse," Frank said.

"We have got to be on the square. You can't hand me anything."

"I told you all. It is the same thing I told him."

"Jesus Christ," Walter said. "I'll just take my little wad right here and you fellows can just get out of this the best way you can. How do I know the whole game isn't a frame-up on me?"

Frank was desperate now. Carl suggested they all write down their crimes, and secure their confessions in a lockbox that all three would have a key to. Frank didn't like that idea. It was becoming clear that Springenberg was just about done with him.

"Frank," Walter said wearily, "suppose you tell us right here everything that happened, and I promise not to mention this thing again."

"Frank will do it," Carl said.

"Just state the facts as they were. Go slow now. Don't talk too fast. I want to hear everything."

Once again, Frank knew what he had to do.

"Now listen," he finally said.

Then he began to confess his sins once more.

*

Sometime later, Ray Schindler heard three flushes. The questioning was over. The stenographer, Ed Handley, and the observer, Reuben Norris, went into the hallway and positioned themselves away from the door to room 200, but near enough to be able to see Carl and Frank leave. That way, Norris could testify in court that it had indeed been Frank Heidemann he heard make the confession.

Schindler contacted Sheriff Hetrick and John Applegate in Asbury Park. He told them he had Frank Heidemann's full, detailed confession. They agreed to meet in Red Bank, a shore town eighty-five miles north of Atlantic City, and just north of Asbury Park, the following morning.

In Red Bank, things happened quickly. The prosecutor, John Applegate, so reluctant to abandon his certainty in Tom Williams's guilt, filled out an application for a warrant for the arrest of Frank Heidemann, charging him with the murder of Marie Smith. A judge in Red Bank signed off on the warrant. It would not work to arrest Frank Heidemann in Atlantic City, since that would create jurisdictional issues. He committed his crime in Monmouth County, and the best thing would be to arrest him somewhere in the county. That meant getting him on a train.

The plan, therefore, was to arrest Heidemann that same day, March 15, as he and Carl Neumeister took a train up the New Jersey coast, straight toward the one town Heidemann wished he would never see again.

Asbury Park.

CHAPTER 37

"It Won't Bring Her Back"

*

March 15, 1911
Red Bank, New Jersey

Once the third confession was in hand, Carl Neumeister, still in character, told Frank Heidemann what he was desperate to hear—that Joe Springenberg had agreed to bring him along to Honduras. Joe would get the tickets, and Carl and Frank would meet him in New York City the next day.

Meanwhile, one day after hearing Frank's confession from the bordering hotel room, Ray Schindler took an 8:45 a.m. train from Atlantic City to Red Bank, ten miles north of Asbury Park. There he and Randolph Miller met with John Applegate, Sheriff Hetrick, and Elwood Minugh, the county detective who earlier in the case had grilled Tom Williams in a long interview. The physically formidable Minugh had always been the one to make the difficult arrests.

Now he'd been selected to arrest Frank Heidemann.

Schindler gave the room an update about the confession. Only days earlier he had nearly come to blows with Prosecutor Applegate, but now Schindler had been proven right, and Applegate dropped his resistance. He could not question the validity of the confession, not after so many people besides Schindler had heard it. After clinging for so long to Tom Williams as the killer, he gave up on the theory in an instant. That morning, Applegate petitioned James H. Sickles, a justice in nearby Red Bank, for an arrest warrant for Frank Heidemann.

While that was happening, Carl and Frank had breakfast at Child's Restaurant in Atlantic City. Afterward, they returned to their rooms to pack for the trip to New York City. They traveled light, with only one small satchel each. They returned to Child's for lunch and finally checked out of Young's Hotel at 1:45 p.m. From there they went to the Philadelphia & Reading Railroad station at Missouri and Arkansas Avenues, and boarded the 2:10 Atlantic City Express to New York City.

They found seats in the smoking car, but not together; Frank sat one row behind Carl. He hung his black coat on a hook by the window and draped it partially across his face for cover. He was nervous. He handled the first part of the trip well, but when the train stopped in the town of Lakewood, just twenty miles south of Asbury Park, he panicked.

"By God, this train may go through Asbury Park," Frank said.

Carl turned around in his seat and told him to calm down.

A few rows behind Frank, Samuel Peterson, one of Schindler's operatives, watched and waited.

Not long after leaving Lakewood, at 3:52 p.m., the train stopped in the town of Farmingdale. Detective Minugh was on the platform and climbed aboard. He walked down the aisle, past Frank Heidemann, half-hidden behind his coat. Frank saw Minugh and recognized him. He whispered to Carl that they had a problem. Again, Carl shrugged it off.

Detective Minugh calmly took his seat next to Samuel Peterson.

"Where is he?" Minugh asked.

Peterson pointed out the target.

The train rattled up the eastern edge of New Jersey. Minugh got up and slowly walked back up the aisle. The seat next to Frank was open. Minugh sat down in the seat.

"Frank Heidemann," he said quietly, "you're under arrest."

The German's instinct was to deny he was Heidemann. But he quickly realized it was pointless. He knew Minugh, and it was clear Minugh knew him. He was trapped. This was it. The end of the line.

"He submitted quietly," the *Asbury Park Press* reported.

*

Ray Schindler was waiting at the Red Bank station when the Atlantic City Express arrived at 4:18 p.m.

He watched as Minugh stepped off the train with the prisoner in his grip. Frank Heidemann had been Schindler's obsession for four months, and here he was, in handcuffs, pale and shrunken. Minugh put Heidemann in a waiting car and drove to Freehold, to the same jail that held Tom Williams. There Heidemann was put in solitary confinement and watched over by guards. His suspenders were confiscated.

Carl Neumeister got off the train, too, and when Minugh drove away with Heidemann, his work for the day was done. He boarded the next train to New York City and slept in his own bed that night.

Word of the arrest quickly spread through Asbury Park. The town was struggling with an outbreak of German measles, and officials were considering closing the schools. But when an *Asbury Park Press* reporter—whom Sheriff Hetrick had allowed to witness the arrest—returned with the news that evening, it seemed no one much cared about measles anymore. The next day "little business was transacted here, for every tradesman, every housewife, nearly everybody else in the town were discussing the arrest of Frank Heidemann," the *New York Times* reported. "Never before in the history of the town has popular interest been aroused to its present pitch."

Before long, Marie's parents, Peter and Nora Smith, heard the news, too. Though they had a new baby now, little Margaret, born two months after Marie's body was found, they had not recovered from the nightmare of losing their beautiful daughter Marie.

"It won't bring her back to me," Peter said somberly of the arrest, "but we will have justice and that is what we ask for—only the justice the law gives, but that in full."

A day after the arrest, Carl Neumeister was back on the job. Ray Schindler, it turned out, wasn't done roping Heidemann yet. He had a solid confession, but he wanted one more thing to bolster his case against Heidemann—the murder weapon. Neumeister, resuming his role as a criminal, visited Heidemann at the Monmouth County Jail and spoke with him through a screened door to his cell. "Subject appeared broken in spirit," Carl reported, "but relieved when he saw me."

"What became of the hammer with which you killed the girl," Carl asked him.

"It must be still in Kruschka's place."

"Joe says we have to get that, and he will pose as a reporter and swipe it. Describe the hammer so he can find the right one."

Carl learned what he could about the weapon, and where it might be found, before Frank became paranoid. He believed a guard spoke German and was listening in on them. Carl promised to send him an attorney, and urged Frank to tell him everything, the whole story.

The attorney would be another Burns operative, Samuel Peterson. The following day, Carl returned to the jail with Peterson and introduced him to Frank. Once again, Frank assembled the grim pieces of the story of how he had murdered Marie Smith. But there were still several unanswered questions—the burn on Marie's nose; the bloody leaves; the role Max Kruschka played in it all. Peterson pushed for more.

"Come on, this will never do," he said. "We can't take a story like that into court—they would laugh at us. Give me the straight story so I can figure out from the facts what arguments would work in your favor."

Frank turned to his friend Carl.

"What does Joe think of this?" he asked.

"Joe thinks it would be for the best to give the whole facts to the lawyer."

But there was not much more that Frank could tell them. He couldn't account for the scattered bloody leaves, because he claimed to have murdered Marie on the spot where she was found. Maybe the wind blew the leaves about. And he didn't know how Marie got the burn on her nose. He denied having taken her into the greenhouse and down in the furnace pit. Maybe, again, the wind had stirred up burning leaves elsewhere in the woods, and landed one on the child's face.

As for Max Kruschka, and whether or not he'd been involved in the crime or in covering it up, Heidemann insisted that he hadn't.

Back in Asbury Park, Kruschka heard about Heidemann's arrest. The *Asbury Park Press* reporter delivered a copy of the rushed evening edition to Kruschka at his home. His reaction was shock.

" 'I can't believe it, I can't believe it,' " Kruschka repeated over and over, the *Press* reported. " 'Frank never did it, it can't be. Never, never. I won't believe it until I hear it from him.' "

Ray Schindler visited Kruschka in his home to ask about the hammer. He got nowhere. Schindler then sent Neumeister, posing as a reporter, to push Kruschka harder about where the weapon might be. Kruschka was friendly enough, until, suddenly, he wasn't.

"He changed to a maniac and told me to leave," Neumeister wrote. "I walked to the door where he blocked my exit, working himself into a passion and saying, 'I know what you are after. You want the hammer that fits the wounds, but you won't get it. You've got the wrong man.' "

Kruschka punched Neumeister on the side of the nose, and kept swinging at him as he chased him out the front gate.

Meanwhile, Samuel Peterson continued his ruse as Heidemann's attorney, visiting him in jail and teasing what he could out of him. It seemed that Heidemann, slowly, grudgingly, was coming around to the reality that he might not be able to escape his predicament, that his shrewdness might not keep him out of the electric chair.

"If all else fails to get me free, and it's certain I'll be convicted and executed, tell Carl to bring poison to my cell," he said to Peterson. "I will take my own life."

Yet he wasn't quite finished looking for a way out. He suggested his friend Carl could bribe the guards, or eliminate the big witnesses against him, Emma Davison and Grace Foster. "He doesn't appear to care what means are adopted to get rid of them," Peterson wrote. Even his friend Max Kruschka could be made to disappear.

"He will drink whiskey with anyone who will pay for it," Heidemann said. "When you get him drunk you can do as you please with him. Anything to get him out of the way."

Heidemann also expressed the rage he felt against Ray Schindler and his detectives. "I'd like to crack their heads," he said, "and I will do so if I ever get the chance."

The roping of Frank Heidemann had now gone on for seventy-seven days. It could have gone on for many more, if it had needed to. But Ray Schindler knew the time had come to end it.

There had been a kind of cruelty to it, especially now that Heidemann was a broken figure in a jail cell—but then the pursuit of justice, Schindler reasoned, wasn't always a pretty thing. Most thought of someone like Heidemann as a monster, deserving of not a single drop of mercy or pity. But Schindler did not see Heidemann as a monster. He saw him as a man who had tipped over to the dark side. Monsters have no interest in redemption. Men do. Men, Ray Schindler believed, want to, need to, be brought back into the fold.

Heidemann did not yet know that he'd been so thoroughly deceived by a Burns detective. Schindler wanted him to learn it directly from him. He wanted to be there when it dawned on Heidemann that he'd been outsmarted, that his every last hope of wriggling out of his reckoning had been extinguished. In that moment of extreme and awful vulnerability, Schindler hoped, he might be able to get what he'd been seeking for so long—the unburdening of Frank Heidemann's soul.

So, on March 25, Schindler traveled to Freehold, to the Monmouth County Jail, to the cell where his target would be waiting for him.

*

Schindler brought Carl Neumeister with him. The two men were taken to Heidemann's solitary cell and led inside. Heidemann looked up at them and, in an instant, realized the deception that had ensnared him.

"He was overcome," Schindler would write.

One newspaper was more descriptive. It reported that Heidemann, realizing Neumeister was working with Schindler, lost all composure and let out a wail of anguish and despair. "It was pitiable," went the report.

Schindler allowed the horrible reality to wash over Heidemann and fully consume him. When he could, he refocused Heidemann on the events of November 9, 1910, the day he murdered Marie Smith.

Heidemann did not resist. He knew now that he was trapped. He admitted that everything he had told Carl Neumeister, and Joe Springenberg, and his attorney, Detective Samuel Peterson, was true. Schindler asked him to lay out the details of the crime once more, this time directly to him. The priest taking confession, the sinner baring all. Whatever he divulged, Schindler warned, could be used against him at his trial.

Frank Heidemann did as he was asked. He confessed again.

"Well," he explained, "I'll go to the chair anyhow."

All told, it was the eleventh partial or complete confession that Schindler had pulled from him.

Five days later, Schindler returned to Heidemann's cell with a typewritten statement. This would be Heidemann's official, final confession. The statement was read to Heidemann, and he was handed a pen. The prisoner signed it, with Schindler and Edward Taylor, a county clerk officer, as witnesses. The roping was over. There was no need for any further deception now.

Freehold, New Jersey
March 30, 1911

I, Frank Heidemann, do hereby voluntarily make the following statement:
    On November 9, 1910, I was employed by Max Kruschka, florist, as helper, and was residing at the residence of Max Kruschka situated

on the northwest corner of Asbury Avenue and Whitesville Road, Asbury Park, N.J.

At about 10:45 a.m. on November 9, 1910, I was at work potting some plants and had stepped inside the entrance of the greenhouse to fix a flower box when I heard the dog bark, and placing the hammer which I was using in my pocket, I stepped over the hot beds until I reached a point on the driveway at the front of the residence near Asbury Avenue. While walking up the driveway, I noticed Mrs. Davison pass the Kruschka residence and she was still in sight walking west on Asbury Avenue when I reached the front of the house. I called the little dog back and as he crawled through the hedge, I noticed a little girl, whom I later learned was Marie Smith, at the point on the Whitesville Road near the first telegraph pole south of Asbury Avenue.

Prior to this occasion, I had never before seen Marie Smith, but when I did, I admired her and made up my mind to get her.

Hearing the dog bark, she turned around and looked back and when I beckoned, she retraced her steps until she reached a point on Asbury Avenue, west of Whitesville Road several feet.

Here I talked to her through the hedge which surrounds the Kruschka property.

I asked her if she wanted to take some flowers home to her father; she replied that she did, and as she turned to enter the yard by the driveway, I told her to go around the corner on Whitesville Road and that I would meet her at the back of the yard. I walked through the yard and met her in the roadway at the rear of the Kruschka property.

I told her I had lost my knife while cutting flowers in the woods and asked her if she would help me look for it.

I took the left hand of Marie Smith in my right hand, and she willingly came along with me.

We walked north on Whitesville Road to Ridge Avenue; crossed the street, and entered the woods at the junction of Ridge Avenue and Whitesville Road [top of Third Avenue].

We walked through the brush some distance, crossing a drift road.

Selecting a spot a short distance from the drift road, I asked Marie to lie down.

As soon as I had unbuttoned her drawers which were of a heavy material, and after turning them down in front, I ran my fingers over the legs and body.

As Marie was sobbing I placed her handkerchief in her mouth. She finally forced the handkerchief out of her mouth as I placed her stocking cap over her mouth, and tied her hair-ribbon tightly around her neck.

I then inserted my index finger into her vagina but as the opening was small I knew I would have some difficulty getting my penis into her vagina, so I took it in my right hand, and while moving my finger around in her vagina, I "spent" on the ground.

During this time I was in a kneeling position, but after taking my finger out and wiping the blood on the front of my sweater, I got up and as Marie was still struggling I grabbed her by the neck and choked her.

I then kicked her in the head, I believe it was the left side, and after turning the body over (face downward) I reached into my hip pocket, took out the hammer, and hit her twice on the head, crushing her skull.

When I left the body the head was towards the drift road and the feet towards Deal Lake. I walked toward the drift road (carrying the hammer in my hand, the handle hanging down between my fingers), turned to the right until I reached Ridge Avenue, thence to Whitesville Road [Third Avenue hill], and entered the Kruschka property from the rear.

After washing the hammer and my hands in the wooden half barrel which stands in the yard, and in which the goldfish are kept, I walked between the house and the barn and entered the greenhouse, where I placed the hammer back in the rack. I do not figure that I was absent from the Kruschka premises for more than twenty minutes.

After returning I went about my work as usual, and at lunchtime I ate with the housekeeper and Mrs. Jackson. There was no one else present as Mr. Kruschka and his son were in New York and Mrs. Kruschka was in Asbury Park at Mrs. Kruschka's store.

I noticed that Marie Smith was dressed in a greenish colored dress, wore a brown overcoat and black stockings. She was slender and not well developed. I do not remember seeing any gloves belonging to her.

The scratches reported to have been on her hands and face must have been caused while she lay struggling on the ground.

I did not aid in the search for the body of Marie Smith at any time nor did I see it again after leaving the body on November 9th, although I went to the spot where it was found on Sunday.

A blanket was over the body, but I noticed it was in the same spot that I had left her after killing her.

Signed, Frank Heidemann

Ray Schindler had one final question for Heidemann, before he left with his signed confession.

"Why did you do it?" he asked.

Heidemann's answer was simple.

"I don't know."

CHAPTER 38

The Fortress

*

April 17, 1911
Freehold, New Jersey

Justice for Marie Smith finally had a time and place—the morning of April 17, in the Monmouth County Courthouse. Willard P. Voorhees, the same judge who handled Tom Williams's habeas corpus hearing, would now preside at the murder trial of Frank Heidemann. At Heidemann's arraignment on March 30, he told Voorhees he had no means to hire an attorney. Voorhees appointed a former judge, William Hoffman, and a former assistant prosecutor, Andrew Stokes, to serve as counsel for the defense.

One problem for the prosecution leading up to the trial was that the murder weapon was still missing. Heidemann insisted he'd put the hammer he used to kill Marie Smith back where it was kept, in a rack in Max Kruschka's greenhouse, and he said he even used it several times after the murder. One of Schindler's men, Samuel Peterson, went to Kruschka's property and retrieved four hammers, and brought them to Heidemann's cell. None, Heidemann said, were the murder weapon. His theory was that Max Kruschka had done away with it.

"Why would he do that?" Peterson asked him.

"He likes to do things his own way."

In the end, the prosecution never produced the murder weapon.

Early on April 17, County Constables William Hulce and Jonathan Ackerman brought Heidemann out of his cell in the Monmouth County Jail and marched him the short distance to the courtroom. Rows of people lined the outdoor path that led to the back of the courthouse and watched silently as the constables pulled Heidemann, handcuffed in front, along the path by his arms. A photographer tried to take his picture, but Heidemann quickly covered his face with his hat.

The constables opened the rear doors of the main courtroom and led Heidemann inside. He was thin and pale, and his mustache was gone. He'd been given a good shave and a well-fitting suit to prepare him for his trial. The courtroom that awaited him had never been more densely packed. Sketch artists, reporters, police officers, curious citizens— including at least fifty spectators from Asbury Park, by one count. Ray Schindler was there and had a seat at the prosecutor's table. Peter and Nora Smith took their places in front, their daughter Margaret, now three months old, in Nora's arms. Outside the room, people crowded the hallways and stairwells and spilled out into the public square.

The prosecutor's office had picked a jury pool of forty-six men. The morning of the trial, the attorneys spent eighty-five minutes winnowing down the pool to twelve jurors. Heidemann, sitting at the defense table, watched nervously, leaning his head on his hand. The jury foreman, John Van Kirk Sr., was a farmer. So were seven other jurors. The rest included a teamster, a lumberman, a painter, and a decorator. Remarkably, all twelve jurors admitted to having formed an opinion on the matter of Heidemann's guilt. To a man, they believed he was the killer. But they also swore they would listen to the evidence impartially.

At 11:15 a.m., Heidemann's lawyers entered a formal plea—nolo contendere. They would not say whether Heidemann was innocent or guilty, nor would they call any witnesses in his defense. No one could recall another such trial where no witnesses had been called. Justice Voorhees rejected the motion on technical grounds, and submitted "not guilty" as Heidemann's official plea.

At 3:00 p.m. that afternoon, the trial formally began.

The prosecutor, John Applegate, stood and read the indictment. It did not take long for Heidemann, somewhat composed at the start of the proceeding, to be overcome. As Applegate described the gruesome crime, Heidemann's body began to shake, and he wept and hid his face in his hands. Neither of his lawyers moved to comfort him. Heidemann sobbed for some time, and when he was done his face was red and swollen.

The witnesses came forth, one by one. A surveyor gave an overview of the woods where Marie Smith's body was found. The coroner, Otto Schultz, discussed the cause of death. Peter Smith took the stand and described the unthinkable events of November 9, 1910. His frail wife, Nora, was the next to testify. She answered questions calmly and slowly, but it was clear she was still sick with grief. At one point, Applegate mistakenly produced the brown overcoat and gray skating cap Marie had worn on the day she was killed. He had not meant for her to see them, but when she did, the sight was too much for her to bear, and she collapsed and sobbed. More than one juror cried along with her.

Voorhees called an end to the first day of the trial. The following morning, the courtroom was filled again. Voorhees warned that the day's testimony would be graphic and disturbing, and advised the many female spectators to leave. Not a single woman got up from her seat.

The star witness on the second day was Carl Neumeister.

Neumeister relayed all the important details of his roping of Heidemann, from giving him his copy of the *Staats Zeitung* in Reinken's Restaurant on Third Avenue, to the staged murder in Yonkers, to the confession in room 202 of Young's Hotel in Atlantic City. The *Press* reported that just as Neumeister recited Heidemann's grisly confession to the silent courtroom, the clock tower bell rang eleven times, for 11:00 a.m.—about the time that Marie had been murdered on November 9.

The bells "had a depressing effect upon the prisoner," the *Press* noted. "He winced and covered his face."

Ray Schindler's brother Walter followed Neumeister to the stand, and after that it was Schindler's turn. He described the circumstances surrounding Heidemann's final confession in his prison cell on March 30. There was much more Schindler could have testified to, but this was enough. The state of New Jersey rested its case. Voorhees sent out the jury to deliberate. The constables led Heidemann back to his cell.

One hour and fifty-five minutes later, the jury reached its verdict.

The *Press* reported Heidemann smiled as he walked up the aisle of the courtroom to his seat. Perhaps he felt that two hours of deliberation meant the jurors had compromised on a verdict of murder in the second degree. That, at least, would spare Heidemann's life. He sat calmly as the twelve men took their seats in the jury box. Justice Voorhees broke the eerie silence in the courtroom by addressing the jurors.

"Have you reached a verdict?"

The foreman, John Van Kirk, rose to his feet and said that they had. Voorhees asked him what the verdict was.

The farmer spoke the words as clearly as he could.

"Guilty of murder in the first degree."

*

The smile disappeared. Instead, Frank Heidemann cried out loudly.

"Prisoner, stand up," Voorhees ordered.

Heidemann could not comply. He didn't have the strength. It took him some time to finally pull himself to his feet, his face contorted in anguish. He kept his head bowed, never looking up as Justice Voorhees pronounced sentence on him.

"You have been found guilty of murder in the first degree for murdering Marie Smith. The punishment provided by law for a conviction of that crime is that you shall suffer death. The sentence of the law is, therefore, and the judgment of the court is that you do suffer death at the time and in the place and in the manner prescribed by law."

The execution, Voorhees said, would be carried out the week beginning on May 22. Frank Heidemann had five weeks to live.

*

Heidemann spent that time in the state prison in Trenton, New Jersey's capital, forty-six miles due west of Asbury Park. It was the oldest prison in New Jersey, and it was a grim, medieval place. Its main compound—high stone walls anchored by turreted block towers—was called the Fortress Penitentiary. Only four years earlier, in 1907, a state appropriations bill set aside ten thousand dollars for the construction of a "death building"— an addition to the Fortress that featured six death row cells and an execution chamber, a starkly bare room with painted brick walls and a wood-planked floor. The chamber housed an electric chair.

Prior to 1906, New Jersey officials carried out executions by hanging. But the advent of electricity and alternating current systems in the late nineteenth century produced, in the minds of most, a more humane method. An electrical engineer, Carl F. Adams, won the contract to build an electric chair for the Trenton State Prison, and delivered a ghastly thing made of wood and steel and rubber—an adjustable seat with leather straps and high-tension lead cables connected to two double-throw switches. The chair cost roughly three thousand dollars, and was capable of pushing 2,400 volts of electricity through a person's body—more than fifty times the minimum lethal amount.

In his small, square death row cell just a few paces from the execution chamber, Frank Heidemann handled his final affairs.

He took care to distribute his few remaining possessions, giving Constable Hulce a silver drinking cup he picked up on a trip back from Germany, and gifting the warden, Edward Cashion, his black overcoat and Ingersoll gold watch and chain. He asked that Max Kruschka be given his gardening shears and a gold seal ring inscribed with the initials "G.L."

Heidemann explained the initials stood for "good luck."

Toward the end of his time on death row, Heidemann asked that a message be sent to Raymond Schindler. He wanted Schindler to come see him in his cell in Trenton.

In New York City, Schindler was surprised by the request. Why would a condemned man ask to see the very person who secured his death sentence? Still, there was no question he would make the trip to Trenton. His curiosity alone was enough to get him there.

At the state prison, Schindler was taken to a meeting room where Frank Heidemann was waiting. He greeted Schindler politely and complimented his investigative skills.

"It was all in a day's work," Heidemann told him. "But I would give anything if I could get my hands around the neck of Carl Neumeister before I die."

Heidemann explained that he needed Schindler's help. He hadn't returned to his native Germany in several years, and he'd lost touch with his family. As far as he knew, they weren't aware of his conviction for murder, and Heidemann wanted to keep it that way. He did not want his mother or sister to learn what he'd done. But he had to somehow explain his disappearance from their lives. That's what he needed Schindler for.

He asked Schindler to write a letter to his mother, posing as an acquaintance. The letter would say that Heidemann had met an accidental death. If, by some chance, his family already knew about Marie Smith, Heidemann asked Schindler to send them another letter laying out some of the details of the murder without making it seem so hideous.

Schindler agreed to help, and that was all Heidemann needed from him. Schindler got up to go. He would see Heidemann again, at the execution, but it was the last time they would ever get the chance to speak. Schindler found there was nothing more to say except good-bye, which he did. Then he was gone. His time with, and attention to, Frank Heidemann was nearly done.

Why had Heidemann asked Schindler for help in these personal matters? He could have asked the warden in Freehold, Edward Cashion, who had been kind to him, or someone else at the prison in Trenton. One of his lawyers, William Hoffman, suffered a stroke and died just a few hours after the guilty verdict, but Heidemann could have asked his assistant counsel for help. Max Kruschka, who had promised to pay for Heidemann's burial, surely would have done him the favor.

Instead, he asked for his capturer, Raymond Schindler.

Did he see some special humanity in the detective, despite how mercilessly he'd been hounded by him? Or did it have to do with Schindler's theories about the relationship between a criminal and his pursuer? Had Schindler taken on, as he hoped he would, the role of Heidemann's spiritual savior—the man who helped him right the awful imbalance in his soul? Had he been the one to bring Heidemann back into the fold, to the side of the good? Was that why Heidemann trusted him with one of his final earthly requests?

It was impossible to say. Nor did Schindler claim any kind of redemptive victory. He did not boast of having saved Heidemann's soul. Whatever understanding passed between them would remain unknown.

But Ray Schindler's view of Heidemann did not change after the capture, or after the trial, or after the meeting in death row. He believed what he believed, and it would guide him through the rest of his career, as he pursued those who had given in to the evil side of themselves.

"We are all potential criminals, all of us," Schindler believed. "We all have criminal instincts to a certain degree. What counts is how we control them."

*

The execution was set for the night of May 23, 1911.

That day, Heidemann spoke easily with his guards. He told one he had fully forgiven both Ray Schindler and Carl Neumeister. What was the point in staying angry at them? He sat and wrote a letter to Prison Supervisor Samuel W. Kirkbride and four other death row officers, thanking them for their kindness toward him. He asked one prison deputy to reach out to Alvin Cliver at the *Asbury Park Press* with an answer to the one question Cliver and so many others seemed haunted by—why did Heidemann do what he did? Why did he kill Marie Smith?

The answer he sent Cliver was the same answer he gave Ray Schindler—*I don't know.*

Heidemann had one final request—he wanted the prison deputy to contact Peter and Nora Smith and beg their forgiveness for him.

Ray Schindler traveled from New York City to Trenton, and at 8:15 p.m. gathered with other witnesses in the prison warden's office. Edward Cashion, the warden from Freehold, was there, and so was Ed Handley, the Burns operative who had taken Heidemann's confession in Atlantic City. There were three doctors and six reporters. At 8:25 p.m., a guard led the witnesses to their seats in the execution chamber.

At 8:27, a door to the chamber opened. In walked the prison chaplain, Aloysius Fish, and Raphael Huber, a local reverend. They were chanting and praying for Heidemann's soul.

Heidemann was right behind them, his lips moving as he silently prayed as well. He appeared calm and steady. Without prompting or help, he sat down in the electric chair, as if taking his place at a dinner table. It took guards less than a minute to tie leather straps around his arms, legs, and chest, and fix a steel cap to his head. Off to the side, an operator stood on a quarter-inch corrugated rubber mat.

Heidemann kept praying until the very last moment.

At 8:34 p.m., the operator sent a charge through Heidemann's skull—1,840 volts at 10 amperes. The charge lasted for a full minute. There was a pause of a few seconds, then the operator sent a second charge—1,890 volts at 10 amperes. After a minute, the electric chair was switched off.

At 8:37 p.m., county physician F. G. Scannell walked up to the chair and placed his stethoscope on Heidemann's chest. He pronounced Heidemann dead. A second doctor, R. S. Bennet, did the same. Then a third, Edwin Fields. Heidemann's body was taken to an examination room, and the witnesses were allowed to observe the body.

Then it was over. The entire procedure, start to finish, had taken less than ten minutes.

The prison chaplain, Aloysius Fish, asked a reporter who was present to contact Max Kruschka in Asbury Park. He needed to discuss

Heidemann's burial. The next day, the reporter got word to Fish that Kruschka had changed his mind. He would not be paying for Heidemann's burial after all.

So the chaplain did what he could, and saw to it that Frank Heidemann was given a burial in a Catholic cemetery in Trenton.

In Asbury Park, state authorities reimbursed Sheriff Clarence Hetrick and Randolph Miller all the fees they paid to the Burns Detective Agency. City Solicitor James D. Carton agreed to release $1,100 in reward money in the Marie Smith case. The bulk of it, one thousand dollars, was split between Ray Schindler and Emma Davison. The remaining one hundred dollars went to William Benson, the florist who found Marie's body in the dark Wanamassa woods, exactly 775 feet from Max Kruschka's home.

In Freehold, the lawyers C. Brooks Ames and Walter L. Glenny stayed involved in Tom Williams's case. The NAACP spent $266 on defending Williams against the likelihood of a questionable murder charge. When Frank Heidemann confessed, Williams was officially exonerated, and relieved by authorities—and reporters—of any connection whatsoever to the Marie Smith case. No one recorded his reaction to hearing that Heidemann had confessed.

Yet Williams did not get his freedom right away. He was sentenced to two years in prison for being a "repeater"—voting twice in the 1910 election—and he served his time.

Once he was let out of prison, Tom Williams disappeared from the public record. There is no evidence he returned to Asbury Park, or moved elsewhere, or did anything at all. He had spent his time in the public eye, and it was his right to live the rest of his life out of it. It appears that's what Black Diamond did. He went back to being a figure of no public consequence, but of some quiet dignity, a man who lived and mattered.

CHAPTER 39

The Lord Has Willed It So

*

March 25, 1931
Chicago, Illinois

For Ida Wells, the battle of her life was against forces far too sweeping and entrenched for any one individual to defeat—slavery, patriarchy, racism, economic suppression. Yet Wells waged that war with both hands, one reaching up to pull down immoral institutions, the other reaching down to lift up the persecuted. She challenged the vast, systemic prejudices of white American society—but she also made the phone calls and collected the dollar bills that saved the life of Steve Green.

Her brave, bold actions, big and small, had rippling consequences. What if Wells hadn't succeeded in ousting Cairo sheriff Frank Davis? Would there have been anyone to pull Steve Green off the train leading him to his death? Would Joel Spingarn have found the cause that ignited his moral fervor and steered him to the NAACP? Would Spingarn have donated the one hundred dollars that paid for two lawyers to defend Tom Williams, and would the NAACP have made the leap to real, effective legal power that it did after Spingarn came aboard?

Wells never stopped fighting for her beliefs, but after her clash with the NAACP, she became less active. So many years of strife and heartbreak, and constant criticism from her contemporaries, had left her weary. In 1920 she was hospitalized and underwent gallbladder surgery. The operation was tricky, and she was kept in the hospital for five weeks.

Many feared she wouldn't survive. When she was brought home, she suffered a relapse, and spent another eight weeks in bed.

"It took me a year to recover," Wells wrote, "and during that year I did more serious thinking from a personal point of view than ever before in my life." Her contemplation led her to a painful discovery.

"All at once," she wrote, "the realization came to me that I had nothing to show for all those years of toil and labor."

This was not true, not by any stretch—but it was how Ida Wells felt. Yet even then, she kept going. She continued to write hard-edged articles calling for action against injustice—enough articles for the U.S. government to classify her "a dangerous race agitator." She covered a race riot in East St. Louis in 1917 and another in Arkansas in 1922. She kept up her work with clubs and reform organizations in Chicago, and she served as the director of the Cook County League of Women's Clubs. She worked with the National Equal Rights League, marched for suffrage, and helped block the segregation of Chicago schools.

In 1930 she even ran for election to the Illinois state legislature. She lost to a white man, but she became one of the very first black women to run for political office in the United States.

This was her deepest belief, and perhaps her greatest disappointment— that the efforts of individuals like her would be the only way to create meaningful change, the only hope for real progress.

"In this work, all may aid," Wells once said in a speech. "Individuals, organizations, press and pulpit should unite in vigorous denunciation of all forms of lawlessness. Nay, more than this, there must spring up in all sections of the country vigorous, aggressive defenders of the Constitution of our beloved land."

And yet, to her sadness, she did not always see this necessary level of urgency in others. "Eternal vigilance is the price of liberty," she wrote in her autobiography, *Crusade for Justice,* "and it does seem to me that, notwithstanding all these social agencies and activities, there is not that vigilance which should be exercised in the preservation of our rights."

*

In the eternal struggle between the darkness and the light, the darkness is mutable. The horrors of slavery gave way to the horrors of lynching and Jim Crow. By one estimate, more than four thousand black Americans were lynched in the United States between 1877 and 1950, the staggering bloodshed forever to be the shame of America. And while the number of lynchings began to drop around 1910, that is when a new practice, known as "legal lynching," emerged—black men given rushed sham trials and sent to die in brand-new electric chairs.

In the same way, Raymond Schindler's desire to wrench confessions from wayward men did not, and could never, curtail the darker aspects of all human nature. The mysterious sinister force that drove Frank Heidemann to kill Marie Smith was as uncontainable and impassively constant as the endless tides in the Atlantic. A quarter century after Heidemann met his end, another German immigrant, Bruno Richard Hauptmann, was convicted of murdering the young son of Charles Lindbergh and sentenced to execution. He, too, was led to Carl Adams's electrified creation in Trenton's Fortress Penitentiary, and died in the very same wooden chair that took Frank Heidemann.

Ray Schindler left the Burns Agency in 1912 and opened his own New York City shop—the Schindler Bureau of Investigation. His father, John, the former minister, joined his sons Ray and Walter there. Schindler cleared an innocent man of murder in the infamous Sir Harry Oakes case in 1943, and cracked several other high-profile crimes.

But he always referred to his first murder case—the Marie Smith case—as the most challenging work of his career.

Schindler also indulged his fascination with crime-fighting machinery, and helped pioneer the use of the dictograph—a telephonic box that could be hidden in a room to pick up sounds and conversations. He collaborated with Walter G. Summers and Leonarde Keeler, the two men who separately birthed the modern lie detector. Schindler used the new device in several cases; in one, he caught the private maid who stole fifteenth-century paintings from her wealthy employer.

Schindler became famous. He loved to dance and he loved the New York City nightlife. He cofounded the Court of Last Resort—a precursor to the modern Innocence Project—and he was the president of the Adventurers Club of New York. He was called the most brilliant and charismatic investigator of his time. Yet he never once used a gun, and never even carried one. He worked in the dangerous underworlds of society, but he was otherwise a peaceful and optimistic man. When he was held up by an armed robber in Los Angeles, "my knees shook violently and I stammered, 'Oh, no,'" Schindler recalled. "I was plenty scared." He got out of it by handing the robber eighty dollars.

Schindler was married five times and had a son, Raymond Jr., and two daughters, Dorothy and Ruth. Later in his life, he took a job as supervisor of security for Ann Gould, daughter of the railroad magnate Jay Gould. She allowed Schindler and his fifth wife, Janice, to stay in the beautiful Spratt mansion, overlooking the Hudson in Tarrytown, New York, and across the way from Gould's own mansion. Schindler lived there until his death from a heart ailment at the age of seventy.

The one murder case he would never have wanted to work happened eleven years after his passing.

In a ghastly echo of the Marie Smith murder, in January 1970, Schindler's widow, Janice, was found savagely beaten to death, her nightgown pulled up, in the Tarrytown rooming house where she lived. Another boarder was arrested for the crime. One of her obituaries carried a photo of her and her beloved husband, Ray, wearing tropical shirts and smiling brightly on a cruise across the Atlantic.

*

After its early struggles, the National Association for the Advancement of Colored People went on to become the most enduring and far-reaching civil rights organization in U.S. history.

After the Tom Williams case, it found more solid footing, opening branches in several cities and growing its membership. By 1919, the NAACP had ninety thousand members and three hundred branches. According to its website, Joel Spingarn, who served as its president for ten years, "formulated much of the strategy that fostered the organization's growth."

The range of matters the NAACP brought under its wing—police brutality, political lobbying, civic engagement, educational equality, criminal justice, health and social issues—is remarkable. Its greatest impact, however, may have happened in courtrooms. The NAACP's lawyers prevailed in a long string of critical legal victories, none bigger than 1954's *Brown v. Board of Education,* argued in front of the U.S. Supreme Court by NAACP chief counsel Thurgood Marshall. The unanimous nine-zero decision established that racial segregation in public schools was unconstitutional. Marshall, the grandson of a slave, became the first African American to serve as a justice on the U.S. Supreme Court.

Today, the association has five hundred thousand members around the world, and an annual budget of $25 million.

In nearly every historical account, Ida B. Wells-Barnett is considered one of the founders of the NAACP.

*

Exactly fifty years after he bought five hundred acres of scrub oak and sand dunes by the Atlantic Ocean, James A. Bradley died in his Manhattan apartment, at 10:00 p.m. on June 6, 1921. He was ninety-one, and the cause of his death was cancer and bladder disease.

The city he created and sought to bend to his will mourned his passing and celebrated his life, and the newspaper he founded devoted its first two full pages to an appreciation of his vision and resolve. Clarence Hetrick, the former sheriff who became mayor of Asbury Park—largely on the strength of his role in the Marie Smith case—eulogized Bradley in the *Asbury Park Evening Press*: "He reared unto himself a monument that is everlasting . . . on the sands of the sea he builded a city. He left us a heritage of high ideals, of character eternal, of work accomplished and things done."

The year Bradley died, officials commissioned a statue of him, lean and bearded, gazing out at the ocean, and placed it in Bradley Park, across from the Convention Hall, in the heart of Asbury Park. In recent years, there have been efforts to have the statue removed because of Bradley's support of segregation. The statue has stayed, though the Asbury Park Historical Society did acknowledge Bradley's history of racism.

So there he stands today, high above his boardwalk, in sight of the stretch of beach where he once sat with his black friend, John Baker, and dreamed of a bright and shining city, godly and free of sin.

As for the city Bradley actually did build, it is but a shell of the glittering resort it once was. The two hundred swank hotels, the carnival rides and dance halls, the Carousel and the Baby Parade—all gone. A shift to the suburbs, a 1970 race riot, new casinos in Atlantic City, crime, and poverty came together to turn Bradley's paradise into something like a ghost town. There have been spurts of urban revival, and today the city has reclaimed some of its vibrancy, but what has been lost will likely never return. America does not spend its summers as it used to, with petticoats and parasols and carriage rides and fortune-tellers.

And the place in the world where Marie Smith's body was found— the gloomy Wanamassa woods on the northern edge of town, by the sparkling waters of Deal Lake—is gone, too. Houses are there now.

Max Kruschka's home and greenhouses are gone as well, replaced by an auto body shop. Whether or not Kruschka knew of Frank Heidemann's crimes, or helped him in any way, remains unknown.

*

On March 21, 1931, Ida Wells-Barnett, then sixty-eight, wasn't feeling well and went to bed early. The next day, she skipped church and stayed in bed. Her husband, Ferdinand, noticed she did not look well—she was restless and burning up. He got her to a hospital, and she remained there, unconscious, for three days.

At 1:00 a.m. on March 25, Wells died of kidney disease.

Crowds filled and surrounded Chicago's Metropolitan Church, where a simple, poignant memorial service was held. Her sons Charles and Henry helped carry her coffin, and a man sang a mournful ballad:

> I've done my work, I've sung my song
> I've done some good, I've done some wrong
> And I shall go where I belong
> The Lord has willed it so.

Long ago, Wells realized her strength lay in her stubbornness, and when the press remembered her, they remembered that strength. "Her militant attitude and uncompromising stand for racial rights made her an outstanding figure," wrote the *New York Age*, while the *Oakland Tribune* said, "she was great because she was fearless . . . she was one of the greatest Negro women the world has ever produced."

The *New York Times* chose not to run an obituary for Wells—a mistake they acknowledged eighty-seven years later, admitting that for more than a century "obituaries in the New York *Times* have been dominated by white men." As recompense, the paper ran a belated tribute:

> Wells is considered by historians to have been the most famous black woman in the United States during her lifetime, even as she was dogged by prejudice, a disease infecting Americans from coast to coast. She pioneered reporting techniques that remain central tenets of modern journalism. And as a former slave who stood less than five feet tall, she took on structural racism more than half a century before her strategies were repurposed, often without crediting her, during the 1960s civil rights movement.

Ida Wells was, in simplest terms, a participant in the battle. She refused to be told how things were, when she could use her own eyes and ears to determine the truth. "When we had a riot in Chicago, she went out every day," her daughter Alfreda M. Duster recalled in an interview years later. "Everyone else was disposed to be holing up and boarding up, but she wanted to be in the action. She wanted to see for herself."

This, too, was Wells's message to the downtrodden—you have more power than you know, and your power is in your individuality, the richness of your divinity, the glory of your humanity. "My mother had a constant drive and desire to make conditions better," Duster said, "so that persons would have an opportunity to fulfill their own potential."

Ida Wells wrote names where before there were none. She demanded the admission that the lynching victims she fought so hard for were once beautiful human beings, with families and dreams and loves and hopes, each a unique child of God, each far more than their struggles and suffering, each flowing with beauty and talent and song. She did this by using the language of her oppressors—who called the black race savage, beastly, barbaric—and flipping it to apply to the practices of oppression. It was the slavers and lynchers who were savages. It was their doings that were demonic.

And the men and women of her race—these were not beasts to be extinguished by "person or persons unknown." There was true greatness and unfathomable grace in what they endured, in what they overcame, in how they grasped at the tools of freedom and pushed their bloodlines through time and history, until their power and culture came to matter, and they began to claim as theirs what rightfully belonged to them.

This was the blessed work of Ida Wells, and this is the brilliant idea that persists:

We are never better than when we give our voice to the voiceless, our strength to the weak, our lives to the battle between the darkness and the light.

Author's Note

*

Seven miles over the Brooklyn Bridge, through the stone arch gates of Holy Cross Cemetery, I found a forgotten grave.

I went there in July 2017 because I'd heard the story of Marie Smith, a young schoolgirl who was murdered in Asbury Park in 1910. Her killing was a notorious crime that was covered nationally, and the defense of the primary murder suspect was the third case ever handled by the National Association for the Advancement of Colored People. The story sat at a historic intersection of sweeping national forces—religious extremism, class struggle, the infancy of criminal psychology, and Jim Crow racial violence. Yet there was hardly any literature about it.

There existed, however, a record of where the young victim was buried in 1910—Holy Cross Cemetery in the Flatbush section of Brooklyn. That seemed like a good place to start learning more.

The grave wasn't easy to find, even with a map of the plots. It was supposed to be in the western end of the ninety-six-acre cemetery, in an area near an old white chapel. I walked along a row of mismatched headstones, many tilting or leaning with age—but I couldn't find the number of the plot I was looking for. It just wasn't there.

I saw a green work truck parked along a walkway and went over. The driver was Fred, the cemetery superintendent. He walked me back to the row of stones and helped me look. About halfway down the row we stopped at a short gray slab with the name O'Brien on it. A few feet to the left was the headstone marked Antoinette Calvello, who passed in

1905. In between the stones, in a space of just two feet across, several clumps of overgrown ryegrass weeds sprouted three feet high. Fred looked at the drooping weeds for a minute before he could be sure.

"That must be it, then," he said, pointing.

"No headstone?"

"No, sir."

I crouched down and pulled the weeds apart. There was a small dirt clearing, the size of a shoe box, where no grass or weeds grew—a spot where a small marker or headstone might go.

But there was nothing there. Just rocks and dirt. All there was in the world to mark that someone's bones lay below. And not just someone—*two* someones. Young Marie Smith, and her brother John, who died of accidental poisoning at eighteen months. Each in their own box, stacked vertically. Buried more than a century ago.

Buried, and now lost beneath the weeds. As close to forgotten as you can get, without having nothing or nowhere at all.

That bare plot of earth is where this book began.

*

A few weeks after the book was finished, in the summer of 2019, I went back to Holy Cross.

This time, it was easy to find Marie's spot. I knelt beside it and pulled up some weeds and dug up three inches of dirt. Then I lay a small bronze-plated marker in the empty space and secured it there. It was a simple marker, the size of a brick, and it was engraved with two names.

John Smith, the beloved son, and his sister, Marie Smith.

The inscription below the girl's name reads:

Marie was the flower.

—Alex Tresniowski, 2019

Acknowledgments

*

Thank you to Lorraine Stundis—I did this book because you believed I could do it, and that meant everything. Thank you to Earlene Williams, who I love and admire so much. Thank you to Tamara Tresniowski, always there for me, my hero and champion at every turn. Thank you to Will Becker, a great guy who taught me what true friendship looks like.

Thank you, Susan Schindehette, for clearing the way for me to do this book. You are and will always be the most beautiful writer I know. To Peter Lucia, the world's top expert on the Tom Williams case—thank you for shining a light on this story. Thank you to my great literary agent, Frank Weimann, who probably has the best left hook among all agents. A big thank-you to the brilliant Dawn Davis, who took a chance on me, encouraged me through all my delays, and made the book so much better than it was. Thank you to Chelcee Johns, for all your help and kindness. And thank you to the incredible historian Paula Giddings, whose definitive book about Ida Wells was my touchstone.

Thank you, Laura Schroff—your support and belief in me means so much more than you will ever know, and so does your unconditional friendship. When I met you, everything changed. Thanks to Mark Apovian, for the golf tips and inappropriate texts. Thanks to the great book lover Lucinda Williams, for always being interested in what I do. Thank you to Jeremy Sabatini, for all your help and support. Thank you to Ricci Adan, for your faith in me, and to Henry Howard, a true badass to the end.

Thank you dearly to all these folks, and to all the people who give my life meaning and joy—to my sister Tam, and Howie; to my sister Fran Lanning, and Rich, Zach, and Emily; to my brother, Nick Tresniowski, and Susan and Humboldt; to Mark Stundis and Janice, Sam, Andreas, Dino, Holly, and Nicky; to Grace Jepson and Rob and Quincy, Henry, and Elizabeth; to Jessie Mignoni and Paul, Celeste, and Charlie; to the one and only Willie Spellmann; to Jordie, Chelsea, and Beau; to Laurentiu, Natalia, and Victor Stroia; to Lindsay, Amy, Neil, and Angela; to Paul Fronczak, Crystal McVea, Steven Carino, Lisa Reburn, Joy Mangano, Roger Woodward, Susie Spain, Nino Perrotta, Maurice Mazyck, Dr. Alan Felix, and Laura Lynne Jackson.

And of course, thank you to all the wonderful little ones who live in my crowded heart—Mischa, Nickie, Billie Boy, BeBe, Nino, She She, Guy, LaLa, Manley, Baby Girl, Bitsy, Pony, Matilda, and Maise. You bring me so much love.

—Alex Tresniowski, 2020

About the Author

*

Alex Tresniowski is a writer who lives and works in New York. He has written for both *TIME* and *People* magazines, handling mostly human-interest stories. He is the author or coauthor of more than twenty books, including the 2005 true-crime thriller *The Vendetta*, which was used as a basis for the 2009 movie *Public Enemies* starring Johnny Depp. For more about this story and the author, please visit alextres.com.